Cooking the Books

Cooking the Books

Mythologies of Money

Anna Kassulke

PRAEGER

Westport, Connecticut
London

Library of Congress Cataloging-in-Publication Data

Kassulke, Anna, 1960–
    Cooking the books : mythologies of money / Anna Kassulke.
        p.   cm.
    Includes bibliographical references (p.) and index.
    ISBN 0–275–97047–7 (alk. paper)
    1. Money—History. I. Title.
    HG220.A2K35   2001
    332.4—dc21   00–061172

British Library Cataloguing in Publication Data is available.

Library of Congress Catalog Card Number: 00–061172
ISBN: 0–275–97047–7

First published in 2001

Praeger Publishers, 88 Post Road West, Westport, CT 06881
An imprint of Greenwood Publishing Group, Inc.
www.praeger.com

Printed in the United States of America

The paper used in this book complies with the
Permanent Paper Standard issued by the National
Information Standards Organization (Z39.48–1984).

10 9 8 7 6 5 4 3 2 1

Contents

Acknowledgments

In many ways I have been thinking about this book since my childhood in Notting Hill Gate. In this part of West London homeless people sheltered in doorways of lavish Georgian buildings, and I saw them on my way to school. Money, I concluded, creates vast ruptures. And so, in a perverse sense, money matters a lot, to all of us. I would not have realised any of this without my mother and father. As Quakers, they taught me to upend entrenched ideas, and to constantly question injustice.

Writing about money is another thing. It is everywhere and nowhere, clear and obscure. Francie Oppel guided me through the mayhem, and I am extremely grateful for her help.

Mark has been a pillar of emotional support, as well as a willing and invaluable sounding board for ideas. Kate and Daniel–thank you–especially for all the sandwiches. I dedicate this book to all six of you.

Introduction

This is a book about money: the stories we tell about it, and the words we use to describe it. Signs of money surface everywhere in our Western culture in advertisements, news reports, political speeches, and fiction; in fact we are bombarded with money and its various value systems at every cultural turn.[1] Because signs of money are widespread in our culture, their representations constitute a mythology, (or sets of mythologies), in a Barthesian sense. Money arguably began as an indifferent concept for exchange, but it has become mythologised in the sense that it is repeatedly *naturalised* and *historicised*. I aim to elucidate how money is seen to have far–reaching cultural effects, even though, or perhaps because, it is poorly delineated as a concept.

Barthes's *Mythologies* (1989 [1957]) provides the principal framework for my analysis of money's mythologies. According to Barthes, the primary aspect of mythology is its inextricable relationship to language. Myth must be conveyed by discourse, and hence it is a type of language (Barthes 1989 [1957], p. 11). Myth borrows signs from the linguistic, or first–order system (Barthes 1989 [1957], p. 126), and gives them a mythological signification, which Barthes refers to as a 'second–order semiological system' (1989 [1957], p. 123). In other words, myth works on and within linguistic signs, because these first–order signs are open to appropriation and new meanings. Barthes explains the openness of language by maintaining that around the first–order sign 'there always remains a halo of virtualities where other possible meanings are floating' (1989 [1957], p. 143), and these are readily turned into myth, depending upon the particular disposition of culture.

Barthes also describes myth as '*a type of speech*' (1989 [1957], p. 117). But he does not refer simply to vocal utterances; he uses speech to refer to a general mode of communication. Speech is anything that *means* something, whether it be in a photograph, a written text, or a gesture, so it is equivalent to 'text'. Barthes's own analysis of mythologies includes texts as diverse as 'The Romans in Films' (1989 [1957], pp. 27–30), 'Operation Margarine' (1989 [1957], pp. 45–47), and 'The World of Wrestling' (1989 [1957], pp. 15–26). It is my contention that money fits his mythological framework more completely than, say, wrestling because money is considerably more ubiquitous, and the reach of its mythologies is global. When Barthes discussed the transactional aspects of language and myth, he could have applied his ideas quite neatly to money, because both are systems of equivalences. Perhaps Barthes's only articulation of the money sign is in *S/Z*: 'In the past money "revealed", it was an index; it furnished a fact, a cause, it had a nature; today it "represents" (everything): it is an equivalent, an exchange, a representation: a sign. Between index and sign, a common mode, that of inscription' (1974, p. 39). Whilst he specifies the representational aspects of the money sign, and its status as a set of equivalences, Barthes also constructs an erroneous temporal distinction between the past and the present, which is essentially a mythological turn in itself, because it historicises. His claim that in the past money had a 'nature' is precisely the kind of mythological construction that I highlight throughout this work.

At their most fundamental level, money's mythologies begin at the level of the sign (or metaphor) 'money'.[2] In the first–order system 'money' is simply a linguistic sign; it is disinterested inscription. But money has numerous sec-ond–order significations that are continually constructed and conceptually mod-ified in our culture. Rather than having a single material referent—which it does not as I elucidate below—money has connotations of power; it is a promise, an object of desire, and as such it structures the way we think, as well as our social systems (such as work, lifestyle, consumption, and government policy). Money plays a central role in our everyday lives, and signs of money proliferate, not only as 'm–o–n–e–y', but as representations of it. We are all acquainted with it in one or other of its guises: coin, cheque, paper notes, stocks, shares, plastic, and recently even digital bits, so that electronic fund transfers bypass the need to han-dle money. But none of these are money per se, they are simply *thought of* as money. Money itself does not exist, because it has no single nature, and no ref-erence outside discourse, it only exists as a series of mythological concepts.

Another central feature of Barthesian mythology is that it 'transforms history into nature' (1989 [1957], p. 140). In other words, myth makes things appear to have justly and nonchalantly evolved, despite any ideological turns and resis-tances that may have accompanied cultural change. But Barthes maintains that mythological signification has to hide its ideological intention in order to remain mythological. So myth is partially clandestine, or covert, because it makes an *instant* impression, forcing the reader to accept it as natural or common–sensical.

Accordingly, mythologies of money make the ideologies of money appear natural, inevitable, and eternal. But no myths are everlasting; they are dependent upon the preoccupations of culture, as well as the availability of signs for appropriation. Therefore there is no eternal myth (Barthes 1989 [1957], p. 118). The idea that money was invented at some particular juncture in history is pure mythological fiction: whilst I am not an archaeologist or a cultural historian, my research has revealed that the myth of money's invention is tenacious, and necessary to the continuation of our money culture. In constructing a past for money (as Barthes does in the quotation cited earlier), texts mythologise money itself, but the myth is purely linguistic so that representations of money in contemporary texts either metaphorise money in differing discursive terms, such as capital or freedom, or embody the money object in character constructs.

In essence, myth is creative, because it gives meaning to words that are otherwise conceptually neutral in the first–order system; it structures the elusive, and gives itself a historical justification. Money's mythology creates an order out of discontinuity, it reifies, but it is not necessarily deceitful. Mythology provides evidence of people's creativity, and attempts to understand its complexity; its behaviour and its contradictory functions are, I argue, recent projects in Western culture, having taken on a sense of urgency in approximately the last two hundred years. Because money is elusive physically, as well as conceptually slippery, it needs myth to contain it in a Nietzschean sense. *The Birth of Tragedy* introduces this idea: 'without myth every culture loses the healthy power of its creativity: only a horizon defined by myths completes and unifies a whole cultural movement' (Nietzsche 1967 [1872], p. 135).

I would suggest that many general readers are unaware of the persistent entanglement of money with culture, because it is often backgrounded, as well as naturalised. However, I reject any conspiratorial elements, preferring to believe that we are all active participants in money's mythologies to some extent. Williamson calls this complicity 'ideology', which is a term I am generally uncomfortable with because of its connotations of manipulation. Nevertheless, I shall borrow her description of ideology to explain my money *mythology:* 'it is always precisely that of which we are not aware, we are active in it, that we do not *receive* it from above: we constantly recreate it. It works *through* us, not at us' (Williamson 1978, p. 41). In other words, as participants in a culture, we construct, relay, and live within numerous myths of money.[3]

The general reader has certain prerogatives when he or she reads in terms of reality, reference, and language. Baudrillard discusses this privilege in 'For a Critique of the Political Economy of the Sign'. He begins by citing Benveniste: ' "For the speaking subject, there is complete adequation between language and reality. The sign recovers and commands reality; better still, it is that reality" ' (Baudrillard 1989 [1972], pp. 83–84). Baudrillard's comment is that 'the poor speaker evidently knows nothing of the arbitrary character of the sign (but then, he probably isn't a semiologist)! Yet there is a certain truth to this naive metaphysic' (1989 [1972], pp. 83–84). My findings are largely interpretations. The validity or otherwise of money's mythologies is for readers to judge.

There is currently a widespread perception that money is disappearing, and that 'somehow, in transition from its economic base, money has lost its intrinsic identity' (Bretton 1980, p. xiv). It seems that technology is largely responsible for this change in money's makeup.[4] There is a sense amongst commentators that our monetary structures are being upended, or transformed, as if money had a natural, or an authentic, existence (sometime) prior to the end of the twentieth century. Furthermore, this existence was not conceptual, it was material. Castells concludes the first volume of his three–volume work, *The Information Age: Economy, Society and Culture,* with the comment: '[We are at] the beginning of a new existence marked by the autonomy of culture vis–a–vis the material bases of our existence' (1996, p. 478). Castells's argument is essentially a Marxist materialist one that attributes *capital* with the ability to transform relations. Bretton, who also shares some Marxist views, maintains that money 'redirected man's purpose on earth. It had accomplished this by bringing within the reach of the individual, material objects and the fulfilment of non-material desires which were absent in the original state of nature' (1980, p. 121). But money itself does not perform tasks; readers and commentators alike confer on it differing kinds of ability.

Two short narratives will enable me to flesh out perceptions of historical and material change, a perception Barthes himself dichotomises as we have seen. The first is from a children's text entitled *The Story of Money*, and it begins as follows: 'A long time ago, there was no such thing as money. The first humans had no need for money. There was no place to spend it' (Maestro 1993, p. 3). The body of this text is an evolutionary account of how trading came to be centralised in markets, and coinage was adopted because it was more convenient than barter. Markets grew in size, until now 'the marketplace has grown to include the whole world' (Maestro 1993, p. 40). The text concludes: 'In recent years, people have begun to use a system of cashless money. Money is a tool that has changed as the world has changed. Now it is changing again. No one knows for sure what the money of the future will be' (Maestro 1993, pp. 42–43).

My second narrative is a very minimal story from the *Australian Financial Review* (25 Sept. 1995): 'Once upon a time, money was measured in pounds, shillings and pence. Then it moved to dollars and cents. Now money is 1s and 0s' (p. 27). Both these stories are written as responses to changes in monetary form. As I read them the stories imply that we are currently in a situation of crisis, because money is breaking down materially. The first story leaves the future of money open and undecided, while the second grounds money in computerised digital networks·(as opposed to traditional national currencies). In the final analysis both stories insinuate that money is disappearing from our grasp, and therefore from its native grounding.

More significantly, as a response to a sense of tangible loss, both narratives construct a history of money with which to contrast a future of cashless money. The narratives appear to be informed by a conservative reaction—as if money historically had a more authentic existence than it does currently—and the inference appears to be that the past can be retrieved through recollection. However, retrieval is solely a linguistic matter: the past can only be constructed in language.

The sentence 'A long time ago there was no such thing as money' can be analysed in order to reveal how language constructs a history. A close reading of the sentence yields a number of interpretations: it begins with a fairy tale introduction, thereby situating the story in pre-consciousness; money's original nonexistence implies transcendence—it was only a matter of time before it would exist (and this is compounded by the reader's knowledge of its existence); and finally money is defined as an object, or 'thing', so it apparently existed previously as a specific material form. Overall these three points raise a question about money, because how money arose is not explained. Was it invented as a concept, or was its inception a literal coining? In fact, *who* invented it in the first place? Is money an object that human beings were destined to have? Levi–Strauss would perhaps be convinced that money is transcendental: 'In the "upside down" world that was the state of nature before the birth of civilization, all future things had to have their counterpart, even if only in a negative form, which was a kind of guarantee of their future existence' (1979, p. 183). Effectively, if this is the case, money began as a concept, and is now returning to its original nontangible state. But because money's material form is becoming increasingly abstract, thanks to technological networks, paper and coin have become dominant icons—symbolising moneyness and suggesting a cultural impulse towards reification. 'Myth is a language,' Barthes writes, and its 'function is to distort, not to make disappear' (1989 [1957], pp. 11, 131). Thus when the forms that we perceive, or sense, such as coin or paper (which are only tokens of the concept), seem to be disappearing, we reinvent them, and their history, thereby constructing whole mythological systems.

Much postmodern interrogation is based upon the idea that there are no universal truths, and that reference is an illusion. Baudrillard, for example, maintains that 'all of Western faith and good faith was engaged in [a] wager of representation: that a sign could refer to a depth of meaning, that a sign could *exchange* for meaning and that something could guarantee this exchange—God, of course' (1989, p. 17). But Nietzsche has declared that God is dead (1974 [1882], p. 167), as does Barthes with reference to the author (1986 [1968], p. 49), so truth is individually determined. Money, like the concept of God, is an invention, but it does not have the tradition of authority that religious dogma has had. Like religion, however, money is partly a matter of faith, because there is no authentic referent for money; it can only exist conceptually, mythologically, and ideologically. Therefore, it is not a question of rejecting referentiality in terms of money's mythologies; because its existence is defined by human beings through language, it is, and never has been anything more than, a system of signs.

Of course, cultures cannot just float aimlessly about without any structure of meaning or delimitation at all. Levi–Strauss points out, 'It is absolutely impossible to conceive of meaning without order' (1978, p. 12). In a structural sense, myth is a mechanism that describes the intangible and the mysterious, and Jackson may be correct when he observes that 'because [money] features so prominently in our everyday lives we tend to overlook its essential mystery' (1994, p. 69). The Greeks converted the elements into gods such as Poseidon (the sea) and Zeus (thunder), but these labels do not explain the phenomena for which they stand. Similarly, mythology does not reveal the nature of money, it merely provides a framework that is necessary for money to continue to function. Money is not an eternal reality, it is not necessarily *necessary,* and it is perhaps for this reason that it is not conceptualised in the same ways universally. Many believe, like Buchan (1997) and Crawford (1994), that our culture has distorted money: what was originally minted in the temple of the goddess Juno *(moneta)* is now a measure of people's lives, characters, and purposes, and therefore it has lost its sacred aspects. Money, then, is fully mythologised, because it is perceived to have slipped from the sacred to the secular. But the construction of historical shifts is indicative of the belief in some circles that change (be it material or conceptual) is accompanied by a negative shift in values.

Whilst I take issue with Baudrillard on some issues, there is one that I cannot fail to mention—the *simulacrum:* 'When the real is no longer what it used to be [or what we believe it used to be], nostalgia assumes its full meaning. There is a proliferation of myths of origin and signs of reality; of second–hand truth, objectivity and authenticity. There is a panic–stricken production of the real and the referential' (1989 [1972], p. 171). Values may not appear to be as fixed as they used to be, because money itself is changing. The consequence of this is that from Baudrillard's perspective, money is the quintessential *simulacrum,* because (as with Barthesian mythology) we seem to need to construct mythologies of money's origin when its material status becomes uncertain.

In the past two decades, innovations in technology, combined with widespread government deregulation of the financial markets in the West, have provoked concern among numerous commentators, and are perceived to be threatening. Millman describes this transformation as a revolution: 'The past two decades have witnessed a revolution in finance comparable to the discovery of nuclear power in physics. Until recently it has been largely a secret revolution, little noticed beyond the financial industry' (1995, p. xi). It now appears to many commentators that the market is more prone to collapse than ever before, and that the effect of a significant stock market crash will affect more people than ever, because more people are investing in stocks and shares (Strange 1989 [1986]; Baker 1995; Kurtzman 1993; Toffler 1990).[5] Evidence of this concern can be found, not just in specific commentaries, but in all manner of texts from the *Economist* to popular fiction. Perhaps the major anxiety that arises from techno-logical systems is that money is disappearing in a material sense: it travels along digital networks, is accessed through plastic cards, and has lost its tangibility. The inference is that new forms of intangible money cannot adequately provide the foundation of a money market system, and so the whole system is weightless.

In July 1995, David Chaum, an inventor of electronic cash, addressed the U.S. House of Representatives about electronic cash (also called digicash, e–cash, e–money, or cyberbucks). He argued that electronic money, which can be exchanged only through computers and digital networks, should be seriously considered as a real payment option (Digicash 1995, http://www.digicash.nl, http://193.78.226.2/, http://www.digicash.com/).

Chaum's company, Digicash, was unsuccessful in its bid, but others such as Microsoft, Citibank, and Mondex have since been attempting to devise a viable way for electronic money to pass through digitalised computer networks without being intercepted or counterfeited. These companies are attempting to create a form of money based on encrypted codes. Concern from the press about this new form of money is on three levels: first, e–cash could facilitate money laundering; second, it could be transferred extremely quickly and therefore be exempt from taxation; and third, this money has no material foundation, and could encourage a 'competitive free–for–all', so that numerous privately owned companies could issue their own money (*Australian Financial Review* 8 Jun. 1995, p. 17). The *New Scientist*'s diagnosis is that 'anytime there is a new financial instrument, people are afraid'. (8 Apr. 1995, p. 29). But what are they afraid of? Essentially it seems that they are resistant to new monetary forms. When the *Australian Financial Review* analysed the issue, it concluded that 'E–cash, Digicash and Cybercash could transform the way we think about money' (8 Jun. 1995, p. 17). Whilst highlighting similar potential changes to our thinking, *Business Week* (12 Jun. 1995) claims that e–cash 'could [also] change consumers' financial lives and shake the foundations of global financial systems and even governments' (p.36).

There is a real sense that our monetary structures are being upended, or trans-formed, as if money had an authentic existence (sometime) prior to the end of the twentieth century, and that furthermore, this existence was not conceptual, it was material. But, economics teaches that money is pure function, it is a medium of exchange, and hence its form is immaterial. It is 'any generally accepted means of payment' which could include 'dog's teeth in the Admiralty Islands, sea shells in parts of Africa, gold during the nineteenth century. What matters is not the phys-ical commodity used, but the social convention that it will be accepted without question as a means of payment' (Begg 1991, p. 402).[6] Similarly dismissive of money's material form, the *Economist* asserts that 'money will be money whether it is constituted as a string of digits or a piece of paper or an entry in a ledger' (26 Nov. 1994, p. 27). It is therefore questionable that changes to its form (the sensible) may transform our thinking (the intelligible) as the *Australian Financial Review* and *Business Week* claim. The belief that money has a conceptual homogeneity is itself a source of alarm, because apparent consistencies are threatened by new forms, and such variances are disruptive to some mythologies.

Therefore, of all the main concerns voiced about e–money, it seems that the physical or material aspects are highlighted above issues of taxation and crime. In effect, the economic definition of money as *anything* that can be exchanged falls short in the case of electronic money, because it is not as tangible as dog's teeth or sea shells. As I perceive it, the problem is essentially one of signification. Because the label 'money' is open, it solicits a range of connotations that in turn dictate cultural activity. If money is conceptualised as power in some cultural circles, then those people who have money are seen to be powerful. But these are not the only readings of money as I shall show. Suffice it to say at this stage that the issue is a *conceptual* one, because money fulfils an exchange function—no matter what is passed on, be it physical (as in coin) or nonphysical (as in e–cash).

Furthermore, the definition of money as *anything* supports the structures of the free market system. The nature of money as a metaphorical concept does have significant implications for money management. The free market philosophy of the Western world essentially loosens monetary bounds, physically and conceptually. Since the large–scale deregulation of the Western markets in the 1970s, the invention and large scale trade in new financial instruments has been unprecedented. In the final analysis, the Western financial markets are founded upon the freedom and manoeuvrability of monetary concepts. Often the objects of financial trade bear very little equivalence to material things (I am thinking here of the myriad of derivatives or futures that are revised continually). According to the economic definition, there is no difference between an index rate future, floating currencies, or dog's teeth—they are all mediums of exchange, and can be called 'money'. The stability of our financial markets then can be analysed by unpicking its mythological structures.

Definitions of 'money' are imprecise, but money nevertheless continues to refer to a widely accepted functional concept. In terms of its exchange function, money is always metaphorical, because it stands for something else. This is the case in both trade *and* language. Economic systems are built upon the concept of money as a medium of exchange that mimics the structure of language, whereby a word represents a thing. Therefore both money and language are representations, and they are both inconsistent. That money can be *anything*—a digital impulse as much as a string of beads or a paper note—means that it is a second–order system; it has no material origin, and so it lacks consistency, except for the fact that it represents everything.

With money's threatening physical disappearance, our culture seems to demand a more structured and even more visible role for money itself, in order to detain both its material form and its value systems. In terms of the media and communication, this can be readily observed: since the late 1980s, financial reports have been a regular feature in news reporting, so that more and more people are familiar with currency and stock market fluctuations. But these reports do not actually provide accurate mappings of monetary movements; they are metaphorical. Money does not actually move *up* or *down* in value, so the reports merely provide a structure that explains what is happening to the money in people's pockets (which is probably more like 'absent' or 'present'). The exposure to monetary configurations also fails to explain the relationship we will have with money in the future.

Money is viewed from many contradictory angles, causing the commentator Gross to remark: 'the bundle of forces suggested by the subject of money and literature is frightening to me both in immensity and complexity' (1980, p. 71). Recognising this complexity, I initially narrowed my scope by limiting my study to an analysis of fictional material published since 1987: the date of a recent major stock market crash. I began by considering how a selection of popular fiction texts discusses the nature of money, thereby exposing some monetary structures to the reader. In some senses, popular fiction texts *write* history, in a Barthesian sense, because they play with the significations of money we have at our disposal. As my work progressed, it struck me that discourses of money *in all texts* are structured mythologically, because collectively they simultaneously represent, contradict, and reiterate. My focus shifted from only so–called fictional texts to encompass a wider textual field, so that this book presents a picture, a bricolage gathered from an eclectic range of texts from the Western financial arena.[7] It was Barthes's *Mythologies* that ultimately enabled me to identify the mythological monetary configuration that I perceive exists today, overtly and covertly, and I re–present some mythologies here.

My approach to money is a new one: I have gathered together readily available material, assimilated it, and then drawn out various mythological threads. In hindsight, I have followed Levi–Strauss's method of gathering disparate material and identifying a structure within that disparity. The material I scrutinise includes popular fiction, advertisements, newspaper articles, biographies, and classic texts such as Marx's *Capital* (vol. 1, 1867; vol. 2, 1885; vol. 3, 1894), Smith's *Wealth of Nations* (1776), and Simmel's (1900) *The Philosophy of Money*. I quote fairly extensively from most of my sources, because the language used is often startling in the ways it describes and structures money's significations, and in my opinion needs to be highlighted. In addition, it is my belief that if language is not questioned, elements of money's recycled mythologies cannot be clarified. I also borrow Barthes's idea that playing with language is an additional means of interrogating it, and so I occasionally use puns in order to illustrate the openness of money signs.

Some texts published in the last five years address the question of money directly: Maestro's (1993) *The Story of Money*, Crawford's (1994) *The Secret Life of Money*, Jackson's (1995) *The Oxford Book of Money*, Buchan's (1997) *Frozen Desire*, Williams's (1997) *Money: A History*, and Rowe's (1998) *The Real Meaning of Money*. It would appear that there has been a surge of interest in the subject recently.

From the perspective of popular narratives, Frey, Ridpath, Parkin, and Bronson have all recognised the potential sales to be gained from novels about the pursuit of money. All four writers have previously worked in the markets: Ridpath spent eight years as a bond trader at an international bank in London, Frey worked in corporate finance as well as in mergers and acquisitions at J. P. Morgan, and Parkin worked in the oil-broking industry and based his *Trade Secret* (1996) on that industry. Bronson too drew upon his knowledge as a trader at First Boston for his text *Bombardiers* (1995).

Frey and Ridpath in particular seem to be cashing in on a fascination with money as a subject for fiction: Ridpath has recently published three novels: *Free to Trade* (1995), *Trading Reality* (1996), and *The Marketmaker* (1998). Frey too has published three novels in three years (*The Takeover* [1995], *The Vulture Fund* [1996], and *The Inner Sanctum* [1997]). All these best-selling novels deal with characters who are willing to kill for a few million dollars. While these texts are classified as thrillers or detective novels, they have a unique factor in common: the murders, disappearances, and chases that characterise the thriller all refer to money, rather than people. Thus, in many ways the thematic concern of these texts is ultimately money's slipperiness and evasiveness.

When purchasing a popular fiction text many readers peruse the reviews, the cover, and the first few lines.[3] The brief statements on these pages are crucial for a sale and need to be overt as well as appealing to mythological structure. The titles also add to their appeal, as well as suggesting their thematic concerns. Metaphors used in some titles reveal a number of openings into the texts. 'Inner sanctums' and 'secrets' suggest that money has a hidden and impenetrable quality. 'Vulture' and 'takeover' imply the greedy and devouring aspects of money. 'Free' is a marvellously open-ended word when applied to money: it recalls money's unfettered flight from material objects, as well as a range of neoclassical economic moves such as deregulation and open markets. 'Reality' seems to conflict with the idea of free trade (as in *Trading Reality*), because reality refers to the reader's world—the everyday and mundane—which is ultimately affected by the money markets. Overall these texts imply a structure whilst simultaneously retaining an openness through which the reader can negotiate meanings of equivalences.

The first lines of these texts often set up a problem solely related to money. *The Takeover* opens: 'Life was good. Andrew Falcon was about to come into a tremendous amount of money—he hoped' (Frey 1995, p. 1). Ridpath's *Free to Trade* begins with the introduction of Paul Murray, the central character: 'I had lost half a million dollars in slightly less than half an hour and the coffee machine didn't work. This was turning into a bad day. Half a million dollars is a lot of money. And I needed a cup of coffee badly' (1995, p. 1). Ridpath's second novel starts with a similar loss: 'It didn't take much to wipe twenty million dollars off the world's bond markets. Just a small sentence' (1996, p. 1). Instantly the reader is confronted with a lack—money is either lost or imminent, which perhaps echoes the monetary mythological structure.

I have turned to Marx, Smith, and Simmel in their (albeit translated) originals, relying very little on secondary material. These foundational thinkers have focused on distinctively different aspects of money, but their influence has been significant in shaping schisms in people's convictions. Often they do not discuss money per se, because they rename it or label it for their own mythological constructions. In other words, money's first–order sign is readily used to structure discursive myths such as Marxism. That money is 'a symbolically generalized medium of communication' is likewise a sociologist's myth (Ganssman 1988, p. 285). It is simply a question of rewriting, or filling the sign with signification. To a large extent the foundations of many of our financial institutions as they exist now are thanks to some aspects of these writers' essential positions. Some of these assumptions may seem common–sensical now, but they too need to be interrogated. The layers of reinscription and revision of Smith's, Marx's, and Simmel's speculations demand an unearthing of the fantastic fictional edifice they have put into place about money, economy, and relationships. I do not wish to claim that there are no other writers who wield this kind of influence, but I am constrained by space to consider those who might be considered the most compelling.

I consider it crucial that context is kept in mind throughout my analysis, because the fictions we have now differ in terms of cultural concerns from, say, nineteenth–century texts, so the majority of my material was first published in the last decade or so. Recent technological innovations seem to be augmenting the distance money has from its natural correspondence to the material world. Money is different now, it has been 'transmogrified' (Kurtzman 1993, Preface), and our perceptions have changed as a consequence of conceptual and cultural layering. It is for this reason that I do not consider nineteenth–century texts by Poe, Austen, or Dickens, for example. These writers did confront the effects of money on their cultures, and studies by Shell (1982), Lodge (1969), and many others have almost exhausted their potential. The anxieties of Austen, for example, could be said to derive from a different cultural sentiment so that industrialisation and the 'gentrification of commercial magnates' arguably structure the central critique (Sutherland 1987, p. 97), whereas Frey, Ridpath, and Bronson critique the new deregulated financial markets.

My theoretical base, it will be noted, is perhaps as eclectic as my bricolage. I do not undertake extensive analyses of these theoretical sources; I simply take their primary tenets, and integrate them into my bricolage, testing their hypotheses against mine. On metaphor I use Lakoff and Johnson (1980) whose work on everyday metaphors is indispensable for a study of representation. Nietzsche's 'On Truth and Lie in a Nonmoral Sense' (1992 [1873]) provides the basis of my argument concerning language, metaphor, and knowledge. In essence, my central theoretical position is that meaning is created by language, not prior to it.

The hypothetical link I have constructed between money, metaphor, and myth needs a single methodological focus, which is difficult for an eclectic study. In order to test my argument that there are numerous prevalent, but distinctive, money mythologies, I have divided my material on myth under conventional literary motifs such as metaphor, narrative, and character, because each of these are representations. In addition, myths share the structures of narratives, and they have characters just as myths do. A brief outline of my chapters will clarify these points, as well as explaining the direction this book takes.

My first chapter, entitled 'Cooking the Books', brings together a range of histories from children's literature, a money gallery, advertisements, and some short narratives from Smith and Marx, as well as single sentences that construct mythological stories of money. The chapter focuses on two mythological aspects of money. The first is that our culture constructs mythic histories of money, largely in response to its perceived disappearance in the present. These histories habitually reiterate the idea that our culture began with barter, proceeded to coin and then to paper money, and ended with money's material disappearance as digital money. This narrative is effectively cyclical, so it also borrows from another mythic paradigm: the myth of the land as the source of all life and ideas, as well as cyclical change, death and renewal. My second aim in this chapter is to show how money becomes ingrained as a cultural object through our narratives, which provide us with a structured teleology or purpose. Essentially this chapter establishes the idea that money is constructed as an indispensable device, and the histories provide a framework out of which this notion of indispensability arises.

My second chapter, 'Money as a Very Important Person', considers how money is vivified in the late twentieth century. My main theoretical sources for character analysis are Amelie Rorty (1990), V. Propp (1968), and E. M. Forster (1971 [1927]). I use Forster's distinction between flat and round characters to illustrate how the reader in economic discourse is flattened into a purely economic agent, whilst money is characterised as enigmatic and lively: round in effect. My analysis reveals that because money is perceived to be dying in a material sense, it is revived as a major cultural protagonist, and hence is characterised. A textual analysis of Maestro's *The Story of Money* (1993) from a Proppian perspective is included in order to demonstrate this point. The principal effect of these two disparate characterisations, I argue, is that the reader is subordinated to the money object, and correlatively to economic systems. A section of this chapter is a consideration of *The Great Gatsby* and *The House of Mirth*, an essential undertaking if I am to demonstrate how characterisations may have shifted since the marriage of money with technology.

My third chapter, 'Heroes of Our Time', identifies how traditional mythic heroes are represented in the late twentieth century. Paradigmatic features of the hero are mapped onto a selection of fictionalised real–life characters whose wealth provides them with the figurehead attribution. Bill Gates, Warren Buffett, Leo Melamed, and George Soros are the characters I have selected for analysis; they have been variously described in biographies and the press as visionaries and gurus simply because of their distinctive relationship to money and (in some cases) the deregulated financial markets. Money is conceived in many stories of the rich as a quest; divinity and lineage are also reworked from the traditional heroic paradigm to suggest uniqueness. I show in this chapter how borrowings effectively authenticate the money myth by reifying the money concept as a figure, as well as deflecting the question of an origin.

Just as myths usually have heroes or figureheads that depict the laudable aspects of cultures, they also have rogues or villains that represent corruption. In terms of the money myth, these characters set out to make a killing on the financial markets, but fail and lose large sums of money. My fourth chapter, 'Making a Killing', outlines the ways in which these characters are condemned in our culture, because they threaten to dismantle some of money's mythological structures. Generally they are traited either as ignorant or greedy; they are characters who fail at a monetary crisis point, such as when a sudden fall in share prices occurs. I focus on two characters in this chapter: Gordon Gekko from the (1987) movie *Wall Street*, and Nick Leeson, a trader who was jailed in December 1995 for dishonest trading practices. Both these characters are constructed as villains, but Leeson is occasionally deemed to be a victim of a corrupt financial system. Because this is a recurrent perception at the moment, the ending of this chapter shifts to a brief consideration of the financial system as villain.

My fifth chapter, 'Money Is No Object' provides some metaphorical bases for money myths. According to Cawelti, 'metaphors are usually quite specific to a particular culture and period' (1976, p. 5), and so it is possible that money metaphors have changed in recent years, because the substance of money has changed.

What interests me is the way that money is represented in everyday language, and how this language may have become modified by shifts in its material form. Money 'is the one true metaphor, the one commodity that can be translated into all else' (Gioia in Jackson 1995, p. xv). It has been 'likened to oil, a cushion, a bridge, a vehicle, liberty, happiness, ritual, art, thought and time' (Jackson 1994, pp. 69–70). It is also metonymic: 'money' stands for a whole range of materials: shells, gold, coins, plastic, and digital impulses, as well as a plethora of new financial instruments such as floating rate notes and index rate futures. But, 'implicit in money's function as a universal instrument of exchange is the worrying possibility that nothing can finally be immune from money's ability to work metamorphoses' (Jackson 1995, p. xv). Once again, money, not people, is perceived to be the creator of change.

A large section of this chapter is devoted to explaining which money metaphors have provided the foundations for influential discourses, such as liberalism, Marxism, and sociology. For this reason, I devote a significant amount of space in this chapter to Smith's, Marx's, and Simmel's money metaphors. I consider (in chronological order) Smith's metaphor of the wheel, Marx's metaphors of transformation, and Simmel's metaphor of money as destroyer. The argument I wish to establish here is that the metaphors these three writers use have—through time—formed the basis of many of our linguistic monetary structures. Three key ideologies are thus identified in this chapter: namely, money is an economic tool; an agent of transformation; and finally a cognitive aid.

Money is a metaphor, which is in turn mythologised, so that we encounter phrases such as 'money is power' and 'money is a bridge'. None of the metaphors considered clarify money in an Aristotelian sense, they merely appropriate and re–present it. There is in fact no stable signified (or concept) behind the sign; there are merely certain knowledges of reality that are 'formless, unstable and nebulous' (to use Barthes's terminology [1989 [1957], pp. 128–29]). The slippage between metaphors of money and money as a metaphor, which will be noted as the book progresses, is precisely what causes myth to arise, because myth continually '[re–presents] itself' (1989 [1957], p. 129). The language of money never rests, it is contradictory, it clarifies, and it obliterates simultaneously.

My sixth, and final, chapter, 'The Discordant Market', focuses on the financial market, an imaginary space that currently structures most of our institutions. The chapter is divided into two main sections. The first continues from where the last chapter left off, and focuses on metaphors, this time of the market. The second section returns to the idea of character, and is an analysis of how the market is personified and characterised. Generally, it is either a mysterious woman (which relates to the Nietzschean idea of the Dionysian), or a rational man (which relates to the masculine Apollinian). My findings here are that the use of oppositional characterisations preclude a unified identity for the market.

The financial market is metaphorised quite diversely, but most metaphors are naturalising. For example, the market is considered to be subject to cycles and harmonious rhythms, metaphors that naturalise by borrowing ideas about the seasons and spiritual vision, as narratives do. Being a good trader means being on the pulse, and being able to predict the market's direction. Metaphors of the market are often designed to delimit, but they fail in some instances, perhaps because the market is not a distinct space. A brief section of this chapter is devoted to spatial metaphors in Bronson's *Bombardiers*, which consistently contradict each other and therefore fail to throw up a single dominant idea, and this causes the reader to recognise crisis, because language alone cannot contain the effects of the structures we have built, which are based on mythologies.

NOTES

1. The Western world as I define it is made up of the countries that operate free markets and complex monetary trading systems; some would call the Western world 'capitalist'.

2. In *Language and Myth,* Cassirer maintains that mythical thinking is metaphorical thinking: 'No matter how widely the content of myth and language may differ the same form of mental conception is operative in both. It is the form which one may denote as *metaphorical thinking*' (1953 [1946], p. 84). Metaphor and myth are characterised as equivalences.

3. The relationship between individual actors and ideology is complex. Briefly, my position echoes Hindess's (1986): 'Actors make decisions and act accordingly, but they do so on the basis of the discursive means and means of action available to them. To a large extent those means are not a matter of choice. Actors can and sometimes do work to change how they (and others) think, but they cannot adopt entirely new discursive forms quickly or at will. Readers who doubt this are invited to try purging their thinking of the effects of literacy' (p. 123). There are, of course, a range of possible responses to all texts, and so the notion of active readers should be considered. Money's mythologies, while familiar because of their ubiquity, nevertheless can be resisted—perhaps by the reader's own identification of unstable significations. In addition, as mythologies work *through* us (as individuals with different backgrounds, concerns, and hence differing interpretive frameworks), they can be opened up, questioned, and modified. Wells's analysis of Williamson highlights the active role readers have in mythological construction: 'Since ideology works through people, surely there must be points of tension between mythological systems and experienced realities which offer possibilities for resistance and change' (1992, p. 173). My overall position considers that readers can resist ideologies and mythologies, but they do so only with the means available to them.

4. I use the terms 'seem' and 'appear' a great deal, because I am identifying perceptions, and it is unavoidable as a qualifying gesture.

5. The cover story of Australia's *Bulletin* (22 Jul. 1997) is about changes to the Australian market since the 1987 'crash'. The article highlights the considerable growth

in share investment whereby 34 percent of Australia's population own shares, and it makes the claim that thanks to extensive media coverage of the financial markets 'Australians have become much more financially literate' (22 Jul. 1997, p. 16).

6. Begg's text is an economics educational textbook. It has also been used as the primary source for defining 'economics', 'economic efficiency', 'monetary policy', 'money creation', and 'money supply' in the *Fontana Dictionary of Modern Thought* (1990). It is thus considered an authoritative and illuminating resource for the clarification of economic ideas.

7. My position on narrative echoes Chambers's, and therefore 'nonliterature' (such as Marx's *Capital*) is considered to be equally fictionalised: 'that one person's "fact" is another's "fiction"; that what is "information," "history," "knowledge," et cetera for one period or culture is read, in another, as "fiction," "literature," "imagination," et cetera' (1984, p. 219).

8. The marketing of books on money begins on the text's surface, and so front and back covers and reviews can plausibly draw on the appeal of money's mythologies. According to Philips and Tomlinson (1992, p. 26): 'The act of choosing to buy or borrow and of reading a book may be a private experience, but the network of publishing hype, library categorisation and criticism within which these choices are made, belong to a wider cultural ideology'.

1

Cooking the Books

Money is primarily a metaphor with inconsistent mythological configurations, so that money can be a tool as well as a cushion, for example. The structures of language hold money's concepts together. The signifiers of money can take a range of forms from coin to sea shells to dog's teeth, but none of these objects are money's sole material referent. In addition, because money's material form is shifting to intangible digital bits, so–called established configurations are threatened. Money is a virtuality or even nonexistent; as a consistent material form it can exist only in language, and this language is readily adaptable and translatable into countless second–order or mythological signs. In this chapter I elucidate some aspects of money's mythologisation in narratives. By consider-ing a selection of (his)stories I will show that money does not have a deter-minable history; rather, it is mythologically historicised: mythological histories make money appear to have been a naturally evolving phenomenon, rather than a concept. Histories of money also naturalise; they construct money as tran-scendental, as well as presupposed and necessary to experience. Considering myth in Barthes's terms, it 'gives [things] a natural and eternal justification, it gives them a clarity which is not that of an explanation but that of a statement of fact' (1989 [1957], p. 156).

The structures of money that we currently participate in are born out of money mythologies that construct money as necessary to culture. Money has a history that we have been in the process of constructing for approximately the

last two hundred years, but a renewed urgency recently has resulted in a proliferation of texts which maintain money's centrality in our culture.

In the main, the histories we construct of money are largely justifications for
money's importance to us; they establish money as a cultural necessity that needs
to be maintained (both in the sense of preserved and overhauled). Attwood quotes
Plumb on the issue of historical legitimisation: ' "From the earliest days of
recorded time" human beings have "used the past in a variety of ways" (and "the
sense of the past [was] usually linked in human consciousness with a sense of the
future")' (1996, p. vii). The histories are mythological accounts that partially
explain why money is necessary *now,* as well as focusing on the evolution of the
money *form* as the basis of these fictions. The meta– (or grand) narrative of these
texts relates to a monetary quest, because money is always elusive. But we continue to pursue it—in our lives and in our stories. Essentially the myth implies
that we need money, but precisely *what it is* and *why it has a centrality* is never
altogether clear. Neither is the outlook for the future, because nobody knows
what form money might take. Several binary oppositions can be discerned in the
money narratives that appear intertextually, such as profit/loss, give/take,
gain/loss, surplus/lack, and excess/absence, to name a few. Money's configurations are always threatened by their opposites.

A recent text entitled *Three Dollars* is an example of a money narrative: the
plot demands a resolution of the initial lack of money that occurs at the beginning of the text: 'Every nine and a half years I see Amanda, each time it is always
and everywhere exceptional. Most recently was today. I had three dollars'
(Perlman 1998, p. 1). The reader is expected to retain the idea of money's
absence and hoped for presence as the plot unfolds. Money narratives such as
these are permeated by commercialism, or a kind of surplus profit, and the redun-
dancy of money signifiers is excessive, persistently serving as a reminder of the
monetary quest.[1]

For some, the money quest is intrinsic to human behaviour. Many texts are
informed by the fictitious notion that money has an eternal signification so that
early people thought of money as we do. For economists, and Adam Smith[2] in
particular, the pursuit of money, and hopefully its capture, is the linchpin of their
philosophy: 'There is scarce perhaps a single instant in which any man is so perfectly and completely satisfied with his situation as to be without any wish of
alteration or improvement of any kind. An augmentation of fortune is the means
by which the greater part of men propose and wish to better their condition'
(1986 [1776], p. 441). It is essential to bear in mind Smith's idea that satisfaction
is rarely achieved, because this idea constructs the quest as endless, and mythologies relating to monetary acquisition can never be finished.

ECONOMIC NARRATIVES

The texts I consider in this chapter are generally nonfictional, because they supposedly deal with historical subject matter. But, as I maintain, these histories form part of money's mythology. The perspective informing these representative texts (which is not conspiratorial, but representative) is decidedly economic: they are accounts that reinforce money's *essential* function in our culture. But they use a formal narrative to structure money's elusiveness, and these two threads, form and function, cause a rupture, because they lead to quite distinctive configurations. In many respects these texts do not require temporal ordering at all, because they enforce money's functionality (or its status as a metaphorical medium of exchange) above its form.

Money (his)stories enforce money's importance to our culture, thereby solidifying relationship structures—especially commercial ones—and they do this in two ways. Some texts I probe in this chapter organise history around a particular money story–which I call *economic* narratives. They are largely speculative (after all no one knows how money actually originated, if it did at all). Their story could be summarised thus: the human race did not originally have money, but now it does, albeit in an incomprehensible form. This type of narrative pinpoints structures on which to hang the origin, and consequently the continued existence of a central character—money. It makes a tradition of a particular fictional chronology: barter–coin–paper–digicash, as I will show below. These are mythological histories of money that deal directly with money as a subject and object, generally stressing money's material presence or form above its transcendent conceptual nature.

Another kind of narrative, which I call a *money* narrative, has money woven into its structure (so that it revolves around the processes of loss and gain). Because money is a quest object, it has a cultural metaphorical status as a bridge (to an ameliorated future), and therefore monetary possession seems to enable the fulfilment of goals. This particular configuration of money encourages and enforces certain cultural desires and behaviours. The proliferation of differing money narratives (particularly in advertisements) *may* be indicative of a cultural need for quests—a search for a purpose in a fractured postmodern world. Conversely, it may also be an ideological mechanism that sanctions the financial leaning of our culture.

We use both sorts of narratives concurrently to establish and retain a historical reality for our current monetary culture. After all, the foundations of our monetary institutions are dependent upon the perpetuation of two ideas: money is transcendental, and money acquisition is essential. In the final analysis, these ideas depend upon the continuing and unquestioned belief in its configurations and endless representations; and translations and signs of money enforce the idea that money is a necessity.

Both money's history and its signs are present in a wide range of texts. In order to sketch some of the ways money is granted a decisive omnipotence, as well as a centrality in many narratives, I consider an eclectic selection of texts in this chapter: single sentence advertisements (which draw upon received ideas, or what Chambers calls 'narrative situation' [1984, p. 4]), short narratives by Marx and Smith (who build their political and philosophical ideologies as they construct their narratives), and some children's stories, that reiterate the economic money myth—including Maestro's *The Story of Money*. These texts constitute a common–sensical, unquestioned, but shaky history of money, and are what Barthes calls 'collective [representations]' (1982 [1977], p. 165). They are culturally determined, and endlessly reiterated, each one configuring and representing money's presence.

Some narratives seek to explain the historical relationship of human beings to money's developing form. It will be shown in this chapter that there is not a single 'abstractable' story of money, which in some ways could undermine my point about money as a linguistic construct or (later) as a fictional character. Because of money's openness, its narratives systematically structure the varying relationships between people and work, people and physical objects, as well as people and money, in many ways, but their overarching discourse currently is economic. Money can be readily assimilated into any discourse, because money is materially nonspecific. It is precisely this indeterminacy that creates tensions in some narratives: the blurring of physical boundaries encourages money to mutate conceptually, which in turn demands a tightly structured rationalised narrative to control its shifting form.

Narrative structures suppress money's physical flight by containing it within a story frame. I concentrate on the tensions in these narratives brought about by the numerous physical forms that money takes, and the implications of these shifts for economics, which endorses change but denies a monetary essence. In the next section I consider two very unembellished advertisements to illustrate my point about common–sensically received ideas. Monetary ideologies and connotations inform the policies, thinking, and construction of our culture, but they are subsumed under disparate modes of presentation or signs as I shall elucidate.

THE GAMBLING ADVERTISEMENT

Money infiltrates an astonishingly large array of texts, and signs of money are naturalised by virtue of their insistent presence, but they may tend to be unnoticed because they appear commonplace or customary. To begin with, there are signs of money (such as images of paper notes) that are omnipresent, appearing in all kinds of advertisements—in banks, on billboards, and on television. It is perhaps because of this omnipresence that money signs are rarely scrutinised. *Mythologies* maintains that the purpose of myth is to distort, and distortion constitutes an ideology: money must be conceptually, and culturally secured (Barthes 1989 [1957], p. 131). Advertisements in particular fulfil this function: 'Ideology is the meaning made necessary by the conditions of society while helping to perpetuate those conditions' (Williamson 1978, p. 13) .

My first example is one I encountered at the end of April 1997 outside a branch of the Australian TAB (Totaliser Administration Board), a government–run gambling chain that is in the process of being privatised. An eye–catching poster outside the shop asserts: 'Some pastimes are more rewarding than others'. It has photographic images of a (fishing) fly, a golf ball and tee, and then, at the bottom, a pile of $20 notes. Barthes maintains that 'captions help [the reader] to choose the correct level of perception' (1982 [1977], pp. 39–40). The pile of money notes is the subject of this ad; it is the interpellator. The reader is expected to reconstruct a meaning based upon the interrelationship of sporting signs, money, and reward.

Essentially, the advertisement implies both that gambling can provide the reader with money and time for recreation, and that gambling is more (financially) rewarding than golf (play) or fishing (food). Therefore money is the primary provider of gratification. Ultimately then, the message is directed at the pile of notes as the source of satisfaction. Statistically, however, it is more likely that the reader would get a hole–in–one or catch a good-sized fish than win a pile of money through gambling. The signification constructed from these signs is a reworking of both the 'time is money' cliche as well as the idea that money is a quest object, but it needs visual signs to be effective.

The image of money notes is compulsive, and to some extent it defers the pursuit of money because it is already there visually; it has a ready presence. Thomson's article, 'follow the money', investigates the image of piles of money in cinematic texts. He writes, 'I have been noticing the frequency of what I take to be the most reverent, erotic, and fatal image on the American screen now. You see it everywhere, not just in movies, but in so many television commercials. It is there, over and over, like the answer, the dream, the destination, and the question. There is a whispered or felt "yes", as if to say, this is it, this is us, and the mystery of the play' (1995, p. 21). It is, he explains, 'the great orgasmic passing of Go' (1995, p. 22). Images of money combat its absence, whilst simultaneously affirming its presence.

My second example is an Australian Gold Lotto [lottery] advertisement that appeared on buses in Brisbane in May 1997. It reads simply: 'STOP WORK!' Underneath this minimal caption is the Gold Lotto logo: a rainbow. The advertisement only needs four signs (stop, work, exclamation point, and rainbow), because it draws upon a range of established concepts about the reader's relationship to money. In fact, the two simple words form a complete ideological fiction, and it is one in which we all participate: that work is a toil, it is not pleasurable, but money can liberate us from the daily grind as well as change our lives—if only we could reach the pot of gold at the end of the rainbow. This advertisement, like the previous TAB ad, is aimed towards the gambling market, and cultivates what Bloom calls 'unearned unlimited wealth myths' (1996, p. 161). Accordingly, working for money is a necessary evil, but the idea of cruising around the world in a yacht, drinking champagne—in short, being the idle rich—is both compelling and overpowering. Money is given a liberating power, a potential to relieve drudgery, and the overall implication is that we are all in the same boat—our lives are dreary, but money can change them.

Ideas about the centrality of *money* in relation to work and people are recent to our culture, becoming entrenched after the industrialisation of the nineteenth century. According to Bauman (1992), 'throughout the first (modern) part of its history, capitalism was characterized by the central position occupied by work simultaneously on the individual, *social,* and *systemic* levels. Indeed, work served as the link holding together individual motivation, social integration and systemic reproduction, as the major institution responsible for their congruence and co-ordination' (p. 49). Bauman goes on to suggest that consumerism has taken over the place of work in 'life-worlds' (1992, p. 49). But both these social configurations are dependent upon the prior existence of money economies.

The idea of work as onerous has been challenged by Lane's (1991) *The Market Experience.* According to Lane, not only can work be satisfying, but it can also organise and enrich all aspects of our lives. Evidence of this sentiment can be found in anecdotal accounts of lottery winners. Hunter Davies's *Living on the Lottery* identifies several people who have become suddenly wealthy thanks to the U.K. lottery, but who choose to continue to work. One winner told Davies, 'People are surprised I'm still working, and tell me I must be mad, but I enjoy it' (1996, p. 290). A similar view was expressed by Sergei Martini, a garbage collector who won A\$ 12 million and told the *Courier Mail*: '"I'm not the kind of guy to stay at home and do nothing"' (29 Jan. 1997, p. 17). Therefore, to some extent, economic theoretical assumptions should be 'more respectful of vernacular accounts of experience' (Jensen and Pauly 1997, p. 167).[3]

Money does not satisfy or humanise, even though we are encouraged to believe so by monetary images and narratives. Many of us may have become consumers of the myth so that, as Bauman validly suggests, 'Reality, as the consumer experiences it, is a pursuit of pleasure [and] seduction may now take the place of repression as the paramount vehicle of systemic control and integration' (1992, pp. 50–51). But, in fact, the promise of money and its effects on the outcomes in our lives has the potential to be repressive, by constructing our needs for us. The spectacle of money as well as its image in the first advertisement is misleading and detrimental; it forestalls critical judgment about real needs and desires. Money can not change our lives, but we can assent to the conceptual frameworks we give it.

Our debt to Adam Smith and Karl Marx for particular ideas about work and monetary renumeration can be made quite manifest. In the next section of this chapter I show how work, money, and 'free' time are tied together by these two cultural analysts, and in so doing I highlight parts of their intellectual legacies. I do not wish to suggest for a moment that Smith and Marx are the *only* writers to wield cultural influence, but they can certainly be accredited with persuasive aspects of our current ideological systems, which are effectively monetary palimpsests.

A PRODUCT OF MY TIME

I have chosen two short extracts for analysis—narratives in themselves—one from Smith, and one from Marx. The choice was largely dictated by a need to be brief, but also by the fact that they share a thematic feature: both extracts are concerned with young people defined by their work. However, these narratives differ quite distinctly in their ideological positions. I turn first to an extract from Smith's *An Inquiry into the Nature and Causes of the Wealth of Nations*, taken from a section entitled 'On Division of Labour':

In the first fire engines, a boy was constantly employed to open and shut alternately the communication between the boiler and the cylinder, according as the piston either ascended or descended. One of those boys, who loved to play with his companions, observed that, by tying a string from the handle of the valve which opened this communication to another part of the machine, the valve would open and shut without his assistance, and leave him at liberty to divert himself with his play–fellows. One of the greatest improvements that had been made upon this machine, since it was first invented, was in this manner the discovery of a boy who wanted to save his own labour. (1986 [1776], pp. 114–15)

Smith's story is clearly rhetorical: it celebrates human ingenuity and inventiveness. The 'boy' is anonymous, and could be taken as representative of the whole human race. But he is also a child, and correlatively possesses naive inclinations. The context of the story is vague—when was this? 'The first fire engines', like first money forms, are subsumed in an ahistorical past, and the character is generalised. The boy who 'loved to play with his companions' is a sentiment we are supposed to share. This characterisation is where the persuasive economic argument surfaces: wouldn't we all rather be playing than working? The reader is left to assume that the boy is working for money, so that he can be fed and clothed. The drudgery of performing his task is reiterated in mechanical language, such as 'open' and 'shut', 'ascend' and 'descend'. The boy is characterised as a reluctant worker, and his suggested innocence makes this characterisation a seemingly   natural one. The resolution, brought about by ingenious forethought is that he is now at 'liberty to divert himself with his play-fellows'—a more rewarding pastime.

The 'discovery' of the labour–saving string device led to the saving of his labour, and he did not presumably have to sacrifice income for this diversion. Invention is inherent to human beings, no more so than with the concept of money. Smith's story grafts the concept of work seamlessly onto the concept of money, so that they are both productive. The story is a model constructed by Smith, that enables him to express the conflict between leisure and work in terms that he needs to support his system of ideas. In addition, the neat resolution makes the story satisfying, inferring that obstacles can be made short work of.

It is worth noting briefly, as a preamble to my focus on character in chapters 2, 3, and 4, that the boy is partially constructed as a heroic figure by the narrative: he has overcome a difficult obstacle successfully, and is rewarded for his hardship. Character constructs such as Smith's are vital to the whole gamut of money mythologies and histories, because they are conversion, or anthropomorphisms, of money's ideologies.

This narrative from Marx is found in the section entitled 'The Working Day' in *Capital,* volume 1[4]:

In the last week of June 1863, all the London daily papers published a paragraph with the 'sensational' heading, 'Death from simple over-work'. It dealt with the death of the milliner, Mary Anne Walkley, 20 years old, employed in a highly respectable dressmaking establishment, exploited by a lady with the pleasant name of Elise. The old, often-told story was now revealed once again. These girls work, on an average, 16½ hours without a break, during the season often 30 hours, and the flow of their failing 'labour power' is maintained by occasional supplies of sherry, port or coffee. It was the height of the season. It was necessary, in the twinkling of an eye, to conjure up magnificent dresses for the noble ladies invited to the ball in honour of the newly imported Princess of Wales. Mary Anne Walkley had worked uninterruptedly for 26½ hours, with sixty other girls, thirty in each room. The rooms provided only ⅓ of the necessary quantity of air, measured in cubic feet. At night the girls slept in pairs in the stifling holes into which a bedroom was divided by wooden partitions. And this was one of the better millinery establishments in London. Mary Anne Walkley fell ill on the Friday and died on Sunday, without, to the astonishment of Madame Elise, having finished off the bit of finery she was working on. (Marx, 1990 [1867], pp. 364–65)

Unlike Smith's story, Marx's is immediate. The story has a specific date (four years prior to the publication of *Capital,* vol. 1), and the character is named. For his contemporaries the story seems to have a real and immediate reference. Marx's text is a story of a story: it relays a news item, but includes ironic narrative comment. The story concerns the death of a young milliner, but it is a sensationalised and 'old, often–told story', and Marx participates in this reiteration. The terms 'highly respectable', 'better millinery establishments', and 'pleasant name' refer to those people who are responsible for Walkley's death. The text contrasts these traits with descriptions of the stifling airless partitioned holes in which the girls work for 16½ hours without a break. Repetition for Marx is related to time (whereas Smith used mechanical description to explain repetitiveness): Walkley worked uninterruptedly for 26½ hours. Thirty hours of work during the season is contrasted with the 'twinkling of an eye'. In addition, the ball and the conjuring trick prompt fairy tale analogies with Cinderella and the glass slipper, so that the text positions the exploiters in a fantasy world. Marx reverses the niceties of fairy tale conventions by inferring that this fantasy world is villainous, through his ironic characterisations, and so the imaginary world of the ball is contrasted with Walkley's reality.

The death of Walkley and her unfinished work is an interesting one in terms of unresolved endings. Marx's story, unlike Smith's, concludes with crisis and irresolution. Like his own work, the story has no conclusive ending. Marx died before he could complete *Capital,* vol. 3, and the final sentence is left open: '(At this point the manuscript breaks off.—F. E.)' [1991 [1894], p. 1026). The reader then is left with a chapter entitled 'Class' that is scarcely begun, therefore the ideology of class conflict from Marx's perspective is left unresolved. The class issue, like the Walkley story, has to be completed by the reader. In terms of grand economic narratives, endings are rarely resolved. It is almost as if money precludes resolution, because it is an inadequate determining vehicle. We really do know—as our stories indicate—that money does transport us to paradise, and that it is not the *summum bonum.*

Without wishing to tread on any essentialist arguments about the value or the division of labour for example, I have to state that 'the bottom line' in both Marx's and Smith's stories concerns money, but its guise has shifted from money to labour. As I shall explain in chapter 5, metaphors of money are merely conceptual, but they provide the building blocks of self-contained ideologies. Whilst money is not mentioned explicitly in either extract, an ideological reading reveals its presence: Walkley, Mme. Elise, and the working boy are all involved in making money. Therefore, even though it is only implied, money is fundamental to the structure of these narratives in terms of plot and character. We could rephrase the ideology as syllogisms such as the following:

People need food,
Money buys food
Therefore people need money.

and

People need money,
Work generates money
Therefore people must work.

Of course, these syllogisms are not stories. They do not contain events, but they are self-contained ideological statements. The idea that money is a necessity (in whatever form) moulds most of the conceptual frameworks noted in this book.

The syllogisms are also logical cul–de–sacs: there seems to be little or no maneuverability within the boundaries of money reasoning. Soros, a wealthy currency speculator (whom I discuss in chapter 3 as a visionary hero), explains that our culture fails to break away from established conventions: 'Changeless society is characterized by the absence of alternatives. There is only one set of circumstances the human mind has to deal with: the way things are. While alternatives can be imagined, they appear like fairy tales, because the path that would lead to them is missing' (1995, p. 255). Ironically, perhaps, Soros himself participates in the way things are: he is renowned in some circles for his ability to profit from our current financial system. Even though he attempts to distance himself from the system, he is appropriated by it, as well as appropriating money from it. From this perspective, all conceptual alternatives are simply exchanges, or substitutions, within monetary systems. Money has become conceptually institutionalised.

Money is a *necessary* object, because it is only with money that we are able to purchase necessities (or luxuries if we are fortunate enough to gather a surplus). Neither Smith's nor Marx's story could be told without the subtext of money: value and labour are determined (albeit randomly) by money. The basic assumption, 'people need money', informs the structure of *all the narratives* I am considering: the only difference being in outcome.

I turn now to some children's (his)tories of money, because these texts are significant in terms of money's socialisation. While Smith and Marx provide the basis for some party-political thinking, children's stories pave the way for money's continued existence. To some extent if we teach children the importance of money, then we are also ensuring that its future is cultivated. How is the relationship between people and money explained to children—to whom we hand down concepts? Is money mythologised in these stories? Does it structure the plot? Maestro considers money concepts to be the same all over the globe (1993, p. 40), but it is not that ideas about *money* are the same, rather the ideologies of free markets and monetary acquisition are incessantly duplicated in texts. Children's stories of money form a vital function in terms of the naturalisation of money.

MONEY'S FAIRY TALE

The children's texts are labelled 'stories' of money. But rather than simply being stories, they are histories–in–the–making, with fabricated chronologies. I will use these instructive texts to highlight the tensions I perceive to exist in money's mythic history: while these texts legitimise money's dominant position, they also vacillate inconsistently between a focus on form on the one hand, and an explanation of the concept, on the other.

A forced chronology is imposed on money by Kain (1994, *The Story of Money*), Maestro (1993, *The Story of Money*), and Cribb (1990, *MONEY*) as part of these texts' mythologisation. These three texts construct a history that implants notions of economic causality in terms of people's developing relationship to money. Readers often expect stories to contain a distinct beginning, middle, and end, but this Aristotelian formula cannot work for the story of money. Money has no single moment of inception, and the notion of its beginnings is erroneous. In addition, the configuration of money's material is never constant, so therefore the chronological structure of these stories is puzzling. If money began as a concept, which was later manifest in coin, then in paper, and latterly in electronic bits, then money is anything and nothing: it is thought reiterated in tangible terms. No evolution occurs.

Despite the fact that these three children's books are ideologically structured around the functional aspects of money, as a medium of exchange, the actual structure informing these stories relates to money's stative, material changes, and this chronology structures the shadowy money concept in an accepted plot progression. The stories trace the development of money from barter to coin to paper to electronic money. Money is conceptually and historically consolidated by the tenacious idea that originally it bore a direct relationship to the land.

It could also be said that both barter and electronic money are synonymous with *no money*, so that these *nonforms* provide evidence of nothing other than money concepts and systems. The effect of this recurrence is that the overall structure of their texts becomes circular, with beginnings meeting ends. Narrative and metaphor in these texts are mutually supportive: both are shaped by the circle, and the origin and the end are deferred. The emphasis on material form has significant repercussions for these narratives. In narrative terms the Aristotelian beginning–middle–end conflicts in these texts with the circular structure of the narrative, and this is because of the subject matter: money. A single history of money (and indeed money itself) is nonexistent outside linguistic structure, and Reid poetically explains the self-containment of stories: 'We make our world go round by chasing our tales' (1992, p. 1).

Kain starts her story with 'long ago' (1994, p. 4), echoing the fairy tale 'once upon a time'. Maestro's text is similarly indeterminate as we have previously seen:

in the dim distant past, money did not exist (Maestro 1993, p. 3). Both stories begin with little definition, but as they progress, they come to be structured by economic concepts. Economic terminology infiltrates without notification. Maestro's tale is essentially an economic story of money, so its new name, medium of exchange, as well as assumptions about its necessary function, is foisted upon the young reader: 'The merchants looked for a new *medium of exchange,* something that people everywhere would accept in trade [my emphasis]' (Maestro 1993, p. 14). The compliant tone suggests universal acceptance of money, so the reader is expected to give an impressed nod to money's cultural refinement.

In Maestro's text, money begins with a mere conceptual shape *by virtue of* its material absence, and the narrative guides us through the increasingly complex manifestations of money's material forms. The reader can rest assured that the absence will be reversed; after all, reading from the present position he or she knows that money eventually surfaces both conceptually and physically. The whole of Maestro's first page works through a number of core oppositions around the contrast between primitive and contemporary states that goad the reader into accepting the advantages of money: early humans wore animal skins, they lived in small groups, they killed for food—but we do not. In this way, the opening of Maestro's text sets up her designated causes of upcoming events: the scale and size of our dealing *has to change,* and the first page anticipates this development.

The function of money in these stories is to sow a seed, or '[plant] an element that will come to fruition later', as Barthes explains it (1982 [1977], p. 89). In other words, the concept of money is introduced and expanded on, and its conceptual connotations gradually multiply. (This is notably the case inside the text, and outside it in terms of money's socialisation.) The nonexistence of money at the beginning of this text is hard to explain without reference to its name. Thus we find that on occasions when money is absent, the imperative seems to be to make its existence felt by naming it, and assuring its presence early on. The beginning of this story is where the tensions between money concept and money form are glaringly obvious. It appears that money has two distinct aspects, one relating to its physicality and the other to its simplicity as an idea, but together they constitute a mythology.

In mythological systems, the signifier becomes both 'form' and 'meaning' (Barthes 1989 [1957], p. 126). Form is 'the letter' or word money (Barthes 1989 [1957], p. 127), whereas meaning constitutes its values. Meaning 'postulates a kind of knowledge, a past, a memory, a comparative order of facts, ideas, decisions' (Barthes 1989 [1957], p. 127). Barthes characterises myth as a 'constant game of hide–and–seek' (1989 [1957], p. 128) whereby 'the meaning is always there to present the form; the form is always there to *outdistance* the meaning. And there is never any contradiction, conflict or split between the meaning and the form: they are never at the same place' (1989 [1957], p. 133). Thus, the tension between money's form and its signification is constantly being played.

The concept of money as a mechanism of exchange *seems* to have always existed, and barter is a case in point. Despite the tactile signs of money, barter continues to be viewed as a 'money system' (Maestro 1993, pp. 21, 30, 38), so that there is nothing contradictory in the rationale that today nations may trade cattle for cars or rice for clothing. No actual money changes hands in these trades, but the monetary concept is still present despite a return to the primitive bartering state. Maestro explicitly states that barter continues to exist in many areas (1993, p. 19). So what is the money system, and could it be said to be the same as the barter system, within which no money changes hands?

Texts do not generally let money disappear altogether, because without some trace money's mythological signification would not be possible. Cribb's text makes the claim that 'it is difficult to imagine a world without money' (1990, p. 6), and this suggestion is endorsed by a page full of money images: a wallet full of various currencies, a credit card, coins, stones, pieces of metal, scales, and weights.[5] The connotation of this remark is that anything can be money, even though the images are based upon the idea of *moneyness*. As an 'eyewitness guide', Cribb's text is heavily reliant upon description and visual imagery to infer money's tangibility: 'Money can be many different things this even applies to things you cannot see or feel [it can be] as heavy as stone, as light as a feather' (1990, p. 8). That money has a weight conceptually and physically can further be implied by this remark. Cribb's image also plays with accepted ideas of moneyness. Because notes and coins are the more familiar signs of money, the reader is forced to undertake a process of sorting the real from the token, so that ultimately the paper notes are the dominant signifiers. The disparate images of forms of money are supposed to illustrate the idea that money can be anything, but the notion is contradicted by a later image of '10,000 one–hundred dollar bills in [a] pile', and so a return to the familiar, represented image is inevitable (1990, p. 26). Cribb implicitly identifies contradictions inherent in the story of money: its form is difficult to totalise and the precise materialisation of money is hard to locate, so his story (as with the others) resorts to 'enforced visualization', a strategy Chatman considers to be intrusive in cinematic character construction, but which seems to be mandatory here (1980, p. 118).

Both Kain's and Maestro's narratives include some rudimentary technical description with their functional analysis, which explains how money is literally made. Next to one illustration, Kain writes: 'The people in this mint are making coins by hand' (1994, p. 13). Maestro describes coining more elaborately: 'After steel presses punch out the blank coin shapes, the design is stamped, or "struck" onto each "blank". All United States coins have two sayings stamped on them: E PLURIBUS UNUM (Latin for "out of many, one"), and IN GOD WE TRUST'

(1993, p. 33). This gesture is a notional acknowledgment of the need to nominate, visualise and understand money's form not just its function—you can not have one without the other. In addition, the stamping of references to the sacred, and to American democratic structures, is ideological overdeterminism.

Representations of paper money are similarly elaborate in some texts. Kain's description, for example, reads: 'The Chinese invented paper money more than 4,000 years ago. It was printed with blue ink on paper made from the mulberry tree' (1994, p. 19). The form of this paper money is shown to be of a specific colour and to have derived from the land (the mulberry tree) as if these factors render the form more cognisant for the juvenile reader. Not only does paper money derive from the land, but it also has an indigenous quality. By implication, national money is special and unique—unlike digital money, which knows no boundaries.

For most accounts, the use of moulded or manufactured precious metals (such as coins or bullion) in exchange seems to mark the appearance of money proper. For Kain the coins first minted about 2,700 years ago mark the beginning of the story of money (1994, p. 10). For Maestro, the Sumerians were the first to make money out of metal, and they did so for reasons of convenience (1993, pp. 18, 15). But as Davies reminds us, 'the question of when coins were "invented" depends very largely on one's definition of a coin' so that economists and numismatists, for example, would each regard coin differently (1995, pp. 55–56). In addition, whether coin is the original form of money is debatable, and depends upon the reader's perspective. But value derives from the scarcity of its material composition, as well as from its convenience in terms of size, and these factors are generally deemed to be intrinsic characteristics of money proper. For these reasons the middle section of most children's stories of money are laden with descriptions of money. Therefore, form gives the concept a structure, but there are many forms. No configuration of money represents money definitively, but all aspects point towards money's ideology: coin is indigenous and convenient, and paper money is national as well as artfully fabricated. But none of these money representations are lasting or determinate.

Maestro devotes a whole page to the disposal of paper money and coins. The illustration features a man throwing wads of banknotes into a furnace, and the commentary explains that old money notes are incinerated when they wear out, and in the same way coins are liquified and reused (Maestro 1993, p. 35). Whenever money is made, destruction is imminent. As Marx explains it, 'For coin, the road from the mint is also the path to the melting pot' (1990 [1867], p. 222). So, each time money is made, it is ready to be destroyed. It could be said that money has an inherent self-destructive mechanism: each time a meaning or form is fabricated, its applicability expires. While money is essentially protean, because its form mutates, its functional aspect persists conceptually.

Most of the children's texts focus on the countries that seemed to dominate the monetary scene in particular epochs, such as Sumer, so their stories establish knowledge about financial hegemony or currency domination. An example mentioned in my introduction can also be read from the perspective of national currency boundaries: 'Once upon a time, money was measured in pounds, shillings and pence. Then it moved on to dollars and cents. Now money is 1s and 0s' (*Australian Financial Review,* 25 Sept. 1995, p. 27). The story is very much like the others, beginning like a fairy tale and then focusing on a specific aspect of money. In this case, the story tracks the historical pattern of currency domination in the pre–decimal era in England (or Australia perhaps) to the United States. But the ending of the story frees money from national arenas as well as people's hands, thereby implying that money has lost its indigenous ties.[6]

Eco believes that reading draws upon a presupposed 'encyclopedia' (cited in Rimmon–Kenan 1983, p. 117), and material from the section marked 'money' is often drawn upon when we read, particularly as adults. So far in this chapter I have attempted to pull together those aspects that could be presented under an imaginary 'money' entry: its images, its forms, and its representations—in advertisements and in informative children's texts. I have tried to bring together bits of information about money that are not generally understood as being unified, but exist in discourse as a *sociolect.*[7] My argument rests upon one central assumption: that texts depend upon certain naturalised cultural assumptions that are either recalled or explicitly restated. These assumptions are an intrinsic part of money's mythologies. Furthermore, these premises are by no means reflective of actual historical reality, rather they are mythological representations.

Presupposed knowledge about money can also work at the level of a single sentence. After all, as Barthes argues in 'Structural Analysis of Narratives', 'A discourse is a long "sentence" just as a sentence is a short "discourse"' (1982 [1977], p. 83). Some examples will demonstrate the interconnectedness and unshakeable tenacity of certain money configurations, that constitute parts of our mythological money encyclopedia.

SINGLE SENTENCE NARRATIVES

One way of illustrating my argument about the interconnectedness of money and narrative is to consider how money unwittingly collaborates in narrative theory itself. Rimmon–Kenan begins her discussion of narrative by setting up the theoretical opposition between state and event in stories. She writes: 'A narrative text or a story paraphrase need not include any sentence denoting a dynamic event; a succession of states would imply a succession of events, as it does in "He was rich, then he was poor, then he was rich again"' (1983, p. 15). The sentence she chooses to exemplify causal sequencing verifies my point: why choose a single-sentence story about fortune—and therefore money—to illustrate story structure? Surely the answer is that readers have become so well acquainted with the monetary story that it serves an explanatory function *in its own right*. Prince formulates a similar minimal story: 'He was rich, then he lost lots of money, then, as a result, he was poor' (in Rimmon–Kenan 1983, p. 18). In effect Rimmon–Kenan has borrowed Prince's story and made it more minimalist than Prince's own (perhaps original) example. Prince however makes his story more concretised and pictorial by adding the redundant trigger 'lots of money' to it. Both Prince and Rimmon–Kenan have tied an inextricable knot between narrative and money, and it is a knot that remains firmly entangled in our cultural cloth. The story *is* a story about our attitudes toward money, but it is one that needs to be unravelled in order to expose how money's mythological significations are culturally ingrained.

Both Prince and Rimmon–Kenan focus on fiction, and its structures of communication. It is an important point to bear in mind here, because, as Gross argues, 'when money's power and significance are central subject matter in literature [fiction] they are virtually always presented critically' (1980, p. 73). From this perspective, narrative fictions as well as histories are informed by conceptual struggle, so that many of our texts perpetually vacillate between the affirmation or the denial of 'the power of money' (Gross 1980, p. 73). The omnipresence of the concept of money, whether it is lacking as in poverty or present as in *richesse*, is that which gives it a cultural omnipotence.

Furthermore, for Rimmon–Kenan and Prince 'rich' and 'poor' are traits with which we evaluate character. Many writers observe the tenacity of this idea. Harvey, for example, maintains that 'money [has become] the means by which we typically compare and assess' (1994, p. 100).[8] Rimmon–Kenan and Prince choose to describe the characters in terms of an attribute extrinsic to character: wealth. The story could have been like the one that Chatman borrows from Forster: 'the king died and then the queen died' (1980, p. 46), but it was a measured choice—designed to be readily understood by the reader. There are, of course, undisputed connections to be made between royalty and wealth—a factor that merely corroborates the point. Being rich is to succeed, and being poor is to fail. I return to this very decisive monetary ideology frequently, and in greater depth in later chapters.

The events in the two minimal stories cited above are structured around loss and gain: Rimmon–Kenan's story permits money to be regained, whereas Prince's is structured around a reversal of states (he started rich and ended poor). The stories then present differing outcomes: they are either concerned with returns or reversals, and these are worked through in economics and popular fiction respectively. Generally the evolutionary money narrative in economic texts is cyclically structured so that money returns to its original—perhaps conceptual—state, as the children's texts imply. The reason for this could be that money is a circulating medium. In popular fiction, on the other hand, the cyclical narrative seems to be unsatisfying for readers, so a conclusive ending is generally found, and winners and losers are specified.

The widespread occurrence of monetary mythologies and narratives closely relates to Genette's ideas about frequency and iteration (1980, pp. 113–27). The power of the iterative statement is that it *generalises* and renders its subject atemporal, thereby making sense of disordered and simultaneously occurring events. For money's history, order is created out of the barter–coin–paper–digicash chronology, even though Western culture often uses all forms of money simultaneously. The iterative statement is that which is able to be taken out of its original (specific) context, and be repeated elsewhere. The mythology of money is not a *single* statement or story found in *specific* texts; it is both a cognitive structure and a system of cultural organisation. Tonypandy's Foreword to Davies's *A History of Money* asserts, 'From earliest times money in some form or another has been central to organized living' (in Davies 1995). Money, in its various representations *is* systemic. But it would be misleading of me to claim that there is a single money mythology that is repeated exactly in each occurrence; rather money mythologies organise, represent, and immortalise money. Tonypandy's statement could be reworked so that money is central to *disorganised* living, for example, but the ideology of money as indispensable is countlessly relayed. The pronouncement that 'money is central to organized living' makes money essential simply by organising the sentence around money as the subject. The single sentences I have considered thus far similarly organise money in tight textual structures.

A number of stories insinuate the move towards money's disappearance as if inscription alone guarantees it a permanent existence: 'Going! Going! Gone!' is the subtitle of Cribb's little story about auctions, and each word seems panic–stricken. Cribb formulates a similar story about loss in gambling: 'if you are clever, or lucky, at cards, your fortune may increase. If you are not clever, or unlucky, it may disappear altogether!' (Cribb 1990, p. 27). Of course, the money does not 'disappear', it merely passes to the winner, and it is then represented, or circulated, as value to another person. In other words, money's material may leave one's hands, but it cannot disappear as a concept—just as money's form as digital bits does not also destroy its signified.

Three sentences (from texts with 'money' in their title) will further illustrate how some money mythologies are reiterated. The first, from Bruce's *Money of Australia* reads: 'Before coins and paper money were invented people swapped or bartered for items they wanted' (1992, p. 3). This sentence draws upon two monetary myths, already discussed, that naturalise the money concept. It does this first by implying that money is transcendental, and secondly by claiming that the money object evolved out of barter. To a large extent Bruce represents

Maestro's argument, whereby money's inception occurred with coin. According to this line of reasoning, money is not a cow, a wampum, or a sea shell, it is coin, and so its a priori aspect is negated. Either 'money' is a concept *or* it is a form. To reiterate: the nebulousness of money, and the constant to–ing and fro–ing in texts between money's conceptual structure (signified) and its form (signifier) seem to be intensifying in contemporary texts, as a response to the view that we are currently living in a precarious time, because money's signifier (coin or paper) is threatening to disappear.

Thomson's *Money in the Computer Age* begins: 'Monetary evolution has been progressing for about 10 000 years and has reached a stage when changes will be as dramatic as when shell and skin money disappeared in favour of metallic discs' (1968, p. 1). Thomson begins his text with an excessive statement, suggesting that the replacement of skin and shell by metallic discs (none of which he calls 'money') had a monumental impact, but on what is unclear. Once again, we find that changes in monetary form are deemed to be extreme and abrupt— an idea that conflicts with Thomson's own notion of gradual, rather than punctuated, evolution.

My final phrase is taken from a politico–economic text called *The Power of Money* and it reiterates Tonypandy's view cited earlier: Money is perhaps 'the most vital ingredient of our social existence' (Bretton 1980, p. xiv). Does this mean that money has a *life,* or that it is *essential*? Bretton maintains that 'somehow, in transition from its economic base, money lost its intrinsic identity' (1980, p. xiv). So 'vital' must refer to its economic origins in the land, or as a barter mechanism—its 'native habitat' (Bretton 1980, p. 105). This view enforces money's mythological history, as well as falsifying our present condition, so that Bretton believes we no longer have an authentic reference for money. I will recall this remark from Bretton in chapter 2, because it could also be interpreted as meaning that money has a vitality and an independent existence, not just that it is necessary.

The three short sentences considered above are all re–presentations; they tell us about money's origins, and its history. More fundamentally, these sentences bind money to our culture through their mythological representations. Money has an imminence in these sentences, but in some it also has a tendency to disappear, or self–destruct. But the stories of money arrest its material development monetarily, and in other ways they emphasise money's arbitrary nature. Money is an inherently contradictory system, and in terms of money's mythologies, money's apparent physical departure ushers in new meanings and concepts. Money's threatened disappearance from our pockets, as well as its mutation into digital bits, is discussed in the remaining two sections of this chapter.

GOING, GOING, GONE!

Several texts conclude by presenting money as if it is heading towards its (speculated) original state, namely, nonexistence. It is here that a glaring contradiction in economic dogma is manifest: if money can be anything, it is really immaterial whether it is a digital bit or a dog's tooth. But we have come to define ourselves and our history in terms of money, and so its appearance as a digital bit is seemingly a threat to the foundations of our culture. The worry seems to be that new money 'cannot be put in a pocket, or even touched, because it exists only as electronic data' (Cribb 1990, p. 58). There is a very real perception in texts, ranging from children's stories to the financial press, that money's material disappearance may be perilous. Crawford, for example, maintains that 'if money vanishes, we will, in a sense, have come full circle. Nothing will be visibly exchanged; the money that we sacrifice to receive our sustenance will vanish. If money vanishes it will be the invisibility, the lack of signs, that will be our greatest challenge' (1994, p. 221).[9] The consequences for the future of the link between technology and money cannot be foretold. Digital technology will literally change the face of money, as well as its use. The feel of money, and the need to retain its tangibility seem to be becoming more urgent as money is transformed into digital bits. Thus the stories and histories of money both reassure and inform the reader simultaneously, because they record, and so they become the annals of money.

Responses to changes in the form of money seem to be either celebratory or alarmist. First, there are those who seem to possess an immense confidence in money and a belief in its generic characteristics (so that money can take any form). Generally speaking, this stance is held by governments, banks, economic experts, and financial market participants—those institutions that appear to be in control of money and its networks. The opposing camp postulates chaos and a lack of control. Books with titles such as *The Death of Money* (Kurtzman 1993) and *Casino Capitalism* (Strange 1989 [1986]) voice dissent. In the main, these latter texts highlight the disparity between (what Kurtzman calls) the 'real' and the 'financial' economies: the first is tangible and the second is dependent upon money's abstraction. The 'global landscape is an abstract land,' he writes, 'a land of description rather than reality, where the real and the financial economies barely touch' (Kurtzman 1993, pp. 164–65). Kurtzman's observations are correct in terms of the disparity between real needs and the fictions upon which the money markets are based, because the conceptual and the descriptive do not feed people. But where the 'real' economy is (as opposed to the abstract one) remains unclear.

As our culture is apparently in crisis in terms of money, technology, and the financial markets, many texts appear to need to resolve the tensions between money's material form and its purely functional aspects. But the tension cannot be resolved, because the money concept is inherently indeterminate. Economic stories can have no resolution because the function of money is presented as eternally necessary, and so the pursuit of money can never cease—and neither can attempts to define its existence.

To sum up, histories of money appear to be ordered chronologically, so that they begin either with primitive money, or barter, or with nothing at all. The questionable assumption here is that money as such did not exist 'in the beginning' or in 'earliest times', but it 'grew' out of necessity or ritual, the idea and form 'emerging' from a naturally occurring need. In addition, metaphors of emergence suggest the existence of a seed, as if the idea was always there, it just needed a metal prototype to get the system rolling. Many texts are heavily dependent upon visual images with which to establish the money concept. An emphasis on material form and/or image means that the narratives have to become circular: beginning with no money and ending with no money.

In terms of the future of money or the ending for the story, nonclosure is very significant. There is a glaring contradiction between the economic treatment of form as insignificant, and the claim that the future is uncertain. Surely the economic narrative should design some picture of futurity? A preoccupation with things as they are now is not a sufficient or complete story. Equilibrium (that is, an exact matching of supply with demand) is the desirable outcome for the economic story, but as this is untenable, discussion is purely speculative.[10] Because the future is unknowable, focus shifts to the state of things as they are *now*. The presupposition is that this is just the way it is; money is here to stay.

THE MONEY GALLERY

Another way for money to be physically detained is to construct a museum, or display of monetary artifacts. On 30 January 1997, the Money Gallery opened at the British Museum in London. It displays monetary curios and collections of archaeological artifacts. The gallery is a 'new departure for the Museum', because whilst other galleries 'look at different cultures, past and present', this gallery focuses on one specific artifact: money (Burnett in Williams 1997, p. 7). In terms of this exhibition then it is money's forms that are privileged. The glossy text that accompanies the exhibition claims to demonstrate that 'there is more to the history of money than just buying and selling'; in other words, money is richer than its concept as a mere tool for trade (Williams 1997, p. 11).[11] The text, entitled *Money: A History,* is based upon two central assumptions: first, that the various forms of money displayed in the exhibition have functions other than as an instrument of exchange, and second, that there is a conceptual gap that the book might fill, because 'as we move towards the end of the second millennium in the Christian era, there is something of a feeling of *angst* in the air, of uncertainty about the future' (Williams 1997, p. 15). Ultimately both the exhibition and the text privilege form, primarily because they are both visual media, and presence is required for monetary texts.

Money: A History describes itself as 'historical' (Williams 1997, p. 10). Rather than being 'a traditional history of money from its "origins" to the present day, it is several histories [because the] real history of money lies in human attitudes and behaviour' (Williams 1997, pp. 11–13). A brief summary of its sections will assist in ascertaining the extent to which Williams's text constitutes a revision of the histories of money, such as those I have discussed so far. The material forms of money are also present, and detain the viewer through their very material distinctiveness.

The first chapters ('Mesopotamia, Egypt and Greece', 'The Roman World,' and 'Medieval Europe') cover various aspects of Western monetary phenomena: the use of gold and silver coins, the increased role of the state in the centralised minting of coins, and the establishment of trade routes, taxation, and credit. The section on Medieval Europe concludes with the comment that 'much of society still would not have employed coin on a daily basis. Most rural daily life would have been based on a large degree of self-sufficiency and small–scale barter the use of money might easily be virtually seasonal' (Williams 1997, p. 84). This is a point unmentioned by the historical accounts considered so far, which maintain that coin was readily accepted by all people for reasons of convenience. In addition, Williams's point negates views such as Thomson's, which postulate that changes to money struck suddenly.

The second section obviates possible charges of Eurocentrism by focusing on Islam, India, the Far East, and China. The section considers the impact that Greece and Islam—as colonisers—had on the coinage and monetary operations in these regions. Prior to various invasions, money used in India, for example, was originally noneconomically delineated: its function was tied to '[religious] and social obligation' (Williams 1997, p. 129), whereby particular rulers as the holders of money were the financial protectors of their subjects: 'The early kings amassed stores of wealth with which they ruled the people, thereby bringing peace to the world' (*Book of Master Guan* [circa 26 B.C.] in Williams 1997, p. 135). Money's use then was not apparently accompanied by a specific character type: the self-interested individual, rather its origins were deemed to be giftlike in Mauss's sense (1967).

Despite Williams's observations about varying attitudes to money, we encounter the familiar (land–coin–paper–digicash) chronology here: money initially derives directly from the land, and in primitive societies barter and self–sufficiency characterise the governor–owned economies. People who worked the land of the ruler or local landowner were protected. Then a change occurred: precious metal as a valued substance was manipulated into coin, a move that freed people from absolute dependency on the land. This shift marks the beginning of money's conceptual independence, because with coin people were able to make money from something else other than the land, as, for example, in the case of usury.

The signalling in Williams's text of money's independence enables discussion to proceed to Western industry. Money is no longer tied to the land, and paper money comes to be made by machines, independent of raw material (unlike Kain's Chinese money). Williams's text ends in the present day, and therefore constructs an ideological path, leading to the present. It focuses on specific events and causes, which are perceived to lead to the present situation.

Not only does the chronology of money narratives need to be questioned, but the construction of the actors in the plot should be too. People seem to be characterised in relation to money forms: 'primitive' people barter, and goal–oriented people work for money. Narratives feature characters who support their connoted ideologies, as we have seen with Smith and Marx. Resistances to these characterisations can emanate from any discourse, and I would suggest that readers do not recognise themselves in many accounts.

The final chapter in *Money: A History*, 'The Modern Period', deals with the intellectual changes brought about by the widespread use of paper money and credit: 'the increasing volatility of money caused by its growing intangibility prompted the realisation that its manipulation could have enormous consequences on the very structure and nature of human society' (Williams 1997, pp. 232–33). The term 'manipulation' is provocative here: Williams attempts to maintain money that can be handled, even though he discusses the intangible. My brief consideration of this fairly lengthy text is designed to demonstrate that there are numerous fractures in our cultural understanding of money. Williams reiterates the prevalent notion that in some ways we are at a crisis point in relation to our cultural development. It is a crisis caused by changes to money's form, which somehow renders money more powerful than it was in the past. So the chase involves pinning down the monetary object, acquiring more than others, as well as *self–definition* through the hunt. But each time readers gain some grip on the monetary concept, myth dismantles it, and this is why money currently 'has a speed', it slips through both concepts and fingers (Bronson 1995, p. 10).

Having established some of the ways that texts make money a constitutive part of our culture, in histories, in advertisements, in children's stories, and in philosophical treatises (in short, these texts have a breadth that envelops both so-called high and low cultures), I would like to address the issue of money's ability to transform itself, and its readers. Williams's text ends with a question: 'How can something that has become so intangible become so very powerful?' (1997, p. 249). The question can only be answered by readers, who as cultural participants, should interrogate the assumptions informing our texts about money. Such an interrogation, or understanding, could lead to a cultural rejection of money's centrality. Dodd suggests that if someone could advance a theory detached from economic reasoning, then 'the very idea of money would be terminally compromised' (1994, p. 162). One of Dodd's primary suggestions is that 'ideas and perceptions of money [such as empowerment] do not merely inform how it is used. They are essential to the possibility of its being used at all' (1994, p. 154). Dodd's view seems to support my mythological perspective, namely, that every individual in our culture complies with monetary systems.

In the next chapter I consider two characters: money and the reader, and how they are perceived to interrelate in some money mythologies. To some extent, money derives its power from mythology, and this power overshadows readers, even though it is perceived to *empower* them. Character is a constituent part of narrative, and in the next chapter I analyse some ways that money mythologies formulate quite distinct characterisations. Economic stories (like any other) need characters. One of these, perhaps the best known, is that of the economic human being: a purely self-interested individual, who pursues money relentlessly, both for its potential to fulfil desires as well as for its ability to define the self.

NOTES

1. This particular text is largely a critique of the Thatcherite era in the mid–eighties, and the first line summons up an anxiety about money that mirrors concerns about the high interest rates, high unemployment, and fiscal uncertainty that occurred during this time. The narrator sarcastically remarks, 'people found it as easy to borrow money as they would find it to lose their homes a few years later' (Perlman 1998, p. 118). The sum, 'three dollars', is persistent throughout the text—not just as its title—but as a recurrent reminder of this apprehension (Perlman 1998, pp. 1, 3, 27, 334, 339, 352, 370).

2. Not to be confused with the 'Adam Smith' who wrote *The Money Game* (1968).

3. Jensen and Pauly in fact discuss the fact that vernacular accounts of experience are lacking in the field of cultural studies, because they believe that a purely textual approach to culture (with readers as textualised constructs) fails to incorporate 'ethnographies of the audience' (1997, p. 166). I find their argument in relation to textual analysis problematic, but I do agree with them about the way readers are frequently constructed, and this is why I devote much of my next chapter to the issue of readers in relation to economic theory.

4. In McLellan's terms, this section is the first 'readable' part of *Capital* (1995, p. 313). If this is the case, and people take up McLellan's suggestion to begin reading the text at this point, the narrative should, or could, be Marx's best known. Of course, this is an unquantifiable remark, but it is worth noting.

5. Cribb is incidentally the curator of the Money Gallery at the British Museum, which I discuss below.

6. It is also significant that the stories are all heavily weighted towards an understanding of the present: they end with the adverb 'now'. This can be interpreted as a

response to the view that we are currently living in a precarious time because money is constantly threatening to disappear into '1s and 0s'.

7. A sociolect is 'the most social, the most mythical [language that presents] an unshakeable homogeneity: woven with habits and repetitions, with stereotypes, obligatory final clauses and key–words' (Barthes 1982 [1977], p. 168).

8. Lane too targets this notion. He notes that in a study by Luft, a social psychologist, '"the hypothetical rich man was seen as relatively healthy, happy, and well adjusted, while the hypothetical poor man was seen as maladjusted and unhappy"' (Lane 1991, p. 90).

9. It will be noted that Crawford's language, like that of many other commentators, encodes the angst. Money as signifier may disappear, but its signified as value may not.

10. Carew notes the view 'that the idea of an economy as a pendulum swinging from side to side is nonsense as there is no fulcrum (fixed point) to guarantee a return to an original position. Those who work in real–world situations should agree with this view: it is probably true that we are rarely in equilibrium because the equilibrium is always changing' (1988, p. 83).

11. Williams is the editor of this text, but each chapter (except for Burnett's Introduction) is written by individual (nameless) curators of various parts of the exhibition, 'specialists in particular areas and periods of the history of coinage and paper money' (Williams 1997, p. 11). Because there is no indication of the writers' names, all references will be attributed to Williams.

2

Money as a Very Important Person

VIVIFYING MONEY

When Marx describes money as a 'dramatis persona', he is inferring that money is a leading character in our culture, as well as an agent of transformation (1990 [1867], p. 206). Of course, 'Money itself has never built a building, manufactured a product or given sound investment advice [it] is valueless paper' (Crawford 1994, p. 3). But, like many other characters, money lives in our minds, because it is *characterised as important*, and this has repercussions in terms of the construction of readers. In other words, money plays a leading role in the construction of character in our culture—we laud the rich, for example, and we also often define ourselves according to how much money we possess. A character in Buchan's *High Latitudes* explains: 'Money is my personality, and without it I do not exist' (1996 p. 187). Rowe recognises this tendency in her psychological study of money in our time: 'Money isn't necessary for physical survival but in most societies today many if not most people regard money as essential for the survival of their person' (1998, p. 36). Davies maintains that money is 'a creature responsive to society's demands' (1995, p. 639). So money seems to be some sort of being that is continually converted physically, mentally, and materially.

In an economic sense, too, money plays the role of a major cultural protagonist: a growing number of nations are adopting monetarist policies that advocate an understanding of the behaviour of money.[1] Texts with titles such as Galbraith's (1975) *Money: Whence It Came, Where It Went* suggest that money's behaviour needs to be analysed. Our indubitable reliance upon money in every aspect of our lives affects a contradictory tension: on the one hand, dependence demands stability (or a sound understanding of money management, such as the control of inflation), and on the other dependence results in multifarious representations of money, that are unrestrained and confusing, but that both question and solidify money's importance to our culture.

Characterisation adds depth and fullness to what would otherwise be simply a name or a function; it encourages character to be mentally abstracted and endowed with meaning independent of the text. The more diversely a character is traited, the more readily it is abstractable beyond the text. Money's character cannot be defined by function alone if it is to be trusted or abstracted, therefore it needs abundant characterisation.

Money performs specific commercial functions, but it cannot act independently, unless it is constructed as a character. Frequently, as I have mentioned, money is characterised as an independent actor, with an 'intrinsic identity' (Bretton 1980, p. xiv), but more often than not, this identity is an anthropomorphism. Readers allow money to be viewed as a character, that is like them, because, as Rowe suggests, without money and its mythologies, individuality is hard to maintain, and so ideas about money as an agent of power continue to circulate. The power of money in terms of character construction is an intrinsic part of our monetary mythologies, providing us with new kinds of heroes and villains, as well as new ideas about the self. Because of the importance of character in mythology, this chapter is the first of three dealing directly with character: chapters 3 and 4 follow up some of the ideas put forward here.

Characterisations play an important part in the construction of money as a character, as I will show. Money is sometimes constructed as a Proppian magical helper, but it also shares features with Rorty heroes, protagonists, persons, and individuals (1990, p. 301). In view of money's currently changing form, we could also consider the ways in which money's character is adaptable to circumstance. More importantly, if money is a character, how does it impact upon the reader? The cliché 'I am not made of money' infers that people are subject to monetisation. The same idea is applied to children when they are labelled as 'good as gold'. As participants in money economies, readers are not only dependent upon the money object, but also upon the signs and stories of money. Economics discourses define the relationship between readers and money quite narrowly in terms of the characterisation of each.

There are two main theories of fictitious characters, and both are applicable in differing degrees to the character of money. The first postulates that 'characters are at most patterns of recurrence' (Weinsheimer in Rimmon–Kenan, 1983, p. 32). According to this semiotic view, characters are not 'imitations of real people'; they are merely textual constructs (Rimmon–Kenan 1983, pp. 32–33).

On a cultural level, the characterisations of money are simply recurrent representations.

For the other main theory of character, such as Bradley's (1971 [1904]), speculation about the characters' (and authors') past, future, motives, and psychological makeup provide the basis for characters to be detached from texts, and for them to continue living in the mind.[2] So, we have two polarised views of character: one that posits that characters are simply constructs, or an assemblage of signs, and the other that believes characters can be interpreted, even psychoanalysed, and so they reach beyond the text, and carry over into real lives. As Zephaniah's poem explains it: 'Money has a habit of going to de head' (in Jackson 1995, p. 264). Money is a construct as well as a concept that resides in the mind, but in terms of the latter, money is only psychologically powerful because it permeates our discourses, and so its centrality is unceasingly repeated.

Mythology depends very crucially upon repetition: it is 'garrulous, it invents itself ceaselessly' (Barthes 1989 [1957], p. 162). The recurrence of money's mythological significations has a cognitive dimension, too. Money is in a sense a 'cultural program' in Geertz's sense; it governs behaviour (1973, p. 44). From Lindemann (1993) I borrow the term 'mindscape', which he defines as a 'cognitive landscape which readers enter from a particular angle, a cognitive scene which they eventually become accustomed to by repeated or prolonged returns' (p. 193). Defined by the knowledges, connections, and inferences it activates (Lindemann 1993, pp. 193–94), the monetary landscape can be distinguished in some ways from other mindscapes. The connections that are particular to one mindscape may not be the same as another, but the connections or metaphorisations are what make up the mindscape. From Lindemann's perspective, money has even *physiologically* entered our mindscapes, by virtue of its cognitive returns. Thus, in terms of money's character, it is sustainable in our minds not because it provides us with an identity, but because it is identifiable through *repetition* and *representation.*

In addition, money needs to be credible in order to be trusted and used, and one of the easiest ways to achieve this credibility is to characterise it anthropomorphically. As Crawford observes, 'money is truly powerless unless we vivify it through our minds' (1994, p. 3). In E. M. Forster's terms, in order to be 'convincing', characters must be 'like' real people (1974 [1927], p. 43), and this may be why we use phrases such as 'money talks'. Character can be reconstructed outside the text (Rimmon–Kenan 1983, p. 31), and correlatively (I would suggest) have implications for everyday experience. The character of money is constantly shifting, and therefore it is not predictable or readily typologised.

To a certain extent, repetitions (despite their variety and shifts in signification) stabilise our perception of money. 'The qualities of characters are the predictable and reliable manifestations of their dispositions: and it is by these dispositions that characters are identified' (Rorty 1990, p. 304). The stable elements of money's character (such as its ability to perform tasks: we put money to work) enable its ideology to be more easily positioned into the reader's construction of reality. Money is dominant in the economic picture, providing all things and people with a relative position. In this chapter, my purpose is twofold: to explain how money is characterised and how the identity of readers' characters is aligned with money.

Before I analyse contemporary characterisations of money and the reader, I feel it is necessary to provide a comparative framework; therefore in the next section, I will briefly outline some characterisations in novels of F. Scott Fitzgerald and Edith Wharton. It will be noted that money does not have an autonomy in these texts, it is not independently characterised, rather it infiltrates characters, and determines their social mobility, so that some could in fact be 'made of money'.

Gatsby and Lily Bart: The Mobilisation of Money in People

Earlier this century, Wharton and Fitzgerald wrote some fascinating narratives involving the interrelationship between money, markets, and characters, in particular *The House of Mirth* (1905) and *The Great Gatsby* (1926). Their thematic concerns focus on the effects of market money on social strata, but nowhere in these texts is money itself characterised; it is merely a measure of social position. Types of money are set against each other, so that market money is set in opposition to old (or inherited) money, and ultimately, in these two texts at least, those who invest in the market are weakened by it. Both texts could be said to be voicing concern about the rise of new types of financiers.

Lily Bart *(The House of Mirth)* and Gatsby and Nick *(The Great Gatsby)* are all involved in Wall Street investment: Lily as a naive investor, Gatsby as an underhanded dealer of securities, and Nick as an unprosperous bond salesman. In many ways, these two texts question the idea that money (or the possession of it) defines character. The narrator of *The House of Mirth* is explicit in this respect: 'The first thousand dollar cheque which Lily received [from her investment] strengthened her self–confidence in the exact degree to which it effaced her debts' (Wharton 1993 [1905], p. 85). In this text, money supports the development of Lily's character.

More significantly in terms of character definition, *Gatsby*'s Daisy is the character through which money speaks, and she is arguably a character representing old money. Her voice is initially described as having 'an excitement that men found difficult to forget: a singing compulsion, a whispered "Listen" ' (Fitzgerald 1990 [1926], pp. 14–25). Later, we find Gatsby making the unexpected observation that 'her voice is full of money' (Fitzgerald 1990 [1926], p. 115). Nick's response to this is that 'that was it. I'd never understood before. It was full of money—that was the inexhaustible charm that rose and fell in it, the jingle of it, the cymbal's song of it' (Fitzgerald 1990 [1926], p. 115). Daisy then also represents the sound of money, the music and siren's call of coined money. Gatsby's money, his 'phantom millions', is contrasted with Daisy's: Gatsby's is silent, shadowy, and has no ring to it (Fitzgerald 1990 [1926], p. 142). The text also aligns Gatsby's money with the 'easy', 'nonolfactory money' of Wall Street deals (Fitzgerald 1990 [1926], pp. 43, 67). Almost all of the reader's senses are summoned up to understand money in this text: hearing, smell, and touch. Gatsby's milieu is characterised as 'a new world, material without being real' (Fitzgerald 1990 [1926], pp. 153–54). The novel then mourns the passing away of so–called real money, that is money that can be smelled, and heard.

Part of the tragedy of the book is the result of distinctions between Daisy's physical possession of money and Gatsby's incorporeal money. He 'was overwhelmingly aware of the youth and mystery that wealth imprisons and preserves, of the freshness of many clothes, and of Daisy, gleaming like silver, safe and proud above the hot struggles of the poor' (Fitzgerald 1990 [1926], p. 142). Gatsby is socially powerless against Daisy's money, so he fabricates himself a monied lineage, telling Nick 'my family all died and I came into a good deal of money' (Fitzgerald 1990 [1926], p. 64). Here we find 'things' as representative of real, material wealth, and wealth as an indicator of character. The idea of monetary possession as a sign of a character's worth still has currency today, and I will discuss some contemporary representations of this idea in the third chapter.

The House of Mirth deals with character slightly differently. Nevertheless, money still has a sound in this text. Lily has been proposed to by Rosedale, and 'the clink of [his] millions had a faintly seductive note' (Wharton 1993 [1905], p. 176). But Rosedale is 'repugnant' to her (Wharton 1993 [1905], p. 176), perhaps because he has 'small stock–taking eyes' that view both money and women as investments (Wharton 1993 [1905] p. 256). 'The contrast [between his clinking millions and his assessing eyes] was too grotesque' (Wharton 1993 [1905], p. 176). Effectively money is appealing to her, but Rosedale's demeanour repels her. This particular text constantly questions the relationship between a desire for money and the upholding of moral principles.

One of the most interesting passages in *The House of Mirth* is the narrator's summary of the New York social 'season'. The season is in autumn, but it is a bad one because people have lost money on Wall Street.

This particular season Mrs. Peniston [Lily's aunt] would have characterized as that in which everybody 'felt poor' except Mr. Simon Rosedale. It had been a bad autumn in Wall Street, [and even] fortunes supposed to be independent of the market either betrayed a secret dependence on it, or suffered from a sympathetic affection: fashion sulked in its country–houses, or came to town incognito, general entertainments were discountenanced, and informality and short dinners became the fashion. But society, amused for a while at playing Cinderella, soon wearied of the hearthside role, and welcomed the Fairy Godmother in the shape of any magician powerful enough to turn the shrunken pumpkin back again into the golden coach. The mere fact of growing richer at a time when people's investments were shrinking, is calculated to attract envious attention; and according to Wall Street rumours Rosedale had found the secret of performing this miracle. [He] was said to have doubled his fortune, and there was talk of his buying the newly–finished house of one of the victims of the crash. (Wharton 1993 [1905], pp. 120–21)

The gist of this passage is the observation that society has an active role in its own characterisation whilst the market, albeit a determinant, is less powerful. Nevertheless, society is seen to be dependent upon the market. But this is a fairy tale dependency that aligns money with magic. The narrator does not seem willing to confront this dependency on Wall Street unless it is in fairy tale terms. The use of the Cinderella story detains the market on a purely textual level, thereby foreclosing realist structuralisation.

Direct references to money are frequently evaded in this text, as if money is somehow soiled. Various characters put forward the view that 'there's one thing vulgar about money, and that's the thinking about it' (Wharton 1993 [1905], p. 176). Lily comes to realise that 'one of the conditions of citizenship is not to think too much about money, and the only way not to think too much about money is to have a great deal of it' (Wharton 1993 [1905], p. 69). Seldon's reply to this remark is that 'you might as well say that the only way not to think about air is to have enough to breathe. That is true enough in a sense; but your lungs are thinking about the air, if you are not' (Wharton 1993 [1905], p. 69). Effectively, money is as necessary as air—and one can never have too much of it.

Characters in Wharton's *The House of Mirth* are defined almost entirely in terms of their social relationships and lineage, so these provide what Wark calls 'the poles of identification' (1994, p. 169). Lily Bart is identified in terms of her relationship to others, gaining friends and losing them, depending upon how much money she possesses. Where money is now excessively characterised itself, it was not so in the two texts I have briefly discussed. In *The Great Gatsby*, rich characters breathe money, their voices are composed of it, and so money is a part of their makeup, but it has not gained an existence or autonomy apart from its host.

Amelie Rorty's 'A Literary Postscript: Characters, Persons, Selves, Individuals' (1990) should be brought in here, because it highlights shifts in cultural ideas about consciousness and character. In this study she outlines the development of different culturally and historically specific views on character that are formulated around notions of political and social enlightenment. Rorty constructs quite specific distinctions between heroes, protagonists, actors, agents, persons, souls, selves, figures, and individuals—each of which, she claims, came to prominence in different historical eras (Rorty 1990, p. 301). 'Heroes', for example, are defined by their lineage (such as Oedipus, the king) (Rorty 1990, p. 303), 'characters' by their 'predictable and reliable dispositions' (Rorty 1990, p. 304). Figures are 'exemplary', they are 'idealizations' and are 'writ large' (Rorty 1990, pp. 307–308). 'Individuals' are centres of integrity and 'resist typing' (Rorty 1990, p. 315). Thus, character for Rorty is not a generalised concept. Specifically, character responds to conditions, rather than having conditions determine character, and it is defined by its 'predictable and reliable manifestations' (Rorty 1990, p. 304). It is at the level of individuation (post–figure) that the 'contrast [between] "inner and outer" becomes manifest' (Rorty 1990, p. 306), 'when *choice* and *intention* come to the fore' (Rorty 1990, pp. 309–11). The distinction or characterisations that Rorty makes between types of 'beings' is indeed forced, as she admits, but the idea of a developing awareness in character is a pertinent point (Rorty 1990, p. 319). As a collection of individuals, readers do have a choice about the extent to which they are typologised themselves in relation to money.

Rorty's delineation of 'selves' is a pertinent one for me, because it isolates the impact that material goods have had on our perception of character. The shift from land–based wealth and power to industrial capital marked a significant adjustment in our concept of character, and it is one we have retained since modernity. Rorty has identified a possible shift in thinking about the character of the self, occasioned by a change in terms of property rights. 'The concerns of selves,' she writes, 'are their interests; their obligations the grammar and semantics of selfhood reveal the possessive forms' (Rorty 1990, p. 314). In addition, 'societies of selves are liable to rapid social and economic change; they are expansive with the ideology if not the actuality of mobility' (Rorty 1990, p. 314). Lily and Gatsby could be the templates for this idea.

The processes of metaphorisation and characterisation are closely aligned: both are conceptual reconfigurations. Once defined by money, as Gatsby, Daisy, and Lily Bart are, many other characters come to be similarly characterised, representing or standing for a particular monetary idea. In addition, both metaphorisation and characterisation have a snowballing quality: they are amenable to layering, as well as intertextual representations. Because the concept of money is not fixed, it is interminably characterised and metaphorised, and hence is increasingly abstracted. I will now explore the idea of money as an abstractable character—often larger than life—that extends beyond its textual and material boundaries.

The Changing Face of Money

The aspects of money and character construction that I focus upon below are naming, traiting, and function, and how any stable aspects of money's characterisations are threatened by its technological transmutation. The first two, names and traits (which include physical characteristics), construct character as an 'autonomous being' (Chatman 1980, p. 119). In my view, character cannot be defined by function alone. The same argument can be applied to money, which is not merely functional as economists believe. According to Baker's reading, 'Simmel argues that money has an existence in its own right [with] its own identity, its own life' (1995, pp. 165–66). This life is perceived to be pre–existent, rather than humanly created, not only because money has a history, but also because money is characterised as a living entity that is hard to pin down. Williams believes that 'the awakening of the separate "personality" of money brought an increasing volatility to its character and behaviour' (1997, p. 248). Effectively, it is money's behaviour or actions that are enigmatic.

I will begin with money's physical characteristics, because they seem to be the most perplexing. The perception is that money's signified is immutable, but responses to digital money are polarised. 'Money Is Dead: Long Live E–Money' declares the *New Scientist* (8 Apr. 1995, front cover), whilst the *Economist* utilises a dismissive headline, 'So Much for the Cashless Society' (26 Nov. 1994, p. 23).

The openness of the money concept is the reason that its material is perceived to be arbitrary. 'Capital' as a metaphor of money, for example, enables any commodity or asset, such as houses, factories, or jewellery, to have a fundamental relationship with money in a metaphorical sense. This represents a shift in perception brought about by (amongst others) Marx's language. Therefore, money's concepts as well as its signifieds alter its form. Over the last two hundred years or so, various money concepts have been devised, resisted, and revived, but money proper has not been perceived to be threatened with invisibility or nonpalpability as it is now (as digital cash), and these changes could potentially impact on money's name, character, and function. Money may not be characterised in the future as it is now.

To the uninitiated the concept of digital technology may be hard to grasp. Negroponte's *Being Digital* (1996) is a very readable account of the workings and potential applications of digital technology. Essentially the digital universe is composed of 'bits' rather than atoms; it is digital (intangible) rather than analog (tangible). A digital bit 'has no color, size or weight, and it can travel at the speed of light' along fibre optic cable at 1,000 billion bits per second (Negroponte 1996, p. 14). The illustration Negroponte chooses is pertinent: A 'fiber the size of a human hair can deliver every issue ever made of the *Wall Street Journal* in less than a second' (1996, p. 23). The consequence of this spatial and temporal compression is that more people have access to more (monetary) information more quickly. Negroponte claims that 'wholly new content will emerge from being digital, as will new players, new economic models' (1996, p. 18). Negroponte is suggesting that our established values should be revised, because they no longer apply to new technologies.

The marriage of money to computers in the 1980s (with Bill Gates of Microsoft as the minister) seems to have enabled money to take new forms, as well as to form new relationships.[3] Not only has their association enabled a whole new range of financial instruments (such as derivatives) to be instantly traded, but the marriage has called into question the nature of money, particularly its physical characteristics.[4] Before digitalisation, settlement in the markets involved the actual transportation of cheques, but now the markets can transfer billions of dollars via computerised digital networks (*Business Week* 12 Jun. 1995, p. 37). Paper (the name for bonds or bills of exchange) has been replaced in numerous cases by digital settlement, so that no material changes hands, and investors are rarely issued with share certificates. 'Money does not have to be expressed on paper' (Gates 1996 [1995], p. 81).

The material of money has changed because of the new networks and relations it is involved in, and these technologies are in turn affected by concepts. In terms of appearance, the perception is that the 'character' of money has changed. Many people are creatures of habit, preferring the tangible reminders of money. They do not want to 'kiss cash goodbye' as the *Australian Financial Review* perceives it (25 Sept. 1995, p. 30). The article postulates that people prefer tangible paper in their pockets to electronic transfers (*Australian Financial Review* 25 Sept. 1995, p. 30). Texts do not seem to be able to abandon references to the tangible: hip pockets will not house digicash.

Not only is money being transferred technologically in the banking and consumer communities, but large corporations have demonstrated a surge of interest in digital money. Since 1995 numerous multinationals (such as Visa, Mastercard, National Westminster Bank, Citibank, and Microsoft) have been working with technology to create digital cash for everyday use. The virtual world is a part of the everyday world. The 'virtual world' is an immaterial, imitation world, a simulation. Digital technology has enabled the development of new trajectories along which money and information can travel in a nonmaterial (i.e., nonanalog or digital) sense, at unfathomably high speeds. It is contrasted with the productive, material world of the nineteenth and early twentieth centuries. David Hollott of Citibank believes that "'*money* will almost disappear in the future. There is no reason [why] technology could not replace *cash* [my emphasis]'" (in *Australian Financial Review* 25 Sept. 1995, p. 30).[5] Once again, money is structured as cash, as if this is its only authentic form. In addition, how can something 'almost' disappear?

According to the Digicash company's internet site, the company had launched a pilot program for electronic money in October 1995. Company officials say that it is 'real money. Real money for your computer', but it is not tied to any 'real existing currency' and it cannot be exchanged for real money (Digicash 1995, http://www.digicash.nl, http://193.78.226.2/, http://www.digicash.com/). The inventor of digicash, David Chaum, explains that his purpose is to replace paper banknotes with numbers. With this system, physical contact with money is eliminated. But these snippets of publicity leave open the question of what real money is. The assumption to be made, in the light of preceding remarks, is that money is cash, and digicash does not share a metaphorical common ground with it because it cannot be exchanged.

The financial press, as well as governments are acutely aware of these changes, and are attempting to prepare for them. 'We're in the beginning stages of a cash–replacement cycle', says a senior manager at Peat Marwick (in *Business Week* 12 Jun. 1995, p. 36). Current technologies enable money to 'flow in and out of countries at lightning speed without being traced', thereby avoiding taxation and being more easily laundered (*Business Week* 12 Jun. 1995, p. 38). In these respects, electronic money can 'do things that paper money could never do' because it is unmarked and unregulated (*Business Week* 12 Jun. 1995, p. 39). New forms of money seem to be given greater autonomy.

A survey in the *Economist* explains that 'to control money, you must know what "money" is—and, thanks partly to innovation and the growth of international finance, that is no longer clear' (19 Sept. 1992, p. 29).[6] The implication of this particular remark is that financial systems are responsible for altering the face of money. In addition, to know what something 'is' implies that one needs to understand it as an 'existence' with a particular makeup. Electronic or digital money has a 'pure, almost conceptual form: [it] has no intrinsic value, and barely even the trace of a physical existence' (*Economist* 26 Nov. 1994, p. 27). This last statement is a reiteration of the inference that money is returning to its fictitious original state: as a concept that existed before coinage. There is a glimmering of recognition here that money does not, in fact, have a single material form. But, as always with mythologies, the form must step in, because it confers a 'literal, immediate presence' upon money (Barthes 1989 [1957], p. 131).

Many of the preceding quotations make the popular suggestion that money used in technological systems is not authentic, and technology has changed money's physical identity. According to *Business Week* (12 Jun. 1995, p. 36), readers' lives will be changed as the result of technological money. But many of these shifts are dependent upon how we read the name 'money'.

The Name

Money is a name rich in variable connotations; it has a suggestive exuberance, metaphorically and psychologically. Buchan characterises money as 'frozen desire' in his text of that name, believing that 'money is incarnate desire [it] has become a sort of railway shunting yard which is forever receiving the wishes and dreams of countless people and despatching them to unimagined destinations' (1997, pp. 19–20). Without more than a passing note of the shunting yard metaphor that concretises a series of abstractions, Buchan's point is that money has an openness, that it has no real content other than individual desire. From this perspective, the sign 'money' is saturated with readers' wishes.

Kermode's analysis of narrative is applicable here in relation to money's character: once given a proper name, character becomes not merely a plot function, but it '[begets] new narrative' (1979, p. 81), such as Buchan's example. The interpretive needs of the reader '[generate] character, and the characters generate new narrative beyond any immediate need' (Kermode 1979, p. 99). We do not actually need to project wishes onto money, we only need it to buy food and shelter. In order to put forward some of the ways in which the word 'money' is not only traited, but is also granted a kind of open independence, I begin with an investigation of its denoted meaning, as defined by dictionaries and economic texts, which fail to adequately define money's cultural value.

By their very nature, dictionaries—particularly economic or financial dictionaries—should proffer comprehensible and integrated denotations of money. Generally however, definitions are synonyms, so they are simply relational. The MIT (1986) *Dictionary of Modern Economics*, for example, is far from exacting; it does not explain the distinctiveness of money, because the task is impossible: money is '*anything* which is widely acceptable in exchange for goods, or in settling debts, not for itself but because it can similarly be passed on, has the character of money since it serves the primary function of money'. This definition emphasises money's conceptual nature, and leaves the concept open to be rewritten by other metaphors such as 'capital'. The corollary of this idea is that if money can be 'anything', it can also be everything. Furthermore, the definition explains that money cannot be valued *for itself*, and that what gives it a 'character' is purely that it can be passed on.[7]

Davies attempts a more rigorous definition in his *History of Money*. Money is:

1. Unit of account (abstract)
2. Common measure of value (abstract)
3. Medium of exchange (concrete)
4. Means of payment (concrete)
5. Standard for deferred payments (abstract)
6. Store of value (concrete)

7. Liquid asset (mostly abstract)
8. Framework of the market allocative system (mostly abstract)
9. A causative factor in the economy (mostly abstract)
10. Controller of the economy (mostly abstract) (1995, p. 27).

Davies notes that accounting or reckoning units (such as measure of value) are abstract in the sense that units have 'no physical constraints' (1995, p. 28). This is undoubtedly the case, because money is an abstract concept. The three 'concrete' aspects of money are also in fact abstract: they do not refer to specific signifieds. Davies's definitions all relate to function and lack any material signifieds or symbolic dimension, such as 'frozen desire'.

Significantly Davies modifies his list of functions by remarking that 'money designed for one specific function will easily take on other jobs and come up smiling' (1995, p. 29). Davies's comprehensive economic definition of money in terms of its functional characteristics has included three anthropomorphisms: points 9 and 10, which suggest that money is in control (it is both a causative factor and a controller), and his qualifier that money has a sense of embedded humour. One can deduce from these slippages that function alone is not sufficient to account for the appeal and persuasive properties of money's signifier. In some respects then the reader's interpretation has no room in this scenario. How does the idea that money is a 'framework for the market allocative system' cohere with the general reader? Readers, as well as writers like Davies, necessarily search for intention and motive, they 'draw conclusions about the psychology of characters from their actions' (Rabinowitz 1985, p. 422). If money 'comes up smiling', then it surfaces as a jolly entity, appealing in its mirth.

In economic terms, money is anything that can be *exchanged*; therefore, the act of exchanging is paramount, and the characters of the agents involved and the physical form are irrelevant. This strategy enables money to be present in any form in countless exchanges, but to 'behave' the same way in each instance. Nevertheless digital money is perceived by many to behave differently from dog's teeth, for example, so this position is frequently untenable. My reading below of *The Story of Money* will demonstrate a similar rupture. The functional, and hence plot-centred, aspect of the economic delineation of money is not comprehensive. It fails, for example, to consider the agents of exchange—people—and their psychological motives. Human behaviour is in many ways defined by the economics discipline almost entirely in terms of our relationship to money, not money's relationship to us. Money may be coin, paper, or digital impulse, but our relationship to it is fundamental to our success as economic beings, as well as to money's continued use. Therefore *how* we think about it, and more to the point, how we describe it, determines how we think about ourselves in relation to money, which can in turn define how we think about ourselves.

Contemporary Characterisations of Money

Readers encountered many muddled characterisations of money in the late twentieth century. *The Wall Street Journal* is an authoritative text for those interested in the financial markets, but its characterisations of money (as opposed to the market) are few and far between.[8] Generally aimed at the professional money–marketeer, what characterisations there are have become market clichés. Soft and hard are the most frequently used adjectives: On 1 November 1996, money is described as 'soft', 'sitting in accounts at Citibank' (front page).

Often the *Wall Street Journal* discusses the U.S. dollar in terms of hyperactivity—rising and falling every day—almost as if the journal is trying to breathe life into currency. On 11 October 1996 the journal described the U.S. dollar as being trapped and 'claustrophobic' (p. C19). Perhaps a swim would help?

On 25 October 1996 money went for a run along Russian rivers with some salmon (p. A9D). On 11 November 1996 money changed its mood again. This time it was apparently annoyed: 'MONEY SPAT' because Greenspan ordered the stock of money in a Los Angeles bank vault to be counted (front page). Money was misbehaving here and being resistant to quantification. Quantification seems to be one way of constructing parameters from within which money can be understood. It is Buchan's view that characteristics or descriptions that money is given merely refer nowadays to quantity, or how much money is in circulation (1997, p. 18). But one of the corollaries of quantification is that money becomes a measure of value, thereby destroying the uniqueness of the measured object.

Simmel's *Philosophy of Money* (1990 [1900]) observed that in modern economies, money had come to quantify all things, as well as de–individuating them. In terms of signification, this idea postulates that money's signifying concept (value) takes precedence over the objects to which it refers (such as a painting or a chair). Money values have come to be similarly applied to people as well as things, so that money is a determinant, and people's idiosyncrasies or differences are undervalued, and this conviction is very much in currency today. Money now provides us with criteria for self-definition or characterisation: 'money [is] the yardstick of success or failure in this society. It [is] the constant against which every individual [can] be measured objectively' (Frey 1995, pp. 151–52). Lane's findings, mentioned earlier, endorse this idea by explaining that our culture judges people according to their ability to procure money, so that 'people use "rich" and "poor" as default values for assessing the desirable personality qualities a person has' (1991, p. 90). A rich person is perceived to have desirable qualities, and many are idolised. Furthermore, this belief has meant that ideas about money have changed in tandem. In some circles, money is now considered to be a positive cultural phenomenon, whereas in the past many stories of money emphasised its destructive or immoral aspects ('the love of money is the root of all evil').

Popular fiction is a particularly loaded textual site to draw upon to provide evidence of prevalent and often clichéd ideas about money. Writing about two decades ago, Gross makes the observation that 'imaginative literature in our time is always responding to money power, either by flight, savage parody, or direct presentation and exposure' (1980, p. 78). But the 'power' that money seems to have is a new kind of power, related to its capacity for self–generation, or 'money's ability to make money [independently]' (Gross 1980, p. 74). The very popularity of fiction that exposes or problematises money enables me to assert the extent of the spread of many of the ideas I am discussing. Popular novels such as *Free to Trade, Trading Reality, The Marketmaker, Bombardiers, The Takeover, The Vulture Fund, The Inner Sanctum, Vanishing Point,* and *High Latitudes* form a new popular fiction subgenre in relation to character construction and monetary/character networks. Each has a key protagonist involved in the financial markets, that is, a character with particular knowledge about the nature and movements of the market. In addition, money has a central role in these texts in terms of plot development. These texts provide an interesting perspective in terms of the dynamics of money and character formation in the late twentieth century.

A brief aside about genre is pertinent here. Cawelti (1976) argues that changes to formulaic imaginative structures (or genres) serve a particular function, which is similar to mythology. He writes, 'formulaic evolution and change are one process by which new interests and values can be assimilated into conventional imaginative structures. This process is probably of particular importance in a discontinuous, pluralistic culture like those of modern industrial societies' (Cawelti 1976, p. 35). In other words, because money is seen to be mysterious, we resort to conventional representational structures such as mythology to control shifting values. But money fits into all genres—adventure, mystery, and romance—because of the ubiquity of its signs. In addition, formulas, be they mythological or formulaic, do not only occur in so-called literary texts. In the concluding remarks of his analysis, Cawelti postulates that similar structures exist outside traditionally labelled imaginative structures: 'Though I have applied the concept of formula and its methods of analysis exclusively to the examination of fictional structures [it would be possible to analyse] popular constructions that do not take the form of stories. I suspect that there are also formulas in the nonfictional literary forms of popular culture such as news, documentaries, and popular history and philosophy' (1976, p. 297).

Popular fiction bridges the gap between the unembellished economic definition and the fantastic definition. Money can be good, that is, it works for us rather than the other way around. Money is 'easy' (Frey 1996, p. 285), a description that has numerous connotations, ranging from sexual availability to convenience. In *Bombardiers* money is described as 'gullible' (Bronson 1995, p. 19), because it is easily adaptable, as well as being uncritically accepting of its position in the market. Characterisations are both determined and influenced by cultural and institutional ideologies, and it is possible to argue that the characterisation of money as gullible is a new one, peculiar to our time, when we are grappling with money in what is perceived to be a new phase of its development. Perhaps we are fostering an adolescent, no longer bound to its readers by an umbilical cord. According to *Bombardiers,* as long as money remains *inside the market,* it is infinitely gullible. Thus, dollars are not only attributed with human characteristics, but they are also given specific traits. The inference to be made from this metaphorical gesture is that money is infinitely malleable, it yields to persuasion and interest.

Conversely money has its own voice, it talks. 'Money talks. But how does it talk? Does it "talk dirty"? Does it swear? Does it mean what it says? Does it mean more than it says?' (Schleifer in Male 1980, p. ix). According to an advertising leaflet recently issued, when money talks it uses a phone card. Thus, the 'money talks' platitude has been reworked so that money has an autonomy, and determines its own language, or mode of communication.

Money is also 'addicting' (Bronson 1995, p. 3) partly because the endless pursuit of money is (as Adam Smith suggests) a natural goal. So why do we treat it as if it were *like us,* functioning as we do? *The Vulture Fund,* a story about greed and a fictional run for the U.S. presidency, often uses parenting concepts to describe money as if we were the guardians of a child that is growing and developing personality. Characters worry about money (Frey 1996, p. 167), and they sometimes play with it (Frey 1996, p. 253).

In terms of plot, a crucial factor is that characters pursue money at any cost: 'she might be willing to relax her morals a bit to get this money' (Frey 1996, p. 136). But the pursuit implies flight, and as we have seen, digital money is wont to disappear or take off. Almost the entire plot of *The Vulture Fund* is based on the obsessive pursuit of money. Money sneaks around throughout the novel, and gets into places without the other characters knowing how (Frey 1996, pp. 251, 262, 307). This particular novel throws up an anxiety about money that is combined with a sense of money's evasiveness. In some ways this text also informs the reader about his or her own character, because part of money's mythology is that it is natural for people to want a successful monetary outcome.

Many popular fiction novels published since the 1987 stock market crash seem to have picked up a number of tensions inherent in free market ideology, some taking a distinctively ethical stance. Some of them are written by ex-traders (Po Bronson and Michael Ridpath) or financial journalists, such as James Buchan, who appear to want to use their own experiences to voice their specialist knowledge about money. They also highlight potential threats that, they perceive, the relationship between money and technology in the markets seems to pose: namely, corruption, exploitation, and easy money. For some readers, these writers' expert knowledge may lend their texts additional judicious credence.

So far in this chapter my focus has been on money: its concepts, its characterisations, and the perception that somehow money is changing. A preoccupation with money's ability to metamorphose independently excludes human intervention to a significant extent. It also makes money appear evasive, hard to grasp, and somewhat magical, or supernatural. But the impression of money's autonomy is made at the expense of the reader—their variable perceptions, and how they relate to money themselves. In the following section, I consider how the reader is constructed as subordinate to the powerful character of money.

DEFINING THE READER

Action and Function

The economic definition of money recounts its function, and the structuralist view of character shares a similar functionality. If we were to ask Propp to define money, it would be a 'helper', enabling convenient exchange between two parties, because for Propp, the only characters that can be nonhuman (i.e., objects) are 'specific helpers, [which fulfil] a single function' (1968, p. 82). Money does help us in the sense that it facilitates trade between remote parties. Money is designed to make our transactions more efficient, but it needs to be passed on, as the dictionary definition cited earlier makes clear.

People too need to have specialised, or instrumental, functions in money economies. As Milton Friedman notes, Adam Smith emphasised the 'specialisation of function as a source of efficiency' (1992, p. 35). In Smith's *The Wealth of Nations*, the butcher, baker, and brewer function as nodes in his conceptual design, so they are merely functional exemplars of instrumentality. In terms of capital generation these characters refine products derived from the land: the baker makes bread from wheat, and the brewer makes beer from hops. But these characters are pure ideological constructs, used to support Smith's call for economic efficiency. We find, for example, that in the beginning (that is, prior to the invention of money proper) things did not run efficiently for people. They used 'cattle [as] the common instrument of commerce' (Smith 1986 [1776], p. 127). In addition, 'beavers [were] exchanged for deer, there [was] a superabundance of materials which [had] little or no value and every man provided himself with food and more clothing than he [could] wear' (Smith 1986 [1776], pp. 150, 266). 'The butcher has more meat in his shop than he himself can consume, and the brewer and the baker would each of them be willing to purchase a part of it. But they have nothing to offer in exchange, except the different productions of their respective trades, and the butcher is already provided with all the bread and beer which he has immediate occasion for' (Smith 1986 [1776], p. 126). However, 'when barter ceases the butcher seldom carries his beef or his mutton to the baker, or the brewer, in order to exchange them for bread or for beer; but he carries them to the market, where he exchanges them for money, and afterwards exchanges that money for bread and beer' (Smith 1986 [1776], p. 135). Money is conceived to be lacking, but its inception is not explained. 'When barter ceases' is scarcely an explanation, and this omission provides economic theory with a certain hollowness in terms of causality, and this has implications for its plausibility.[9]

A second important development of character in terms of function in *The Wealth of Nations* concerns the impact of the division of labour on the functional aspects of the characters. 'Originally' each person 'unites three different characters in one person' (Smith 1986 [1776], p. 156); 'every farmer must be butcher, baker, and brewer for his own family' (Smith 1986 [1776], p. 122), whereas 'in every improved society, the farmer is generally nothing but a farmer' (Smith 1986 [1776], p. 111). Effectively Smith has flattened people into purely functional constructs to illustrate his hypotheses concerning economic development and efficiency.

We also find that the butcher, baker, and brewer have one specific universal motivation, and this is the only attribute Smith gives them. He writes, 'it is not from the benevolence of the butcher, the brewer, or the baker that we expect our dinner, but from their regard to their own interest. We address ourselves, not to their humanity but to their self–love' (Smith 1986 [1776], p. 119). Prior to the advent of commercial society, optimum efficiency in exchange was needed, but now the exchange process becomes heavily motivated by self–love, which in turn becomes more acute and displaces the action of exchange for an insatiable pursuit for more goods or wealth. Economic theory is based almost entirely on these two premises. Heyne's (1994) economic textbook reiterates Smith's view for students: 'The fact that almost everyone prefers more money to less is an enormous aid [to the economic way of thinking], an extremely important lubricant, if you will, in the mechanism of social coordination' (p. 6).

According to Propp's structuralist reading, motivations 'belong to the most inconstant and unstable elements of the tale they represent an element less precise and definite than functions or connectives' (1968, p. 75). For Propp, the relationship between character and function in terms of the narrative is an important one: 'Function is understood as an act of character, defined from the point of view of its significance for the course of the action' (1968, p. 21). Furthermore, 'functions of characters serve as stable, constant elements in a tale, independent of how and by whom they are fulfilled. They constitute the fundamental components of a tale' (Propp 1968, p. 21). In addition, labelling characters with proper names is unimportant (indeed it may even undermine his own formalist argument). Function comes first and differences in tales are only expressed by differences in actions that are developed from within the 31 functions he proposed (Propp 1968, p. 64). Therefore, 'The sphere of action exactly corresponds to the character', and any implied motives are highly questionable, because they are unstable (Propp 1968, p. 80).

Proppian theories of character bear a remarkable resemblance to economic functionalism, because people are simply functional in the economic story, and they have a single selfish motivation. Being centred on the functional, both the Proppian and economic stories have profound consequences in terms of the narrative outcome of our relationship to money. Economics defines people with universal and consistent behavioural characteristics (self-interested, rational, maximising, or 'calculating machines', as McCloskey [1996] calls them), rather like Propp's functional narrative agents. This position is resisted even by some commentators from within the economics discipline itself. As Klamer notes, the economic model is frequently criticised for 'projecting a one–dimensional, solipsistic, characterless "unity" with no social bonds' (1987, p. 179). Individual difference does not seem to matter in the economic model; people are merely characterless respondents to the monetary carrot.

Readers appropriate many cultural myths in the act of reading, but they are also at liberty to assimilate and/or resist them. While Rabinowitz suggests that readers hold the 'key' to genre, they also hold the key to character construction. Reading is subject to a certain number of rules, as Rabinowitz suggests: rules of 'notice', 'signification', 'configuration', and 'coherence' (1985, pp. 421–43). The reader's ability to draw conclusions from recognisable patterns is essential for the perpetuation of economic mythologies. A financial novel such as *The Vulture Fund* is based on a plot of monetary pursuit, and relies upon the reader's ability to draw conclusions about the character of money, as well as the relationship of the fictional characters in the text to money. This is where the reader is expected to bring certain knowledge to the text, and this is generally knowledge, however sketchy, of economic plots.

Brummett observes that 'the stock market "crash" of October 19, 1987 demonstrated at least one fact clearly: Discourse about economic matters has moved from dismal science to popular culture increasing economic awareness makes people understand that the value of the dollar in Tokyo affects whether one can buy that stereo or not' (1990, p. 153). Over the last decade or so economics has had to enter into new fields, such as the analysis of newly invented financial instruments, but according to Friedman, new subjects are analysed with 'recognisably similar components of pure theory, descriptive statistics and econometrics' (1992, p. 39). So for the reader received economic wisdom is partially anachronistic. Nevertheless, the prevalence of economic mythologies means that many readers feel equipped to enter the economic debate. Davies believes that at no previous time in human history have economics and monetary theory been so widely and hotly disputed (1995, p. 4).

The abundance of texts available on the subject of money from the economic perspective perpetuates its ideologies, which include money's power as well as ideas about instrumentality. Maestro's (1993) children's book is a fitting story to consider here from the perspective of Propp. It is an economic-centred text with money as the central character. But it is also a new text, so I analyse it in this context in order to ascertain how money may currently be seen to function differently from money, say, in Smith's time. In this text money is (to a certain extent) an autonomous character because the notion of human agency in the development of money is conspicuously lacking: the text suggests that money spontaneously emerged, that it created itself. Focusing on the changes in money's material form, the book presents an interesting perspective in relation to character, because it adopts an unconventional economic approach to money. Moreover, as a flat character, defined by function alone, money should not need to be watched for developments, neither should it be hard to recognise (Forster 1974 [1927], p. 47).

The story is also provocative because it is not in fact a 'story' in the theoretical sense of the word: it is a carefully devised narrative, focusing on the financial hegemony of the United States. Schleifer would consider this strategy to be legitimate, because 'money is perhaps the great American fiction' (in Male 1980, p. x). The Appendixes, along with the satellite events, such as the use of wampum in trade right up to the seventeenth century, are predominantly American. Many of the events are supported by fictional incidences, which masquerade as history. The text suggests, for example, that George Washington donated his own heirlooms to the Philadelphia Mint in 1792 (Maestro 1993, p. 30). But, with reference to this incident, 'no one knows if this is true' (Maestro 1993, p. 30).

The story begins with a lack (in Propp's terms): 'A long time ago there was no such thing as money' (Maestro 1993, p. 3). 'An initial shortage or lack represents a situation. One can imagine that, prior to the beginning of the action, the situation lasted for years. But the moment comes when the dispatcher or searcher [the human being] suddenly realizes that something is lacking causing an immediate search' (Propp 1968, p. 76). But Maestro presents us with a double lack situation; the reason there was no money apparently was that there were no shops in existence (1993, p. 3). The inference is that early humans were short sighted, because they had neglected to create money or shops, and furthermore that money is humankind's crowning imaginative discovery.

For Propp action can proceed as follows: 'the object lacking involuntarily gives away some bit of news about itself by appearing momentarily, leaving behind some clear trace of itself, or else appearing to the hero in certain reflected forms. The hero loses his mental equilibrium and is seized with a longing for the beauty which he had once beheld' (1968, p. 76). This is an idea that echoes Levi–Strauss's thought about all objects having a counterpart in the past that ensures their future existence (1979, p. 183).

To Propp, situations of lack demand a hero 'who agrees to liquidate the misfortune or lack of another person. In the course of the action the hero is the person who is supplied with a magical agent (a magical helper), and who makes use of it or is served by it' (1968, p. 50). Applied to Maestro's story, we can only infer that the hero is the human race as a whole, but as yet it is unconscious of its purpose. Therefore, the acquisition and pursuit of money is a collective exercise, and relates to human creativity. The next chapter, however, will indicate that in fact only an elite selection of characters are currently labelled heroes by our culture; they are the men who possess vision and single–mindedness in money matters, who stand apart from the rest of the human race. So money, in fact, only figures in particular people.

Maestro introduces money to her characters by formulating the search around food, whereby nomadic peoples pursued wild animals, cattle, and the like (1993, p. 4). Thus, 'rationalized forms [such as] money, the means of existence, etc. are lacking' (Propp 1968, p. 35). The hero is allowed to depart from home to track down the needed object (Propp 1968, p. 37). Often he meets other, unfamiliar groups of people along the way and performs some exchanges: 'Any object could be exchanged for any other object if the two traders agreed. *Pretty* shells might be swapped for *bright* feathers [my emphasis]' (Maestro 1993, p. 5). Has the lacking object now appeared momentarily in this story, or has 'the hero [simply acquired] the use of a magical agent' (Propp 1968, p. 43)? Will it cause the hero to 'lose his mental equilibrium', as Propp suggests (1968, p. 76)? Reflected forms, such as 'bright', appealing things seem to have an impact on our conceptual control.

According to Blanchard, 'the narrator is at liberty to forget about the end, to be purposeless and to become a descriptor: to let himself be taken by the context and his reactions to it' (1980, p. 210). Description, as an interruption in narrative (in Blanchard's terms), '[represents] a genuine desire to return to or to remain in a nonnarrative state of association and nonobjectification, [but] it also fosters a desire to prepare for that very objectification' (1980, p. 214). Maestro's pretty shells and bright feathers seem to function in this way: they demand that the reader slows down, contemplates the object, possibly aestheticising it. We need descriptions to protect objects from 'disappearing into nothingness' (Blanchard 1980, p. 215). 'Not only can a description be made of [objects] (their shape, their color, their weight), but they have their own story to tell (where they originated, who used them first), and this story in turn, becomes our own (how we use them, how we live). We should thus be prepared to admit that descriptive-associative processes contribute to the elaboration of narrative' (Blanchard 1980, p. 212). Perhaps then, the multitude of sometimes conflicting delineations of money, such as bright feathers and symbolic coins, are manifestations of a cultural need to aestheticise money as a response to cashless (i.e., weightless, colourless, and shapeless) systems?

Maestro is in full flight: 'About ten thousand years ago, people began to farm the land people had time to learn new skills—to specialize in other jobs. Herders raised meat animals for butchers to kill, farmers raised grain for millers to grind into flour. Potters weavers carpenters, boat builders, and metalsmiths could be found in most big towns' (1993, pp. 6–7). Smith's story about the brewer, butcher, and baker are echoed here, so some sort of division of labour can be anticipated. Maestro's characters are members of a township, identified only by their trade or profession—a specialised performative function that delimits spheres of action (in Propp's and Smith's senses). Aside from the fact that this narrative is exclusively white Anglo-Saxon (the Australian aborigines, for instance, did *not* begin farming 10,000 years ago), the characters and their actions are beginning to be forced into the grand narrative of economic progress as if it were an inevitability.

'To make trading easier', Maestro continues, 'people began to use certain objects [such as salt]. Salt was valuable to people because they needed it to preserve and flavor food' (1993, p. 11). At this point in the narrative money is still awaiting its streamlined function, and even though Maestro has named the object, she has not yet delimited its signifieds: a wide range of other things were also used 'as money' (1993, p. 12). Salt or feathers, which were both used in exchange, can serve more than one function—we eat salt, use it as a preservative, and we can write with, or decorate, ourselves with feathers. Is this where money appears momentarily, perhaps conceptually, so as to reinforce the notion of lack to the hero? Salt was valuable because of its scarcity (Maestro 1993, p. 11). There is a very dominant idea about pursuit here, as if money is always playing hard to get. In addition, convenience and ease are also necessary prerequisites for the money object, but these ideas were still unrecognised by people at the time.

Eventually, as we have seen, the Sumerians discovered that metal could be used as money (Maestro 1993, pp. 14–15). This is a sudden unexplained action, and for Propp this is the climax of the narrative: 'The initial misfortune or lack is liquidated. The object of search is obtained by several personages at once, through a rapid interchange of their actions. The narrative reaches its peak in this function' (Propp 1968 , p. 53). But of course, money's story continues, in the minds of people *despite* its materialisation as metal, so the concept of money overrides its coining, and people continue to pursue it.

'Trading brought about more than an exchange of goods. It also brought about an exchange of ideas. The idea of money made from a precious metal spread', and by about 700 B.C. coins were relatively commonplace (Maestro 1993, pp. 16–17). Why? Because coins were '*easy*', '*popular*', trustworthy, and furthermore they '*worked* [my emphasis]' (Maestro 1993, pp. 18–22). Once again money is anthropomorphised.

Coining marks the climax of Maestro's narrative, and from this point on she begins to make sweeping statements. It seems that the arrival of metal coins brought about an erasure of difference amongst people. Maestro claims that everyone thinks the same way about money (1993, p. 40), and that they value money notes for what they represent (1993, p. 38).[10] Once again economics utilises universalisms, so that historical, social, and cultural specificity is ignored in favour of cultural generalisations. In addition, marginal or satellite stories are instantly effaced.

The book ends with the already cited conclusion: 'Money is a tool that has changed as the world has changed. Now it is changing again. No one knows for sure what the future of money will be' (Maestro 1993, pp. 42–43). Money is granted an autonomy at the end of this text that coincides with Forster's idea that characters 'try to live their own lives' (1974 [1927], p. 46). From the point of view of narrative, the ending is left open: changes to the material of money are rationalised in this text from the position of an open–ended present, and to me, the lack of an ending to this story signals crisis: *The Story of Money* leaves the future of money uncertain, unpredictable, beyond the realm of human agency.

Money is our co–dependent; we need it as much as it needs us, but the relationship is 'dysfunctional', as Blanchard suggests: 'Because the subject, the hero, is dependent on the world for the determination of his own identity, he cannot simply own or use objects for their own purposes; and because he must derive from them the meaning, the purpose of his own life, this relation often turns into a neurotic dependency' (1980, p. 211).

Money is largely destabilising in a psychological sense, as Lane's research in *The Market Experience* reveals. Money, Lane argues, complicates human reasoning, because it causes irrational behaviour and initiates moral uncertainty. The idea of the inherent rationality of the market, as expounded by many economists, is discredited, because from Lane's psychological perspective money can preclude rational calculation.

My whimsical combination of the ideas of Propp and Blanchard could lead to the conclusion that as soon as money appears, it disturbs us mentally, turning human beings into neurotic dependents, and hindering rational judgment. But then again, the idea may not be so frivolous after all. So far in this chapter we have seen that money can change us: digital money is a threat, because we have a new money form, and it is independent. Money speaks, spits and grows. It is an invisible yardstick, that sanctions and defines our individual and cultural purposes. Money is addicting, gullible, and hard to get (or evasive). But these characterisations are purely significations that infer a chaotic dependency. 'Money functions as an autonomous, perhaps rather frightening, language. It is a language of more than symbolism. There is a living, interactive code of metaphor implicit in money. Given the weird, surrealistic, metaphorical qualities of money, it's hardly surprising that both the markets and the people in them behave most of the time as if they were stark, raving mad' (Baker 1995, p. 167). Money significations are confused, and hence confusing. They provide little stable foundation for subsequent actions in the (self–labelled, turbulent) financial markets, and in Baker's terms could lead to a state of cultural schizophrenia.

Flat Money or Flat Readers?

Assumptions about readers are made in all texts that characterise. Jensen and Pauly maintain that cultural theory itself 'invokes an image of the audience. For the researcher the audience may appear as a market of consumers, a jaded mob, a nascent public, a lumpen proletariat, textual poachers, situated spectators, "the people" ' (1997, p. 155). No text is exempt from this practice. Furthermore, because we are culturally determined by our stories, the degree to which we consider ourselves to be individuals or types (such as the lumpen proletariat) is dictated by 'our knowledge of character codes' (Kermode 1979, p. 77), and currently these are generally borrowed from the mythologies of economics.

In a postindustrial world, character is a complex and torn ideology. Money and readers have both lost any sense they may have had of integrated essence. The question of a fractured individuality, defined by a fragmented monetary system, is perhaps unique to the late twentieth century. Many popular texts explore the interrelationship between the self and money, as if money were now the maker of character, so that we can consider ourselves to be partially made of money.

Litt's 'Adventures in Capitalism' is a text that deals with postindustrial identity. It is a short story that begins, 'After I won the lottery and jacked in my job at the Lab, I decided, in a spirit of scientific enquiry, to spend a year and a day believing everything the ads told me' (Litt 1995, p. 409). This first sentence plays with the economic assumption that once money is effortlessly won, work should cease. In addition, the juxtaposition of (scientific) *enquiry* and *belief* calls enquiry into question, but ultimately privileges belief. The text implies that money is a matter of faith rather than rational enquiry. Through the course of the narrative, the narrator finds that 'the whole world competed for my body and my cash', and this assertion culminates in a complete physical make–over (Litt 1995, p. 411). It is at this point that the relationship between the self (or the body) and money (as the definer of character) is called into question: 'Though enabled by money, I was created by myself. Even Max, my chief surgeon, will admit to that' (Litt 1995, p. 418). Money and plastic surgery are called into question in this text, because they are deemed to be similarly artificial conversions. Thus, in Litt's terms, there is nothing natural about character or money, and this view may be a symptomatic late twentieth–century view.[11]

Hunter's 'Reading Character' explains that the context of reading is important. 'Characters are read not only by comparing them with so–called real personalities, but by applying the norms and rules of characterisation current at the time' (1983, p. 230). Therefore, Hunter claims, 'character in the nineteenth–century practice of reading is primarily a moral object' and this 'dramatic characterisation [is] a systematic projection of the reader's moral character' (1983, pp. 230–33). For his argument, the institutions of the academy and the Church have traditionally organised concepts of the self via education and popular moral texts (Hunter 1983, p. 233).[12] Hunter contends that the reader's character is moulded, as well as restrained, by norms, so the reader becomes the constructed subject, and manoeuvre is precluded.

Undoubtedly, institutions such as the Church play a vital role in the dissemination of ideas about character and the reader's position. Allport and Odbert take a similar stance:

> It is the tendency of each social epoch to characterize human qualities in the light of standards and interests peculiar to the times. Historically, the production of trait names can be seen to follow this principal of cultural determination to a striking degree. Presumably human beings through countless ages had displayed such qualities as devotion, pity, and patience, but these terms were not established with their present meanings until the Church made of them recognized and articulated human virtues. (cited in Chatman 1980, p. 13)

This extract unwittingly touches upon some mythological aspects of character. It postulates a history behind 'articulated' values, and it is precisely in this type of narrativising that mythologies begin to surface. The impulse to draw on an apparently determining history in character analysis is widespread, but no more so than with the economic actor.

Institutions and their ideologies insinuate themselves into popular culture. The financial markets are beginning to dominate our so–called traditional power structures, such as the Church, the government (or ruling body), or the nation (an imagined community of people). Therefore it would be viable to assume that the mythologies that form these markets as institutions are to be found in popular texts, and are arguably worshipped. This chapter has outlined a few characterisations of money found in novels, the financial press, and a children's story. But these ideas derive from a collection of unstable signs, which in turn connote a sense of loss and recovery in relation to money. Money is characterised with qualities alien to its material existence, such as dependability and trustworthiness.

Buchan argues in *Frozen Desire* that a number of historical occurrences (such as double–entry book keeping, paper money, and credit) have altered our perception of money. Accordingly, as the material and management of money has changed, so have cultural relationships. 'The relations of human beings, both to one another and to the world of things, took on some of the character of money. They became fluid, temporary, indifferent, unstable' (Buchan 1997, p. 269). But in some ways instability can be desirable, because it has the capacity to clear the dogmatic ground. Once again, a fictional, more authentic past (such as Smith's where beavers were exchanged for deer) is brought to bear against the perception of an immaterial nullifying present. Money and people do share some indeterminate features, as Buchan suggests, but the development of the relationship does not seem to me to be so clear–cut. What is 'the character of money'? Buchan suggests that it is a yardstick and an end in itself so that money has 'passed from being a mere conveyance of desire to the object of all desire [whereby men have] lost sight of the natural sources of their existence' (1997, p. 269). The analysis he presents frequently characterises money as an agent of change, free of human intervention. Phrases he uses, such as 'money has spread out to colonise the world' (Buchan 1997, p. 268), continue the characterisation, constructing money as both imperialistic and a power.

So what do these characterisations contribute to our understanding of money, and of us as individual characters? Flat characters are 'constructed round a single idea or quality' (Forster 1974 [1927], p. 47). Flat characters are 'easily recognized', 'they never need reintroducing', they 'never run away', they do not need to be 'watched for development', they 'provide their own atmosphere', and they are 'easily remembered' (Forster 1974 [1927], p. 47). In Rimmon–Kenan's terms, flat characters consist of a sparse set of habitual, predictable actions that 'reveal the character's unchanging or static aspect' (1983, p. 61). Thus flat characters are limited, and little is expected of them developmentally. Applying this theory to the economic story, we find that people as rational, self–interested beings fit the flat picture, rather than money.

Round characters, on the other hand, are 'highly organized', 'they function all round', and they 'are ready for an extended life' (Forster 1974 [1927], p. 52). Even though money in economics has a purely functional character, it is *not* a flat predictable character, because it can be 'anything'. Money totally lacks specific, consistent traits or distinguishing features. The unexpected is the key to this type of character: 'The test of a round character is whether it is capable of surprising in a convincing way. If it never surprises, it is flat' (Forster 1974 [1927], p. 54). In the economic model, people are flat characters, whereas money is surprising and unpredictable.

So how do the characterisations of money as an independent actor function culturally and in texts? Why watch the money markets? Clearly they *do* need to be watched for development. In addition money has a directional dimension: implicit in its construction is the idea of its autonomy. In relation to Forster's view of character, I believe that money is given more animation than readers, and the very real implication of this is that readers become subordinate to money's functions. It is in the reader's perception of money as a character that monetary ideology is most threatening, because it destabilises the reader's perception of himself or herself. While the reader's identity is stabilised around a few key signifiers in economic theory, money's disappearance seems to solicit more open meanings. Nevertheless, the predictable and reliable aspects of character, as Rorty perceives it, 'stabilize the structure of a society' (1990, p. 304).

Of course, money is not a person with physical capacities. Neither is it a person in Rorty's sense: it does not possess an awareness of its rights or obligations. Physically it possesses no limbs or brain and therefore (though not necessarily correlatively) has no intrinsic ability to make moral or political choices. In Rorty's terms, money is in fact a 'figure', because figures function as 'idealizations' in which 'one or two physical details are focused upon, to make a presence salient. Vividness is often taken to be a mark of the real' (1990, p. 308).

Rorty concludes, 'we might do well to inquire into the ways various traits support different conceptions of responsibility. If Venusians and robots come to be thought of as persons, at least part of the argument that will establish them will be that they function as we do' (1990, pp. 321–22). By making money appear to be independent, and resemble us behaviourally, we are overemphasising its importance and limiting our ability to see things as they might be otherwise. At some stage in our history, money came to be attributed with human characteristics, and these characteristics are becoming increasingly obvious in the signs we encounter. The recognition of the idea that money could behave like a human being encourages the idea itself, so that rather than being simply a measurement, store of value, or exchange tool, money is permitted to extend beyond its purely instrumental boundaries.

My strategy for analysing money as a designator of character has had two distinct, but connected, aspects. In order to ascertain how money has often become more powerful than people in our society, I have shown in the first part of this chapter how money is constructed as an autonomous character, frequently with human characteristics, but always inconsistently. In the second part I explained how the vivified construction of money in turn defines the reader as a purely economic agent subordinate to the money concept. Both these ideas relate to notions of transformation and money as a dramatis persona. The *New Scientist* makes the arresting claim that because the character of money has changed, *all other parts of our lives* will change as a consequence: 'if the visionaries are right, e–cash will transform every aspect of our lives' (8 Apr. 1995, p. 29). Basically, money's character brings about a crisis of identity in the reader—regardless of its form.

Money's evasiveness and power to transform work in numerous ways, and some of these I have already outlined. Another way that money is attributed with power is in the notion that those who possess large sums of money are somehow superior to those who have little, such as the average reader. Contemporary characterisations of the rich redefine the archaic idea of the hero, so that we now construct cultural favourites who are visionaries, who quest for money. Possessing large amounts of money has somehow become an attribute, increasingly accentuated towards the end of the twentieth century, so that money actually seems to define a character's moral worthiness.

NOTES

1. The central belief amongst monetarists is that controlling the money supply is the best way of stabilising the economy, and controlling inflation.

2. Bradley's aim in *Shakespearean Tragedy* is to 'learn to apprehend the action and some of the personages of each [tragedy] with a somewhat greater truth and intensity, so that they may assume in our imaginations a shape a little less unlike the shape they wore in the imagination of their creator' (1971[1904], p. 1).

3. Gates acknowledges, however, that 'a complete failure of the network is worth worrying about' (1996 [1995], p. 301).

4. Many developments, such as twenty–four–hour trading in the financial markets would have been almost impossible without the PC, according to the *Australian Financial Review* (25 Sept. 1995, p. 28).

5. The *Australian Financial Review* is here explicitly stating that money is cash, a position that the paper's ideology would not generally endorse.

6. Some would say, incidentally, that human beings have 'so far been unable to master money' (Davies 1995, p. 4). And according to the Nobel–Prize–winning champion of monetarism, people have 'not succeeded in evolving a satisfactory monetary system in several millennia' (Friedman 1992, p. 39).

7. Noneconomic texts are similarly vague. The *Oxford English Dictionary* cites 'current coin; metal stamped in pieces of portable form as a medium of exchange and measure of value' as its first definition. Its second reads: 'applied occasionally by extension to other objects, or any material, *serving the same purposes as coin* [my emphasis]'.

8. Of course, in its own terms, the *Wall Street Journal* is not concerned with money per se, but with its mechanisms, its discourse, and its culture: in short, the systems constructed by the concept.

9. Kermode's investigation into versions of the Passion puts forward the idea that for the sake of 'sequentiality or plausibility' other narratives need to be brought to the fore (1979, p. 86) His example is a consideration of the motives behind Judas's betrayal for

thirty pieces of silver. Strictly speaking this is not an intrinsic part of the Passion, but it is a question the reader seems to need to have answered. The reader similarly needs to know how money came to surpass barter, not just *why* the change occurred.

10. Crawford would not agree, because to him, 'money is valueless paper' (1994, p. 3). Are ideas about money the same all over the world then?

11. According to Barthes, plastic too is mythological: it seems to have few boundaries, it is 'in essence the stuff of alchemy the transmutation of matter' (1989 [1957], p. 104). It is 'ubiquity made invisible it is less a thing than the trace of a movement' (1989 [1957], p. 104).

12. Rorty would perhaps describe this character construct as a 'person': 'In fusing the legal and dramatic concepts of person, Christianity made every human being with a will, qualify as a person' (1990, p. 310).

3

Heroes of Our Time

Like traditional myth, money's twentieth–century mythologies construct heroes, characters that are the focus of admiration. Throughout time, cultures have constructed heroes based on what Eliade calls an 'archetype' (1971 [1954], p. xiv). Whilst I reject Eliade's notion of an origin in terms of heroic representation, character typologies nevertheless do exist, but on a purely cultural level, and these typologies are recycled in different cultures with variations.[1] In addition, as Cawelti observes, the appeal of heroes 'is probably greatest at a time when neither tradition nor some concept of a future goal adequately defines what is virtuous for a man' (1976, p. 250), and our time is arguably directionless in Cawelti's sense. The hero is a character endowed with unique qualities (or gadgets) whose function is to restore order out of chaos. In the case of mythologies of money, chaos is money's perceived mystery.

The late twentieth–century hero is assisted by the belief that value derives from money as a measure; therefore money itself is a measure of distinction (Simmel 1990 [1900], p. 444). Each of the characters considered in this chapter has been associated with incalculably large sums of money, running into the billions of American dollars, and this is the fundamental criterion for my examination of heroes here. In some cases, money has become a trait of the hero, replacing traditional notions of valour and divine lineage. 'When Buffett made the Forbes list of billionaires', he became a 'folk hero' (Lowenstein 1996, pp. 265, 275; *New York Times* 5 Apr. 1998, p. 3). Undoubtedly there are other kinds of heroes constructed in our culture such as the sports hero. But where the sports hero depends upon his own body for success, the financial hero is decidedly different; he depends entirely upon an external entity (money) for his accolades.

Being rich or having an affinity with money are the central reasons for his success, and without it his hero status is nullified.

Heroes have a place in every society; they are symbolic models of conduct (*Encyclopedia of Religion* 1987, p. 302). In order to be a hero, a character must fulfil certain criteria: he should be born of a divine heritage (such as Jesus), and/or possess a magical tool (such as Perseus' magic wallet and helmet of invisibility), and he should perform outstanding deeds. Generally expected to complete a quest, such as slaying a monster, the hero should exhibit single-minded vision and fearlessness in the face of danger. The restoration of order also plays a fundamental part in the mythic story, because it reestablishes cultural systems and organisations. Perseus' slaughter of Medusa is mimicked in the late twentieth-century West by a selection of characters who make a killing on the financial markets, thereby to a degree solidifying our monetary systems.

MONIED AND MONETARY HEROES

J. P. Morgan, John D. Rockefeller, and Henry T. Ford are arguably the first three money heroes of the twentieth century, but others have followed in their footsteps. For the sake of clarity I have divided my four chosen heroes into two types: monied heroes and monetary heroes. The first, the *monied* hero, refers to the rich character who possesses, and is defined by, his wealth. Generally this label could currently be applied to Warren Buffett and Bill Gates. Buffett is a multi*billionaire*, one–time holder of the Forbes title richest man in America. Lowenstein maintains that *super*wealth is the defining characteristic of Buffett (1996, p. 415). Aside from once being America's richest man, he is distinguished for his wisdom concerning the financial markets, and he is often consulted by journalists for his view on market movements. Gates took over the title of richest man in the United States from Buffett in 1994. He is lauded for two things: his technological innovations, mainly computer software, and the vast wealth he has made from them. Gates surpassed the merely rich mark in 1993 by also becoming 'the *youngest* billionaire in the history of America [my emphasis]' (Wallace and Erickson 1993, p. 81). 'According to 1997 data, the Sultan of Brunei has been toppled as the *world's* richest person. His successor is software genius Bill Gates, 41' (*Money of the World* 1998, p. 1).

The second term, the *monetary* hero, I use to refer to the visionary character who utilises or invents new money tools. Soros is not an inventor, he is a hedge fund manager who uses the markets to his own financial advantage. Soros first came to the public's attention when he made a '$1.5 billion profit by betting on a weakening British pound in 1992' (Baker 1995, p. 145). As a consequence of this action, he is now commonly labelled '[manipulator] of the foreign exchange market' (Baker 1995, p. 146), or more simply, as the man himself expresses it, he can 'move markets' (Soros 1995, p. 85). My second monetary hero is Leo Melamed, who launched the International Money Markets in Chicago, which now trade financial instruments (including futures) rather than physical commodities such as pork bellies and soya beans. Melamed invented and popularised financial futures trading.[2] These heroes are often the originators of self–generating systems, and in this respect Gates too fits into this category with his PC and software innovations. As with all heroes, Buffett, Gates, Soros, and Melamed are all partially reconstructed from earlier mythic models, which is consistent with the repetitive turns that characterise mythology. All four characters are admired and discussed in terms of their unique relationship to money, as if money were a trait, but they are in turn traited in heroic commonalities, that do not always cohere with my own typological distinctions.

There are many common links forged between these characters in texts, whether they are monied or monetary heroes. Of these four characters, Melamed and Gates are represented as visionaries, Proppian heroes who recognise that something is lacking and bring it to us: Gates popularised the personal computer and software, and Melamed popularised financial futures. On the other hand, Buffett and Soros are loners; mistrustful of the herd, they go against the grain of their cultural milieux. Melamed and Soros are also outsiders from another angle: they are both of middle–European origin, whereas Buffett and Gates are 'home–grown' Anglo–American talent. Alternatively we find that it has been said of both Gates and Buffett that money making was in their genes, that it was a biological inheritance. This is a new idea about money, drawing upon our cultural preoccupation with genetics, and can be compared with ideas about old money and blue blood.

Monetary and monied heroes are constructed as out of the ordinary, or distinctive. On the back cover of Melamed's (1996) book, wittily entitled *Escape to the Futures,* we find the idea of revolution enveloping three of my chosen heroes: 'There are only a few people who have revolutionized big portions of the business world. Warren Buffett did it in investing, Bill Gates in software, Leo Melamed truly revolutionized futures trading in the United States'. Another circle is formed around business people by virtue of the fact that they are unconventional. Known as 'Crazy Henry' (Gross 1996, p. 77), Ford '[ignored] conventional wisdom' (Gross 1996, p. 81). Bill Gates, we find, 'was not cut from the usual executive cloth' (Gross 1996, p. 342). In *Buffett: The Making of an American Capitalist,* we have Buffett characterised as a man who 'stands alone' (Lowenstein 1996, p. xiii), exhibiting a 'habit of independent thought' (Lowenstein 1996, p. 11). Effectively these kinds of constructions prohibit the reader from aligning himself or herself with heroes, because they emphasise the characters' inherent distance from general, everyday cultural practices.

Soros explains his singularity in terms of investment dilemma. He claims that the knowledge investors use in the financial market is not original, rather it is unimaginative and undistinguished. Therefore, because his fund operated against the grain, anyone with accepted ideas was not welcome in his team (1995, p. 48). Soros is an exceptional investor because he rarely follows the crowd's wisdom. Buffett also explains his oppositional investment characteristics as being 'out of step' (in Lowenstein 1996, p. 96). Accordingly, 'Buffett's reaction [is] instinctive: *Be greedy when others are fearful* [Lowenstein's emphasis]' (1996, p. 150).[3] Both Buffett and Soros are perceived to play the financial markets successfully, because they have unique approaches to the financial world. Monied and monetary heroes are admired for their prophetic, almost divine qualities, so the market and its successful players take on the appearance of a quasi–religious fellowship.

According to Eliade's *The Myth of the Eternal Return*, 'for the traditional societies, all the important acts of life were revealed *ab origine* by gods or heroes. Men only represent these exemplary and paradigmatic gestures *ad infinitum*' (1971 [1954], p. 32). For money's mythology, there are no historical monetary precedents, so heroic models are borrowed from other mythologies, such as the religious mythology. The repeated idea that money has a historical foundation that can be recovered seems to give the heroes of money an authenticity. It also implies that the money–making quest has a quasi–religious element. In Eliade's terms, 'an object or an act becomes real only insofar as it imitates or repeats an archetype. Thus, reality is acquired solely through repetition or participation; everything which lacks an exemplary model is "meaningless", i.e., it lacks reality' (1971 [1954], p. 34).

The mythic hero of all ancient cultures has special links to divinity, either through his parents, or as Eliade maintains, through his deeds, which have a religious significance: 'All religious acts are held to have been founded by gods, civilizing heroes, or mythical ancestors any human act whatever acquires effectiveness to the extent that it exactly *repeats* an act performed at the beginning of time by a god, a hero, or an ancestor' (1971 [1954], p. 22). The borrowing of ancient myth for twentieth–century constructions of money heroes implies an originary divine plan, but the idea is untenable, because money is an entirely human venture; we are its god—as its creators and preservers. Nevertheless ideas about heroes sharing features with the gods persist. In addition, money's mythology constitutes a partial surrender to history and fictional monetary cycles, so that attempts to control money are destined to be thwarted.

There is a claim, popular in many texts, that the instinct for successful investing comes from the gods. Soros says that 'by entering the fray as an investor, I descended from Mount Olympus and became a flesh and blood human being' (1995, p. 143). Soros makes claims on history, (Greek) myth, and simple clay–footed investment. In a similar vein, Bill Gates, the Microsoft hero, is constructed as a godlike visionary. When he visited Australia in 1995, *Business Review Weekly* labelled him 'the richest evangelist' of the 'information age' (30 Jan. 1995, p. 28). Furthermore, 'Rumor has it that the Pope has timed his visit to Australia to be closer to God [read: Gates]. Such is the type of hype, sometimes mania that surrounds Gates' (*Business Review Weekly* 30 Jan. 1995, p. 28). And, of course, the journalists on *Business Review Weekly* themselves participated in this adoration.

An article entitled 'Interest in the Divine' (*New York Times* 9 May 1997, p. B1) makes a similar analogy between Buffett and god:

One man speaks to God. The other speaks to the stock market. Both of them hear things that no one else does. The rabbi knows precious little about business and is fine with that. The investor, an avowed agnostic, bought his first stock when he was 11, and his acumen for making money seems divine. Pretty much every one knows the gilded story of Warren E. Buffett, the investor from Omaha with the otherworldly nose for stocks, the man of gold who is now worshipped on Wall Street as the god of stock pickers.

Of course, according to my argument, there is nothing godly about gilt-edged investment. Buffett is simply being constructed as a representative character. The flowery terminology in this piece contributes to the illusion that Buffett's money sense *seems* divine, and so he is worshipped.

Before I turn to my four specific contemporary examples of the rich hero, I will first consider an earlier model in order to highlight some paradigms and distortions of traditional heroes that we construct today. Monetary heroes are partially authenticated by historical precedents, and this point can best be illustrated by considering a character that emerged in the early eighteenth century, along with paper money.

JOHN LAW—SWINDLER OR PROPHET?

John Law (1671–1729) has been variously described as 'swindler and prophet' (Marx 1991[1894], p. 573), 'the greatest financier of history', and a 'gorgeous sinner [a] paragon of masculinity and finance' (Buchan 1997, pp. 133, 131). There is a certain fascinating complexity to the way this character is constructed, as well as to the fact that he is hauled out of the annals of financial texts in moments of monetary crisis (such as when money changes form or monetary management is questioned). The infatuation derives primarily from the fact that Law was responsible for the first banknote issue in France in 1716, so he effectively '[created] a new medium of currency' (Williams 1997, p. 182). Despite the fact that Law's 'System', as he called it (Davies 1995, p. 554), went disastrously wrong, he is given many labels, some from the traditional heroic paradigm—

hence Marx's swindler *and* prophet. From any perspective, Law is constructed as an enigma.

We encounter the attribution of heroic traits in passages such as Davies's summary of Law's early life: 'He was born in Edinburgh, where his father was a goldsmith and a banker. The son showed an early proficiency in mathematics and worked in his father's bank from the age of fourteen until seventeen, when his father died. He then moved to London and got involved in a duel with a certain Mr. Wilson, whom he killed. He escaped from prison by fleeing abroad' (1995, p. 553). First, we find that Law has a monied lineage as well as a kind of genetic aptitude for money making. According to Rorty, 'the fate of heroes is their parentage. To be the child of Athene fixes the major events of one's life, determines one's tasks, and even one's capacities to meet them' (1990, p. 303). In other words, the heroic destiny is pre–determined. In addition, Law has an aptitude for mathematics, which could be interpreted as a type of mastery, or at least a capacity for rationalisation. Successful money makers are considered to be careful—calculating and mindful of mathematical formulae—model economic characters. Law leaves home (albeit as an escape), and in Proppian terms, departure from the homeland is vital to the hero's story. Law demonstrates a capacity for slaying, and proves himself to be roguish (like Robin Hood). And the roguish characterisation is a 'popular [expression] of the valuing of individualism above the limiting structures of society' (Hourihan 1997, p. 150), but once again the reader is precluded by economic characterisations from achieving similar recognition, and so ambitions are partially fulfilled through textual gratification.

Law's issue of paper money initially seems indicative of creative mastery. Law starts up a system of banknote issues from France's 'first public bank'— Law & Co—a bank he owned with his (insignificant) brother (Davies 1995, p. 554). At first the banknotes were a success, and appeared to solve the problem of France's national debt. In the process, Law himself became very rich indeed. But all went sadly wrong. Greed overtook the French populace and 'by December 1720 he had long since lost the backing of the Regent, and the bank and his Mississippi Company had collapsed, shattering public confidence and earning him international and lasting notoriety' (Williams 1997, p. 182). According to Davies, 'Law's system had gone into reverse. [He] left France and nine years later died in poverty in Venice' (1995, p. 555). When Law died he left his son and daughter as well as their mother—Lady Catherine Knollys—almost penniless.

Law's character is constructed around contradictory characterisations, because he was a failure and a success. Buchan draws some characterisations together: He was 'a Protestant [who was goaded into converting to Catholicism by the Regent], a gambler, adulterer, convicted murderer, slaver, and coward (also the handsomest man in Europe and possessed, as even his enemies conceded, of peculiarly beautiful manners)' (Buchan 1997, p. 128). Above all, for Buchan and Williams, Law is a 'monetary hero' (Buchan 1997, p. 272), because he invented paper money, and is therefore deemed to be 'imaginative, clever and idealistic' (Williams 1997, p. 182). The establishment of paper money, as an imaginative venture, constitutes to some extent mastery over nature—that is, if we concede that money is a naturalised concept.

Hourihan's study of children's stories in Western culture, *Deconstructing the Hero*, makes the claim that 'the story of the hero and his quest, the adventure story, is always essentially the same' (1997, p. 2). She lists what she calls the 'invariable pattern' of the hero story in Anglo cultures (which I condense here): 'The hero is white, male, British, American or European', he leaves home to 'venture into the wilderness', which may be a 'fantasy land' where 'dangerous and magical things happen'. The hero 'is determined to succeed' and 'may receive assistance from benevolent beings'. 'He achieves his goal which may be golden riches', and 'returns home rewarded' (Hourihan 1997, pp. 9–10).

Much of Law's story is constructed along these lines: he is a white British male who leaves home to live in Paris where he sets up a fantastic monetary scheme with the assistance of the Regent. According to Williams, who clearly relishes Law's imagination and idealism, Law's theories 'were based not on short-term expediency, but on a long cherished theory of promoting domestic industry through the provision of credit in the form of paper money backed by the value of land' (1997, p. 182). If paper money is overissued (or as current parlance has it, 'printed'), the paper comes to have a value *higher* than the value of the land on which it is based, and uncontrollable inflation occurs (according to some monetarist arguments). Correlatively the land, which is the material foundation of all monies, comes to be *under*valued, and money is more *highly* valued for itself. The unanticipated overspeculation and oversubscription of shares in Law's later Mississippi project was incredible. The appeal of paper money, and the potential wealth to be derived from it was unprecedented in France. Mackay's *Extraordinary Popular Delusions and the Madness of Crowds* maintains that 'the people were rapidly approaching the zenith of their infatuation. The highest and lowest classes were alike filled with a vision of boundless wealth' (1996 [1841], p. 36). Because the Mississippi share issues were not tied to land, they were, according to Mackay, a 'departure from sound principles' (1996 [1841], p. 33). Sound principles bear a metaphorical relationship to the land and nature, as they are part of the solid foundation of all that is concrete and tangible in money matters. This solidity is generally contrasted with the intangible, virtual, and airy–fairy makeup of new forms of money, a contrast we have encountered in relation to Daisy and Gatsby. Discussing Law, a Dutch satirical cartoon of 1720, for example, claimed that his paper money with its promise–to–pay–the–bearer–on–demand was 'based on nothing more than wind, smoke and deceit' (in Williams 1997, p. 183).

Law's status as a true hero is threatened according to Hourihan's account, because Law does not return home rewarded. Therefore it could be said that Law was partially a failure, falling short of the heroic in a monied respect. The implication of this is that while the paradisical is appealing, it is a largely unrealisable quest. Nevertheless, as Buchan notes, Law continues to surface as an exemplar in economic and monetary discussions, and so it is his financial innovation that characterises him (1997, pp. 132–33). Law, like Melamed and Soros in our time, perceived a lack in our monetary tools, and they all became monetary heroes whether or not they had money (as is the case with the *monied* hero). Some, like Mackay, consider Law to be a victim of circumstance, and so he retains hero status as a masterful individual despite his losses: 'How was he to foretell that the French people, like the man in the fable, would kill, in their frantic eagerness, the fine goose he had brought to lay them so many golden eggs?' (Mackay 1996 [1841], p. 21). The perception of Law as a financial innovator overrides his failure in many commentators' perceptions. For example, according to Mackay, Law was 'more deceived than deceiving, more sinned against than sinning' (1996 [1841], p. 21). A vision of boundless wealth came to be inextricably linked to Law's character. Other characters have similarly come to be perceived as monetary heroes in popular perception because of their unique capacity to generate money.

In effect, I concur with Buchan's observation that 'the rich are loved for making actual the wishes of everybody' (1997, p. 152). But the wishes are not fulfilled in any real sense, they are merely constructed by and reproduced in texts, and so they remain unrealised, or even 'frozen', as Buchan expresses it in his title (1997). Monied heroes structure relationships, in the sense that the hero forces readers to define themselves in terms of rich or poor, haves or have–nots. The stories of these heroes also foist a desire or need for money upon us, thereby '[impoverishing] consciousness' (Barthes 1989 [1957], p. 154). To borrow Barthes's terminology, they delimit thought as well as ambition.

Messent's (1990) *New Readings of the American Novel* questions the notion of individual sovereignty. He claims that his 'critically destabilizing notion of character as similarity [is] a powerful textual thrust which radically undercuts and questions the notion of the sovereign self' (Messent 1990, p. 127). Characters, deemed to be alike, dissolve the boundaries of difference and uniqueness. Unashamedly rewriting the context of Messent's remark, I would say that like metaphor, character is a 'connective principle [hinging] on an awareness both of similarity and difference' (Messent 1990, p. 81). In other words, some heroes in this chapter share some cultural territory with the reader, but they are more often distinct from the reader.

The stories of monetary heroes that we have today in the press and in biographies share many features of the Law story. Monetary and monied heroes are visionaries, innovative and unswerving in their monetary quest. However, Buchan suggests that with new forms of money, we have new kinds of heroes (1997, p. 128). The late twentieth–century virtual money world is characterised by a sense of infinite duplication, reproduction, and representation. Abstract financial instruments, known in market discourse as 'paper', seem to generate more heroic constructs as a way of concretising or giving a face to our financial culture.

The monetary hero leads me to dispute Calder's assertion that 'the heroic idea [has] lost currency' in the twentieth century: heroes such as Soros are actually defined by currency (Calder 1977, p. xi). Calder further maintains that the hero's 'most notable twentieth century function appeared to be to entice us away from reality, rather than to confront all its difficulties', a point I agree with to some extent (1977, p. xi). It is precisely because mythology is a second–order system that it is removed from reality, and the hero is an intrinsic facet of this mythological structure. Even though myths traditionally deal with fantastic subject matter, both myths and Barthesian mythologies are used to define and maintain cultural order, providing the basis of many truths by which people live. 'The hero story is a myth in both the traditional sense and the sense in which Roland Barthes uses the term to describe the way certain stories and images function to shape our perception of reality' (Hourihan 1997, p. 12).

THE TWENTIETH–CENTURY HERO

Twentieth–century monied and monetary heroes embody many facets of traditional and mythical heroes, but these are modified, because 'the hero changes with his surroundings, his time and his sociocultural environment' (Lash 1995, p. 27). The aspects retained from archaic constructions serve two functions: they authenticate the monied hero, and they also demonstrate a cultural inclination for past (mythical) values. Unlike Walter Benjamin, who believed that reproduction assisted in the release of art from ritual and tradition, I argue that reproduction is precisely that part of financial discourse that encourages a revitalisation of ritual and tradition (1969, pp. 217–51). The seeming artifice of money causes us to make increased references to historical stories and myths. Effectively, mythology has a cyclical nature; it is continuously turning towards *and away* from reality.

As new money comes to be regarded as artificial, the impulse is to reconstruct character types as well as history mythologically. While monied and monetary heroes are inconsistently shaped, the conventional elements that are incorporated into their construction make them resonant and recognisable. The construction of the late twentieth–century rich as heroes authenticates their achievements in mythological terms, as well as providing readers with a quest object: money.

The Quest

More than any other characteristic they share, Gates, Buffett, Melamed, and Soros are rich, and therefore in traditional mythic terms they have been rewarded (either for their valour or their vision). The hero gains his status through the completion of a quest. According to Hourihan, 'the quest story is implicit in the nature of the hero. He strives towards his goal never doubting the rightness or the primacy of his cause' (1997, p. 58). In general terms, the quest is about triumph over 'chaos, nature, evil, [and] death itself' (Hourihan 1997, p. 27), and involves the suppression or slaughter of primeval forces. Therefore my focus in this section is on both the money quest and the heroes' (metaphoric) death.

Heroism is 'about mastery' (Hourihan 1997, p. 11), and 'the hero story celebrates the conquest of nature the transformation of nature into "shape and meaning" ' (Hourihan 1997, pp. 6–7). The irrational, the formless and the unknown are mastered by the hero according to Hourihan, and in some instances this configuration is female. 'Women are regarded as closer to nature' (Hourihan 1997, p. 161), and the financial market, as I note in chapter 6, is frequently described as female, mysterious, and often uncontrollable, similar to Nietzsche's concept of the Dionysian nature.[4] Money management is deemed to be a rational pursuit, and consequently a male prerogative. In Plumwood's terms all nonrational (i.e., feminine) elements need to be excluded from the heroic paradigm (cited in Hourihan 1997, pp. 16–17). It is partially then a feminine market that is first naturalised, and then tamed, by the hero. Where dragons or barbarians were the objects of the hero's conquest previously, the structures of money (such as the metaphorical market) and the nature of money itself now become the focus of heroic activity.

When a market player such as Buffett or Soros is constructed as a hero, his character contributes to a heightened sense of money as a monster to be tamed. Conquest is intrinsic to the hero; he must be able to master 'an excess of force his challenge is to face forces gone out of control' (Lash 1995, p. 6). Soros's currency trading is effectively a struggle with a vast financial market. Buffett too masters market movements, which to some observers seem random and uncontrollable. Several of the monied heroes experience adrenalin rushes, risk, and potential monetary downfall in their dealings with the market monster. They exhibit fearlessness in the face of risk. The threat of losing money is stimulating to the new hero: 'going to the brink serves a purpose. There is nothing like danger to focus the mind, and I do need the excitement connected with taking risks in order to think clearly' (Soros 1995, pp. 15–16). The risk entails a potential loss of money; it does not entail a physical threat of any kind. The hero can be a 'monster slayer' (Lash 1995, p. 10), and Soros's trading is seen to be the result of a killer instinct: 'like sharks, hedge funds would sniff in the water the slightest trace of blood from a potential victim' (Gapper and Denton 1996, p. 244). Soros made a killing out of a weak pound in 1992.

Monied heroes are always purposeful, pursuing money against all odds, leaping over all hurdles. Upward or downward movements in the market can emotionally affect some, but 'Buffett's rare ability to separate his emotions from the Dow Jones Industrial Average was a big part of his success' (Lowenstein 1996, p. 156).[5] Consistency, self–control, focus, tenacity, and an unnerving calmness are further characteristics of the monied hero.

Hourihan summarises the following primary traits for the typical hero: will, ambition, activism, and rationality, but 'his [overall] mode is domination' (1997, p. 58). The linearity of hero stories, namely, the quest–struggle–success plot results from these traits, and Hourihan considers the heroic paradigm to be one that reinforces the structures of Western patriarchy. Furthermore, 'to many readers [the hero's] certainty is enormously attractive because it reinforces established views of the way the world is' (Hourihan 1997, p. 58). For money's mythologies, Buffett, Gates, and Soros fulfil this function, validating money as a quest object as well as reinforcing the apparently common–sensical financial structures of the West. Furthermore, the triumph over money these characters accomplish is perceived as 'the infinite power of man over nature' (Barthes 1989 [1957], p. 77), because the chaotic market is naturalised and womanised.

The hero cannot be a woman. Whilst this seems self–evident, it cannot be over-stressed. The hero must be manly, drawing upon a whole range of so–called masculine traits. In her study, *The Hero: Manhood and Power*, Lash observes: 'Foremost in the heroic configuration is virility, the essence of the masculine sex ideally the hero incarnates masculinity at its best' (1995, p. 5). Virility and money making may seem a problematic analogy, but not so in Buffett's case. Buffett's biographer, Lowenstein, maintains that 'the market collapse of 1973–4 was the *ideal* time to be a hero' (1996, p. 157), and at that same time Buffett was telling *Forbes* that he felt like 'an oversexed guy in a whorehouse. This is the time to start investing' (in Lowenstein 1996, p. 161). The parallel between prostitution and money is replete, yielding a number of readings: availability, pleasure fulfilment, and exploitation (amongst others). More significantly, Buffett infers some sort of biological compulsion and mastery in his description, suggesting that like women, money can be dominated. Therefore Buffett shapes money very much in terms of patriarchal ideology.

Whether Buffett's position is determined by psychology or instinct is undecidable. He fails, however, to disassociate himself from the female aspects of money as I have explained them so far. Lash makes the further point that the hero 'displays exclusively one dimension of our common endowment: *the full ripening of the aggressive instinct which assures survival by the mastery of overwhelming forces rather than by adaptation to them* [Lash's emphasis]'

(1995, p. 10). According to this view, the female is somehow naturally bound to nature and is resolutely bound to an acceptance of her condition. Lash brings scientific discourse into the equation by pointing out that 'modern studies of embryonic development confirm how the higher degree of masculine self–definition is claimed by arduous disengagement from a female "ground–plan" ' (1995, p. 12). The problem of how the 'ground–plan' invades the foetus will have to be left unsolved in this work, but it should be noted that the female/male opposition is occasionally ushered into monetary discourse.

The construction of the quest has been significantly modified from ancient models. Nevertheless, as with 'early legends [the hero's] quest involves [the people's] aspirations' (Hourihan 1997, pp. 62–63). To a certain extent readers expect heroes to identify and fulfil their wishes for them, as Buchan contends (1997, p. 152). In a sense mythical heroism is also about problem solving; it restores order to contemporary chaos. A significant shift occurred in the nineteenth century when 'commerce and industrialization seriously threatened the heroic idea through their inevitable fragmentation of society' (Calder 1977, p. ix). As a consequence, Calder argues, the heroic 'Man of Enterprise' entered the fictional scene. He is the hero who 'worked and won success, which usually meant money and recognition. Achievement and money were usually things the Victorian public found it hard to ignore' (1977, p. 51). If Calder's analysis holds sway, then the hero gradually came to be lauded for the spoils of his success, rather than for resolving an ethical struggle implicit in the quest itself, and yet Calder intimates a contrary position: 'the best men of enterprise were more interested in what they accomplished than their lifestyle or the symbols of what money could buy, although most relished the kind of heroic symbolism success could bring. Most of them enjoyed making money, they enjoyed that very concrete recognition of their achievements' (1977, p. 54). This analysis is consistent with Lowenstein's diagnosis of Buffett: 'Wall Street interested him merely as an abstraction—the money meant nothing to him' (1996, p. 37).

Generally the heroic goal is monetary 'success', but according to numerous texts, the pursuit of money is not an end in itself. Money is 'proof' of ability or participation in the game; it is not designed to change lives (Lowenstein 1996, p. 87). Merely a passport, or ticket, to better things, money is seen here as the means only to an end. This perception conflicts with the views of many modern social theorists from Simmel to Veblen: 'The possession of wealth, which was at the outset valued simply as evidence of efficiency, becomes, in popular apprehension, itself a meritorious act' (Veblen 1970 [1899], p. 37).

The monied hero is to a certain extent a necessary construct for the placing of readers economically, encouraging a sense of inferiority and inadequacy, and it is through comparative difference that the monied hero exists as a cultural, but more importantly monetary, spur. Drawing upon a range of heroic characteristics

such as vision, lineage, and quest fulfilment, the monied hero reproduces the traditional mythic hero. In this sense, the monied hero as he is constructed (by the
press in particular) is a re–presentation of an earlier model.

Visions, Oracles, and Windows

Many heroes are constructed around the idea that they had no *choice* but to
fulfil their destiny. According to Gross, Roy Kroc, the Hamburger King saw 'his
destiny', and he set about 'fulfilling his vision': to make McDonald's a 'global
institution' (1996, pp. 180–88). In Proppian terms the hero becomes obsessed by
a momentary vision that he feels he has to concretise. The implication of this for
me is that the economic ideal, or quest, is deemed to be predetermined; it merely
needs to be realised. Monetary and monied heroes are somehow tied to another
world, an ideal world where the vision and purpose of money are clearly represented.

Being able to predict the movements of the financial markets, or to go against
them as Buffett and Soros do, is deemed to be visionary. But, as Spooner
explains, '*the stock market is a state of mind* [Spooner's emphasis]' (1985, p.
13). This argument is a prevalent one in texts that resist the concept of trading as
rational (Fay 1996; Baker 1995), and it is a position I find incontrovertible. 'The
market has nothing to do with housing starts, money supply or interest rates. It
has to do with emotion' (Spooner 1985, p. 13). If Buffett buys shares in, say,
Coca Cola (which he has done), hoards of investors mimic his purchase, thereby
artificially, and maybe only briefly, driving the price up. Buffett is then lauded as
a visionary for predicting a surge in price. It is not the hero then who should be
accredited with vision.

There is an implicit idea in some texts that money can only be viewed
through a certain lens. Investors are constructed as visionaries as we have just
seen, but some characters are constructed as unique, because they understand
business 'through the keyhole of finance' (Lowenstein 1996, p. 101). But the
keyhole restricts, making the hero's focus solely monetary. Money is the goal,
the attribute, and the object that defines success. Soros asserts that if you want to
be rich, you should direct your attention solely at the 'bottom line' (1995, p. 245).
The bottom line here is the heroic goal; it is wealth to be pursued against all odds,
like a Holy Grail.

Gates and Melamed are visionaries, who see the world as it should be. 'Bill,
certainly, always had the vision', and the vision indicated that he 'was clearly
thinking in the right direction' (Wallace and Erickson 1993, pp. 95, 110). Wallace
and Erickson maintain that, thanks to Gates, 'Eventually, everyone would own a
computer' (1993, p. 90). It is because Gates is perceived to be a visionary that his
text *The Road Ahead* actually sells. The text is full of constructions of Gates as a
visionary. 'When I was nineteen,' Gates writes, 'I caught sight of the future and

based my career on what I saw. I turned out to have been right' (1996 [1995], p. 4).[6] (I wonder if there is any significance in the fact that Gates is looking backwards on the cover of his book, rather than at the road [future] ahead?).

Let us take a closer look at Leo Melamed, a man Milton Friedman (the monetarist and Nobel Prize winner) considers to be 'imaginative' (Melamed 1996, p. 176). In the early 1970s Melamed initiated a market in financial futures in Chicago, and finally launched the International Monetary Market (IMM) on 16 May 1972. It was the first time that financial instruments rather than physical commodities were traded in the Chicago Futures Exchange. The project was backed by Milton Friedman, who compiled a feasibility report for the idea and was paid $5,000 for his efforts (Melamed 1996, p. 177). Of himself, Melamed says, '[I] wasn't blind to the fact that by introducing a financial instrument to the futures world, I would be blazing a new trail' (1996, p. 171). He has also been described as 'one of the most powerful figures in the world of finance—a visionary' (front inside cover). These attributions are reminiscent of the Law construction. Again, Melamed is an exaggerated character, godlike in his capacity to use the future to his advantage, and he has been excessively praised for his financial prowess. 'As his reputation as a financial genius grew, so did the tales of his larger–than–life personality' (front inside cover). 'I was an evangelist, a dreamer, a Don Quixote, half crazed with the belief that financial futures were an idea whose time had come' (Melamed 1996, p. 183). Melamed, like Gates and Soros, participated in the cultural construction of his own mythical character.

Because its construction is 'invisible', money has been let off the reins and is now self–generating. Governments and indeed whole groups of people, such as the IMF, the World Bank, and others, have no control over monetary spread or loss—the Asian economic downturn of 1997 being a recent example. In an age of corporate rotundity, it is now possible for corporations and individuals such as Soros to control vast proportions of the world's wealth. Furthermore, because money is based on abstract concepts, it encourages the niche–creating entrepreneurial spirit. Without a material substance, constrained by physical laws such as gravity, the form (or nonform) of money now enables people like Melamed to invent instruments that 'shed the straitjacket of physical delivery' (Melamed 1996, p. 334).

Monetary heroes are frequently intertextualised. In a speech on Melamed's retirement, for example, a close colleague made the following remarks:

to the world you have given an idea, just as Newton, Galileo, Copernicus, Euclid and a great many other great thinkers and innovators did before you. Your idea, ultimately, like theirs, has and will continue to spawn many others that will have an immeasurable impact on the world. In our lifetime, because of you, we will see international trade burgeon, time zones disappear, and cooperation between countries flourish. (Melamed 1996, p. 420)

Aligned with the 'great' scientific thinkers, Melamed's financial inventions have allowed money to defy gravity and time, and this bears a direct relationship on his characterisation. Furthermore, his invention spawns others, and it is therefore a self–generating tool. I now turn to a related idea: genetic inheritance—an important factor for the heroic character.

Money Making: Genetic Inheritance or Cultural Mastery?

Monied and monetary heroes achieve their status either because of their achievements (vision, inventiveness, or money making schemes) or their inherited qualities (mathematical genius, parentage, masculinity). Superman has inherent characteristics: x–ray vision and he can fly, and this makes him a superhero rather like Soros and Buffett. Batman on the other hand (like Gates and Melamed) has many gadgets to assist him, which makes him a hero dependent upon his deeds. In terms of background, Superman hails from Krypton while Batman comes from a wealthy family (remember the hero's lineage is generally considered important).

Soros likes the figurehead attribution, because it paradoxically frees him from bondage, financially and character–wise: 'In some ways I am an exception. Having more money than I need, I have been liberated from the law of gravity: I can afford to stand up for abstract principles' (1995, p. 247). The implication of this view is that only the monied person is free to pursue philosophical concepts, whereas the unmonied are tied to lowly pursuits and pragmatic calculations.

According to Rorty's interpretation: 'The fate of heroes is their parentage. Yet at the same time the hero is known by his deeds: setting himself superhuman tasks' (1990, p. 303). This short phrase encapsulates several of the aspects I have attempted to differentiate: the fulfilled quest, the setting of his own tasks in the absence of natural threat. But the issue of parentage and genetic inheritance is a pressing one, particularly in view of genetic engineering. After all, if we can cure alcoholic tendencies, for example, by manipulating DNA, can we not also create a world of money makers?

Being reproducible also equates with cloning: we now have the technology to clone sheep like Dolly, why not people, why not those people who have some 'innate' capacity for reproducing money? A genetic capacity for money generation situates the majority of people outside the bounds of monetary reproduction, so that the periphery is merely a cultural bondage, tying those who have no money gene to the mythologies of money's culture.

Twice Lowenstein implies that money–making is in Buffett's genes (1996, pp. 5, 366). Of Gates we encounter a slightly different perspective on inheritance: 'If bloodlines are an indication of future success, then Bill Gates was born into a family generous with its gifts' (Wallace and Erickson 1993, p. 8). The implication of these two remarks is that money is a part of the body's makeup.

The movie *Trading Places* (1983) presents the money–making gene argument as a challenge. Duke and Duke, a pair of wealthy and elderly futures traders, construct a 'scientific' experiment. They bet each other $1 that a young black conman named Valentine, who is 'a product of a poor environment', can not run the company as well as Winthrop who has money in his genes. The outcome is a triumph for the cultural argument. Both characters fall into the pattern of their new environments, but eventually turn the tables on Duke and Duke by causing them to lose a significant sum on frozen orange juice. Essentially the thematic concern of this text is with the cultural construction of 'human nature'. The establishment is represented by old money: pork bellies, soya beans, and heritage clubs. One of the Duke brothers is resistant to scientific progress: 'I don't care about heredity versus environment. I only care about how much we'll get for pork bellies'. Ultimately, the movie suggests that *anyone* can make money, 'given the right surroundings'.

Notions of Darwinian selection or evolution frequently surface in texts. Buffett, for example, wrote the following confusing remark in a report to his shareholders: 'I had this idea that some sort of economic Darwinism would work and that if offers were made, it was the invisible hand working and that it would improve the breed of managers' (in Lowenstein 1996, p. 268). Clearly trying to express ideas about financial 'survival' in the marketplace, he refers to a complex range of issues—badly. Related to the Lamarckian concept of striving, we find the argument tenable in social terms, but not biologically. Striving for things, like the giraffe does for leaves, could increase our neck length. The Lamarckian promise of social evolution and learning is an appealing one in relation to money, but it is generally foreclosed because its tenability is shaky. Furthermore, an aptitude for striving alone does not constitute a monied hero. Wisdom, analysis, and vision are also prerequisites. The door leading to wealth is not open to all readers despite the claims in self–help texts to the contrary. 'The constituency of the leisure class is kept by a continual selective process, whereby the individuals and lines of descent that are eminently fitted for an aggressive pecuniary competition are withdrawn from the lower classes' (Veblen 1970 [1899], p. 158).

REPRESENTATION AND INTERTEXTUALITY

More than any other factor, it is representation that constructs the mythic monied and monetary heroes: they are represented with variations from earlier models (such as Law's), their stories are reproduced in the press, and they are constructed as the products of monied blood or vision. It is, however, methodologically difficult to separate the varying facets of representation, because the notion has complementary as well as contradictory effects.

Let me explain, using the example of pictorial reproduction: from one perspective reproduction brings objects within reach, giving them an immediate presence. It also instigates a sense of proliferation: multiple copies give the impression of abundance. On the other hand, reproduction is a falsification, because it infers that an original existed and is merely lost in the (mythic) mists of time. Representation and reproduction both play with the idea that an original can be discerned or unearthed. Likewise, paper money (which is easily reproduced) functions as part of the mythic money system. It holds a promise of materiality: its definition as an abstract medium of exchange is forgotten when it is conceptualised as the means to obtaining a more sturdy object such as a loaf of bread or a gold nugget. The hero, too, appears concrete and real (in photographs and textual characterisations), but he is only a cultural representation. In addition, according to Spooner, heroes must remain physically distanced: 'Heroes and heroines we have never met can always remain heroes and heroines. But once we realize that Robert Redford is shorter than we are, Faye Dunaway in the flesh is quite plain, it is the beginning of the end' (1985, p. 35).

The text, *Soros on Soros*, consists of a series of transcribed interviews, with two appendices consisting of some philosophical extracts written by Soros himself. The question/answer format of the main text makes Soros's character seem more immediate, responsive, and authentic: words of wisdom direct from the horse's mouth, unlike the distant Buffett.

The interviewer introduces Soros on the first page: 'There's a story going around Wall Street these days that opposite Mount Rushmore, there's another mountain, and its devoted to the world's greatest money managers. Two figures have been chiseled into the face of the mountain, Warren Buffett and your own' (1995, p. 3). Noting in passing the question of the story's circulation around Wall Street as part of the myth's dissemination, we find an interesting physicality to the Soros myth. His persona is engraved on the landscape: figuratively, mythically, and physically, which contrasts with his abstract postulating.

The repetition of mythic paradigms in monetary discourse establishes a sense of money's permanency in the annals of human thinking, and this operates in a number of ways. Monied and monetary heroes—characters constructed out of actual, living people—are compared with fictionalised figures, an alliance that infers uniqueness, but also places these characters within a homogenous heroic frame. The monetary and monied heroes borrow certain paradigmatic elements from the traditional hero, masculinity, vision, mastery, fearlessness, and independence, as I have noted. Despite, or even because of, this last characteristic, independence, the hero becomes fully absorbed into cultural myth.

All heroes are culturally constructed. They have no foundational point of reference, and so they are constructed comparatively. In a sense, mythologies mimic the idea of eternal return. According to Eliade: 'death is inevitably followed by resurrection, cataclysm by a new Creation' (1971 [1954], p. 102). In terms of heroes, the original or ancient model may die out, but it is recycled when chaos or death is immanent (as seems to be the case at the moment, with lack of monetary control). Thus, in the final analysis, mythology is purely intertextual, and surfaces when culture is in crisis, and the persistence of the intertextual turn indicates the absence of an origin.

Two brief examples of such contemporary representations come to mind, and serve to briefly introduce the character types found in my next chapter. The bond trader from *Bonfire of the Vanities* appears in *Business Review Weekly* as a prime example of the 'boomer executive [who shows] little anxiety and uncertainty about the future' (20 Jan. 1997, p. 33). This quotation draws upon established perceptions of the hero as fearless and adventurous. Similarly, Gekko from the movie *Wall Street* has become an intertextual financial type. In condemning the often–made connection between economics and selfishness, the *Economist* writes: 'Adam Smith was no 18th–century precursor to Gordon Gekko, pronouncing "Greed is good" '(21 Dec. 1996, p. 17). Of course, Smith did not advocate greed per se and the *Economist*'s point may be valid, but the anachronistic imposition of present values onto centuries–old texts is characteristic of the mythological construction of money and its effects. Intertextuality is simply another form of secondary representation, or self–multiplication, and what these two quotations once again demonstrate is the fact that fiction provides support to ideas with which we structure culture.

More importantly perhaps, the parallels drawn between Gekko and Smith confer a degree of timeless significance on money–making activities:

We perceive a second aspect of primitive ontology: insofar as an act (or an object) acquires a certain reality through the repetition of certain paradigmatic gestures, and acquires it through that alone, there is an implicit abolition of profane time, of duration, of 'history', and he who reproduces the exemplary gesture thus finds himself transported into a mythical epoch in which its revelation took place. (Eliade 1971 [1954], p. 35)

In effect, the myth of the monied hero reproduces heroic intent, but the quest is merely related to monetary acquisition (an otherwise lowly pursuit in Smith's terms).[7]

The tensions between heroism and economic power are abundant, but they remain conveniently contained within the stories of which they form a part. In essence our mythologies are vicious circles; the financial character unites heroism of mythic proportions with money (an abstraction), thereby somehow authenticating both. Monied heroes are the characters idealised in popular texts; they possess some traits and sums of money that the reader lacks, but they are also like the reader in some ways, as I will indicate. Heroes need to be identifiable for readers and in the next section I will highlight some of the ways they are constructed as both exceptional and unexceptional.

Perhaps the most visible and talked about new monied hero currently is Bill Gates. Like money, Gates sneaks up in the most unexpected ways, featuring in court cases, Australian Federal Cabinet meetings, popular fiction, and several Internet Web sites. *Trading Reality*, depends upon the Gates phenomenon in two respects. First, the novel's central plot centres around a battle for the rights to a virtual software program, and second, the image of Gates occurs twice in the novel, causing the central character to focus on his investigation: the murdered brother was reading his biography before he died, but he only made it to chapter 3 (Ridpath 1996, p. 66). Later the main character 'saw the weedy image of Bill Gates staring up from the book Richard had left open on his sofa' (Ridpath 1996, p. 237). Gates also features in *The Vulture Fund* when Kathleen Hunt suggests that she will approach Bill Gates for money for their fund (Frey 1996, p. 97). She does not approach him, as it turns out.

It is not only Gates's achievements as a software nerd that are noted. Readers of the *Wall Street Journal* will know that Gates undertook to spend U.S. $30–40 million on his new house. But, according to the sardonic *Journal,* '$30 million Doesn't Buy Much Today' (*Wall Street Journal* 25 Oct. 1996, p. B10). Gates's house in Medina, Washington, is arguably the most famous house in the United States—perhaps even the world. It has the 'gee whiz factor' (*Wall Street Journal* 25 Oct. 1996, p. B10), aligning Gates with monied heroes of both the present and the past. As it turns out, Gates spent much more than the U.S. $40 million forecast in 1996. Seven years and over U.S. $60 million later, Gates has nearly moved into his 'waterfront techno–palace' (*Australian* 15 Jul. 1997, p. 14).

The *Wall Street Journal* feature also draws a parallel between Gates's and Randolph Hearst's houses. The feature quotes Gates from *The Road Ahead*: 'the technological innovations I have in mind for my house are not really different in spirit from those Hearst wanted in his. He wanted news and entertainment, all at a touch. So do I' (1996 [1995], p. 248). Gates is thus intertextually likened to an earlier financial magnate, thereby becoming encircled in a mythological financial realm.

The feature directly following this, on the same page of the *Journal,* narrows the gap between the reader and Gates. It reads: 'You, too, Can Live Like a Billionaire. Your last name may not be Vanderbilt, Hearst or even Gates, but even if you don't have $30 million to spend, you can pick up a mansion fit for a robber baron' (*Wall Street Journal* 25 Oct. 1996, p. B10). Here we encounter the seductive interpellation that summons the reader into believing that significant wealth is a possibility, a gesture that cancels out the voyeuristic aspects of the beginning of the article.

Buffett's (unauthorised) biography also presents an excessive number of intertextual character references. The dominant analogy with Buffett in this text is that 'he resembled the magnates of a previous age, such as J. P. Morgan, Sr.' (Lowenstein 1996, p. xv), because like Morgan he believes that the 'principal judgments in business are those concerning character' (Lowenstein 1996, p. 250). In addition, 'Buffett's emphasis on reputation was oddly reminiscent of Morgan's testimony that character—not money—was the basis of credit' (Lowenstein 1996, p. 395). It could be said that how people represent themselves is a vital factor to the Buffett construct. According to Lowenstein, Buffett courts many friends, and one of them is the author Adam Smith, but not '(the original) Adam Smith' (1996, p. 255). Not only can the reader never be certain of an original referent, but the unrestrained comparisons between Buffett and other characters bring about Buffett's de–individuation.[8]

There are, however, a number of differences drawn between Buffett and other prolific money makers, differences that emphasise his 'Garbo–like loneness' (Lowenstein 1996, p. 66). Being parsimonious, Buffett disapproves of Randolph Hearst's squandering 'on the grandiose San Simeon, thus diverting "massive amounts of labour and material away from other societal purposes"' (Lowenstein 1996, p. 334). In addition, unlike superwealthy characters, Buffett did not design or produce anything specific, he simply moved his money around the market (Lowenstein 1996, p. 413). Does the idea that Buffett is a *pure* investor make him more interesting, less 'nerdy', and less or more individuated?

These heroes seem to have exhibited abnormal behaviour in childhood. Two of them did not play, like their friends; they preferred instead to study numbers. In fact, a passion for numbers seems essential, as we saw with Law. Warren Buffett 'lived and breathed numbers' (Lowenstein 1996, p. 12); he 'had a thirst for numbers as though they held the key to some Euclidean riddle' (Lowenstein 1996, pp. 12, 3). Buffett's passion for calculation led him to describe himself as 'a computer' (Lowenstein 1996, p. 276). Gates's school friends claim that 'when you are a kid, if someone is good at math, that's what sets them apart. We all know Gates was very, very good at math' (in Wallace and Erickson 1993, p. 17), and this made him 'smarter than us' (in Wallace and Erickson 1993, p. 16).

Hard work—an apparent anathema to the average reader, according to the economic argument—is that which brings success for all these heroes, so the reader is again excluded. Gates does all–nighters, never putting his feet up, and Buffett is rarely out of his office. Apparently Gates's dislike of time wasting was inherited from his mother (Wallace and Erickson 1993, p. 17). Gates not only has *Hard Drive* (the title of Wallace and Erickson's book), but 'white–hot drive' (Wallace and Erickson 1993, p. 117). In fact drive seems to frame his existence, whether it be floppy disk drives, ambition or fast cars: 'Gates liked to drive fast, testing the limits of himself and his machine' (Wallace & Erickson 1993, p. 129).

As the two richest men in America, Gates and Buffett also suffer from a unique monetary disease that only the rich can be prone to. It is called 'Rhinophobia' and is 'an investors' disease meaning "the dread of ever having any cash"' (Lowenstein 1996, p. 354). Thus, the acquisition of assets such as cars and houses is essential, whereas cash is a liability. The need to get rid of cash may seem startling to the reader, particularly considering that money is the quest object. But ruptures such as this are essential to the distorting structures of money's mythological discourse.

Buffett and Gates lead a simple lifestyle, which brings them back to the reader's cultural level, and encourages identification. 'Even with his immense fortune, Buffett continued to live simply' (Lowenstein 1996, p. 234). He was 'the last person in America who ate sausage' (Lowenstein 1996, p. 277), and Lowenstein takes this as an indication that Buffett has a need to uphold an 'idealized past against a rootless and too hurriedly changing present' (Lowenstein 1996, p. 277).

Gates and Buffett both have a penchant for junk food: burgers, delivered pizzas, and caffeinated drinks (Gross 1996, p. 345). Buffett '[drank] about five bottles of [Cherry Coke] a day. He stocked the office with potato chips and what a visitor described as "thousands" of bottles of Cherry Coke' (Lowenstein 1996, p. 278). At Microsoft headquarters, 'there was always a supply of free Coca–Cola around' (Wallace and Erickson 1993, p. 127). Gates was always 'working with a Coke and a hamburger' (Wallace & Erickson 1993, p. 135). Abstemious they are not; these men are like over–sexed rhinos with the constitutions of oxen. Nevertheless some of their behaviour is quite modest, considering their wealth. Buffett has stayed in his original home in Omaha, and so there are facets of their characters that readers can sympathise with.

GREATEST BUSINESS STORIES

One of the primary functions of the hero is to encourage imitation. A brief survey of bookshop shelves will show that there is a conspicuous popular fascination with these characters; authorised and unauthorised biographies proliferate. Alongside self-help titles such as *Money Made Simple*, and *101 Ways to Make Money* can be found a text entitled *The Richest Man in Babylon*, which is aimed at helping the reader understand money's mysterious workings (Clason 1988). One can also find what Gross calls some 'personality stories' (Gross 1996, p. 1), which may include books with titles such as *The Warren Buffett Way* (Hagstrom 1994) and *Warren Buffett Speaks: Wit and Wisdom from the World's Greatest Investor* (Buffett 1997) and *The Road Ahead* (Gates 1996 [1995]). The multibillionaires are also habitually lauded in the press, their whereabouts and actions are monitored. But what is the appeal? How can a computer nerd like Bill Gates become a feature of the popular fiction landscape when nerds are foolish, feeble, and uninteresting? Perhaps the belief is that by reading their stories some of their success can rub off or be passed on to the reader.

Soros, seemingly the most self–reflective, and certainly the most outspoken of the heroes I am considering, concedes that his status as 'a guru' (Baker 1995, pp. 146–48) is not of his making: 'It was my killing on sterling that gave me a high profile. I think that's a commentary on the values that prevail in our society' (1995, p. 238).

Mythologies touches upon the issue of the 'norm as dreamed, though not actually lived a whole section of humanity cannot live up to it except in imagination, that is, at the cost of an immobilization and an impoverishment of consciousness' (Barthes 1989 [1957], pp. 153–54). Behind the construction of the rich hero is an implicit idea about the reader's own potential and destiny. As a participant in Western culture, the reader is provided with a dream of wealth, which has a latent sense of realisability. Microsoft's advertisement on television for the Windows 98 update initiated a significant turn in terms of who or what the actual hero is in relation to this company. The soundtrack was David Bowie's song entitled 'We Can Be Heroes', which implies that the reader too can be heroic if he or she uses the software program. Heroism is at all our fingertips. Heroes are sources of inspiration; they provide goals for cultures, as well as highlighting those goals. But it is a dream impossible to realise in a world of unequal distribution of wealth. The rich mythological hero serves two functions: he contributes towards the authentication of money in mythic archetypal terms, but also precludes participation.

In 1996 *Forbes* magazine published a book entitled *Greatest Business Stories of All Time,* which attempts to explain what 'Bill Gates, Henry Ford, J. P. Morgan and Walt Disney have in common' (frontispiece).[9] Judging by the title, the factor these characters have in common is their part in the development of large businesses. The text purports to be full of inspiring tales and 'lessons' for attaining success (Gross 1996, p. 2). The Introduction constructs its mythological position:

This is a book of heroes. Make no mistake about it. The people whose stories are collected here earned that status as surely as any soldier or athlete or explorer or statesman you can name. By making and selling, by organizing and financing, by discerning and serving the needs and desires of others, they have done more to affect who we are and what we are today than all but a handful of history makers. In doing so, most of them got rich; some, very rich. Indeed, names such as Morgan, Rockefeller, and now Gates are virtual synonyms for vast wealth. But for all of the success told of here, these are far from tales of greed and avarice. (Gross 1996, p. 1)

These characters make, sell, organise, finance, discern, and service our needs, and therefore they are worthy of their status. But we have a definite trait for the monied hero here: a disregard for greed and avarice. So Gross touches upon a moral dimension, new to the hero apparently, because in 'archaic and legendary accounts, the moral dimension of the hero is not an issue' (Lash 1995, p. 21).

Generally these great business stories are fairy tales, in the rags–to–riches genre: from 'office boy to chairman of the board' (Gross 1996, p. 155). These heroes are often from a 'poor' background: Rockefeller's father was an 'occasional farmer, small-time entrepreneur and scam artist' (Gross 1996, p. 43); Ford's was also a farmer. Kroc, the founder of McDonald's, started out in life as a 'milkshake salesman' (Gross 1996, p. 179), and John H. Johnson (one of the richest black Americans, founder of *Ebony* magazine) 'had been laughed out of a loan office in 1942 [but by 1970 was] a member of the nation's elite' (Gross 1996, p. 154). Once just the boy or girl next door, they have achieved the economic ideal, and are a part of a social and cultural circle out of most readers' reach. But their stories are also about possibility: there is a rich hero in all of us. In this respect, the money myth is powerfully creative, but inconsistent: it supports the money system as well as nominating the Deserving.

The *Forbes* book tells the stories of twenty wealthy, successful Americans whose business dealings have shaped readers' lives, sometimes irrevocably. Of Henry Ford we read that 'no other individual in this century so completely transformed the nation's way of life' (Gross 1996, pp. 75–76). Kroc is 'the king of the hamburger [who] transformed the nation's cultural landscape' (Gross 1996, p. 178). Gates's Microsoft corporation has 'done more to change the world than any other' (Gross 1996, p. 349). Powerful claims indeed.

These particular characters are not just the heroes who have recognised a 'lack' as the Proppian economic story goes, but they are people who have in fact *created* needs: fast food, cars, the trappings of wealth and conspicuous consumption; they have transformed 'luxuries to necessities' (Gross 1996, p. 76). Johnson's *Ebony* magazine (from which he made a fortune) is described as a necessity: 'Black America needed a magazine of its own' (Gross 1996, p. 146). But aren't needs questionable? Heyne's *The Economic Way of Thinking* hammers home the point that 'entities like states or cities never really want anything' (1994, p. 21) and furthermore, 'the concept of "needs" implies a perfectly inelastic demand curve—an extremely rare phenomenon' (1994, p. 39). 'Do people in wealthy nations like the United States "need" air conditioning more than people in hotter but also much poorer nations, such as Bangladesh or Niger?' (Heyne 1994, p. 40). Monetary heroes often create a demand for products that nobody *really* needs; therefore, in some ways their achievements constitute a myth of necessity.

Because the concept of the hero embodies ideas about success and mastery, the hero is flattened into a simple conqueror, rather than being an exceptional or unique figure. Therefore the hero, like the reader, is a character at the mercy of the quest object, which is money in this case. In addition, the notion of the hero as an individual (as distinct from the group) is bound to self–destruction. In other words, the hero starts off as a character of difference, but ends up absorbed in an ideological, fictionalised typology. According to Lash, 'In all cultures and traditions, the hero is defined by how he faces death' (1995, p. 84). In terms of money's mythologies, death often entails the loss of individuality; heroes can be swallowed up by their business.

Hinckley and Hinckley notice a tendency in character construction that seemed to become more accentuated towards the end of the period they investigate. There are not many villains anymore, they write, 'much more commonly evil is shown as a collective force' (Hinckley and Hinckley 1989, p. 188). Their hypothesis is clearly aligned with their analysis of multiple characters, although they fail to pursue the implications of this finding. Currently, this collective force could be the faceless financial market, and Castells would agree: 'Above a diversity of human–flesh capitalists there is a faceless collective capitalist, made up of financial [electronic] flows' (1996, p. 474). Hinckley and Hinckley continue: 'We see that many books feature no individuals at all. The group or society is the real protagonist. If villains have turned into faceless enemies, the protagonists also have dispersed and multiplied, becoming rather faceless themselves' (1989, p. 188).

Nonetheless, we maintain a degree of dependency upon the individual. Individuals, faces, and names are precariously placed in *Greatest Business Stories*. As businesses become increasingly aggrandised, the position of the hero seems to shift, but the name remains as residuum. For Rorty, 'the concept of a figure introduces the germ of what will become a distinction between the inner and the outer person. An individual's perspective on his model, his idealized real figure, is originally externally presented, but it becomes internalized, [becoming] the internal model of self–representation' (Rorty 1990, p. 308–309). In this way, Gates re–represents himself as Microsoft. In *The Road Ahead*, Gates constructs Microsoft as alive and active: 'Windows is not invincible, and neither is Microsoft. Someday Microsoft will die. Somebody at a conference asked me, "What operating system will replace Windows when it dies?" I said, "Tell me where I'm going to die, and I'll make sure not to go there"' (1996 [1995], p. 321). Gates is clearly being identified with his business here, and even though he has resigned as CEO, his name remains synonymous with the company. The cultural perception is that Gates *is* Microsoft.

Soros recognises this duplicitous relationship: 'There is a two–way reflexive interaction between the personal me and the public persona. Obviously, I have a role in shaping that persona, but the persona also shapes me' (1995, p. 249).

To some extent, great businesses as conglomerates contribute towards the death of the hero in our culture, so that Kroc (for example) cannot be a hero, because his McDonald's chain with its golden arches has effaced his identity. Similarly, it could be said that Microsoft is more suited to the Hinckleys' idea of the protagonist, and if this is the case then individuation is a thing of the popular fiction past.

It is my additional contention that metaphoric death actually threatens the very existence of the notion of the monetary and monied heroes. Our monied heroes are to some extent threatened by extinction by the very monsters they have created. Calder is concerned that heroes may become extinct, and her fear is caused by her belief that heroes signify an imaginative need, fulfilling a purpose as illustrators of human potential (1977, pp. 200–201). But an intrinsic element of the narrative of the monied hero as I perceive it is that their success in business heralds their individual demise, whereby their presence is threatened by overwhelming corporate identities.

Titanic growth and consumption in gargantuan proportions are characteristics of these characters' financial landscapes. Their businesses seem to reproduce themselves indefinitely so that even the world is not big enough; many business empires are described as the 'world's largest' (Gross 1996, p. 159). It is not inconceivable that one of these world leaders might eventually swallow up everyone else. Soros takes up the destructive (devouring) consumer metaphor: '[My] Fund was an organism, a parasite, sucking my blood and draining my energy' (1995, p. 55). Microsoft's 'character and flavour' is such that it has 'a vision of where it wants to go', 'sucking in everything around it' (Wallace and Erickson 1993, pp. 109, 125, 422).

More than any other, Gates is seen as a threat, perhaps because he is a newcomer to the arena of the wealthy, but also because his company has been labelled a monopoly. By way of contrast, the monied heroes of the past, such as J. P. Morgan, have become comfortably distanced and culturally appropriated. Nevertheless, this does not stop *The New Republic* from identifying a parallel between the two characters: 'Bill Gates' character and career reveal continuities with Morgan's. For both Napoleon was a boyhood idol' (18 Oct 1999, p.29). Wallace and Erickson choose to focus on industrial growth: 'Gates had started out as only a tiny player in the new revolution of the information age. Now he straddled the industry like a colossus. He had obtained the kind of power and influence that John D. Rockefeller held over America's oil industry at the turn of the century' (1993, p. 422). But parallels often seem to be instructive in terms of lessons to be learned from the past. Gates shares many experiences with John D.

Rockefeller: they both controlled 90 percent of their industry, they are both billionaires, and both their companies have been subject to antitrust cases. Both apparently suffered from 'selective amnesia' (*Business Week* 22 Nov. 1999, p. 48).

Perceptions of Gates are mixed—sometimes he is a vampire, in the light of his recent court case, and a book by Rohn entitled *The Microsoft File: The Secret Case against Bill Gates* (1998), but at other times he is heroic: he works hard, deserves what he gets, and is a model of so–called capitalism. The *Australian Financial Review* (14–15 Mar. 1998) makes the claim that Gates's wealth 'endears him to most of the world's heads of State. Recently, he has been entertained by the ruling parties of Britain, France, China, Brazil, India, Malaysia, South Africa and now Australia. The only country where he is less than welcome is his own, given that the US authorities are increasingly treating Microsoft as a monopolistic anti–competitive evil empire' (p.6). The press and the World Wide Web are full of texts on Gates, all of which lay claim to some special understanding of the man behind the myth. Without doubt, the Gates character is the most enigmatic, as well as the most mythologised, money hero of the new millennium.

Vast sums of money and huge businesses undoubtedly impact upon these heroic characters, but initially this impact is resisted, as Soros explains:

> At first, I didn't want to identify myself with my business career. I felt there was more to me than making money. I kept my private life strictly separate from my business. Then I went through a rough patch. I had some psychosomatic symptoms, like vertigo. It made me realise that making money is an essential part of existence. I realize that I cut a larger–than–life figure. (1995, pp. 145–46)

It seems that success of heroic proportions can derive from the business itself, not solely from the hero's abilities. Soros is identified with his business—the Quantum Fund. Money has taken over from the gods as far as missions are concerned. In addition, Soros describes money as *essential* to existence. In historical terms the technologies of Industrial Revolution partially tamed natural threats, and so, as Lash suggests, man 'resorted to inventing his own ordeals', namely, money management (1995, p. 42).

Big business and multinationals contribute to the effacement of the hero, extinguishing him from the public eye, and even rewriting his character. In many respects, money's mythology is always awaiting its own destruction, so that it can be rebuilt, or shifted slightly. In the next chapter, I consider annihilation from a different perspective, focusing on the rogue. In some respects the rogue is a potential hero at the outset, but he fails to exhibit diligence, restraint, and rationality as Soros and Buffett do.

NOTES

1. Eliade maintains that 'all religious acts are held to have been founded by gods, civilizing heroes, or mythical ancestors. It may be mentioned in passing that, among primitives, not only do rituals have their mythical model but any human act whatever acquires effectiveness to the extent that it exactly *repeats* an act performed at the beginning of time by a god, a hero, or an ancestor' (1971 [1954], p. 22).

2. Briefly, futures are essentially 'bets on the future price [of a] financial instrument in a number of months' (Baker 1995, p. 149). One could, for example, bet on the level of the Dow Jones index in six months' time, and stand to make a gain or a loss on the prediction. This is known as an index rate future, and measures virtually nothing but activity in the market.

3. Greed is a complex attribute, sometimes perceived to be a positive prerequisite for activity in the financial markets, and at other times it is decidedly negative. Often the privileging of greed can go awry, as I will explain in chapter 4, 'Making a Killing'; in fact greed (as well as fear) can be destructive traits, and they are generally applied to characters antithetical to heroes: villains.

4. This idea contrasts with the economic belief that the market is a collection of rational beings, ultimately self–regulating.

5. The imposition of an indicator of share trading into people's lives is nicely satirised in *Three Dollars*: 'It was nineteen eighty–five, the first year of the second Reagan administration, the sixth year of the Thatcher reign. It was the first time we had ever heard a report of share movements on the radio. The interminable repetition of share market indices thereafter did not leave us unchanged. I would call Tanya at work and get a quotation of her "all ordinaries index" '. Was she up or down today?' (Perlman 1998, pp. 87–89).

6. The text is co–written: Gates is assisted by Myhrvold and Rinearson.

7. According to Smith's dictum, it is not the money that people desire but the goods they can purchase with it. A quest defined by the pursuit of money alone is historically deemed immoral—after all the love of money is the root of all evil—so it is somewhat against the Christian tradition to label the super–rich folk heroes. I would suggest that their wealth—which often far exceeds their needs—should make them villains when measured against the millions of hungry and homeless in the world.

8. Rowe clearly does not know where to turn for reference in her *The Real Meaning of Money*, because each time she discusses Warren Buffett, she calls him William (1998, pp. 96, 443).

9. This text will be referred to simply as *Greatest Business Stories* from this point on.

4

Making a Killing

Money's history, its autonomy, and its heroes each contribute to money's mythology, and most of these stories are taken for granted, or left unquestioned, because their separate facets are perceived to exist naturally. They are all however fictional; they are reconstructed from received linguistic and cultural significations. That money has a real history, and that it is a knowable character, which can elevate those knowledgeable to heroic heights, is—in Nietzschean terms—a lie. Truth is nothing but 'a movable host of...anthropomorphisms: in short, a sum of human relations which have been poetically and rhetorically intensified, transferred and embellished, and which, after long usage, seem to a people, to be fixed, canonical and binding [society lies] according to a fixed convention' (Nietzsche 1992 [1873], p. 84).

Like language, money has a moral dimension that is purely anthropomorphic: both are human constructs with no reference outside language. In short, our monetary concepts as well as our financial systems have an 'unstable foundation [they are built] as it were on running water' (Nietzsche 1992 [1873], p. 85).

In addition, money like language encourages human beings to be creative, to instigate self–multiplying systems (such as the financial markets), and to be deceived by these creations. Money is no more than a structured abstraction that designates and supports various cultural relations. Human beings have created both language and money, not just as mediums of exchange, but also as signifiers of moral worthiness. (The idea that the word 'honest', for example, refers to no essential quality [Nietzsche 1992 (1873), p. 83], and the further inference that people can be honest in their monetary practices, is simply a layering of this fallacy). These evaluations were accentuated in the late twentieth century partly because our monetary systems as well as our language are perceived to have liquidated 'all referentials' (Baudrillard 1989 [1972], p. 167). The false idea that money has an identifiable and distinctive origin encourages moral judgments about its use: it has specific functions designated to it. Two ideas surface with a moral inclination here: first, that money is becoming displaced from its material base (and is therefore inauthentic), and second, that it is a crime to lose it.

THE MONEY ROGUE

The repertoire of heroes established in the previous chapter has shown that these men are perceived to move markets, they are creative, they possess vision, and they make enormous amounts of money. Whereas the heroes of the last chapter either possess monetary vision or money itself, the characters in this chapter— the rogues—set out to make a killing, but fail. The rogue is the figurative opposite: he is not a prophet with profits. In broad terms, the characters I am concerned with in this chapter are constructed as either immoral or amoral: they refuse to partake in money's fixed conventions. Effectively, it is the rogue that supports the hero in money's mythology: heroes have a moral dimension that gains additional credence when it is supported by its antithesis: the rogue. Difference is as much a feature of structuration as similarity, because distinctiveness cannot be understood without recourse to its opposite.

Temptation, greed, and ignorance are all aspects of the rogue's character, and they serve a moral cultural function. 'The function of villains in formulaic structures [is] to express, explore, and finally reject those actions which are forbidden, but which, because of certain other cultural patterns, are strongly tempting' (Cawelti 1976, p. 35). The central character in *The Marketmaker* makes a similar judgment: 'I had always put loyalty [to a financial institution] down to greed, or at least ambition—the ambition to make a fortune, which was almost the same thing' (Ridpath 1998, p. 275). And, according to this same character, some traders 'follow the doctrine of whatever institution [they] are in' (Ridpath 1998, p. 275). In this respect, we are all the victims of financial systems, because the temptation of money is hard to resist.

Money and its heroes are powerful motivators. Because rogues have not achieved hero status, but believe it to be achievable, they are arguably defined by a sole motivation: to acquire vast sums of money. Characters, as well as readers are encouraged to emulate the very rich, because 'money [has] become the main, perhaps the sole, standard of judgement of a person's value' (Fay 1996, p. 68).

As with the hero, I have identified two types of rogues in the texts I have analysed. Despite their differences, both types are villainous because they are both imprudent, as well as push the boundaries of money market convention. The first is characterised as greedy, ruthless, and lacking compassion, and Gordon Gekko from the movie *Wall Street* is an exemplar of this type. In a sense, Gekko is a failed hero, and so his character is somewhat enigmatic: he blurs the boundaries of monetary integrity. Like Buffett, he has an appetite for playing the market, but he falls short. Buffett does not care about the money (Lowenstein 1996, p. 37), whereas Gekko does: 'it's all about bucks, kid' (*Wall Street* [motion picture] 1987); Buffett continues to gain money, whereas Gekko ultimately loses; and finally, Buffett depends on analysis for his market activity, whereas Gekko depends upon insider information.

The second type of rogue is also a potential hero at the outset, but because he deals *in other people's money* (whereas Gekko uses his own), losing it incites all kinds of moral judgments from observers. Nick Leeson, a real trader, has been the object of scorn in many popular texts because of his failure to act with financial honesty, and with a disregard for restraint in his trading practices.

The perception of traders as corrupt is fairly common, because they mediate between investors and the market. Heyne's *The Economic Way of Thinking* contains a chapter entitled 'Information, Middlemen, and Speculators' in which he attempts to balance the 'public's deep–rooted suspicion of middlemen' (1994, p. 174). Nevertheless, their culpability for monetary damage and loss is real, as Heyne obliquely acknowledges, and in a sense it is an acknowledgment that nullifies his own defence of them: 'Because of all the interdependencies that characterize our highly specialized economic system, mistaken decisions will often have costly consequences for many more people than the ones who made the decision' (1994, p. 173).

Brokers, traders, portfolio managers, booth molls, runners and strappers—those people whose business it is to deal in other people's money—are positioned culturally several steps down from the heroes on the ladder of monetary success (or 'the hierarchy of money', as Baker calls it [1995, p. 48]).[1] Because it is not their own money, their position in terms of success is precarious: a single trade can break their reputation, and earn them the title of rogue, villain, or lowlife. Baker considers job titles to be irrelevant: *anyone* involved in the markets, in any capacity, is low life (1995, p. 48). When compared with animals such as tracker dogs, foxes, horses, or reptiles, as they often are, traders are positioned on the lower rungs of the monetary hierarchy, with little ability for articulation: 'Salesmen and traders are wild, cunning, aboriginal creatures their favourite phrase is, "Fuck you" ' (Partnoy 1997, p. 50). Partnoy perhaps pushes the debasement to extremes: 'the fact that we [derivatives traders] were the richest assholes in the world didn't change the fact that we were assholes' (1997, p. 247), and this attack is unsurprising, because Partnoy's text is an explicit attack on money market culture.

A converse view is articulated by supporters of the money market system, such as Lowenstein, who claims that 'traders merely [do] the work of Adam Smith's Invisible Hand' (1996, p. 307). In other words, they use their knowledge of shifting financial values to match buyers and sellers in the market; and this is a 'mechanism of co–ordination', otherwise known as the invisible hand (Heyne 1994, p. 4). According to Heyne, 'the common habit of viewing the middleman as an unproductive bandit on the highway of trade stems from the erroneous assumption that information is a free good' (1994, p. 191). And because they have knowledge, traders are interpreters of the market, convincing the lay person that obscure financial instruments represent something tangible. But there are good and bad traders: while Soros 'has an impeccable and justified reputation for the probity of his dealings', others are perceived to be 'playing the game of being gods of the investment world' (Baker 1995, pp. 145, 158), believing sometimes that they have unfettered power. But, 'money is a Very Serious Business', and 'the stewardship of capital is holy, and the handler of money must conduct himself as a Prudent Man' (Smith 1968, p. 9). In terms of the specifications for their work, traders are information providers, advising monied investors where to put their money. But their decisions are generally made on the basis of behaviour, not market indicators, because the market is simply a collection of people.

Above all, 'money players' are described as 'money–hungry' (Frey 1996, pp. 235, 268). Gekko's description of ideal traders as 'guys who are poor, smart, hungry, and [have] no feelings' (*Wall Street* [motion picture] 1987) is greatly intertextualised, particularly in relation to hunger—but, it is hunger for money, not for food: in *The Marketmaker*, the head trader explains that he likes 'people who are hungry, people who *need* to make money for themselves. But I don't think it's greed, exactly' (Ridpath 1998, p. 90). The juxtaposition of hunger, money, and greed infers that traders are responsive to bodily needs (just as Buffett has a thirst for numbers), a strategy that provides money with a necessary, natural foundation. In our monetary culture, the signifier greed is coming to be reworked, largely thanks to the Gekko mythology.

An insatiable desire to make money pushes many traders into situations where they are forced to make split–second decisions on their trading positions. How are traders characterised as distinctive types? Leeson claims that traders have 'the fastest brains and [are the] most highly–paid people in the world' (1996, p. 99). These two factors, the ability to think quickly and to be paid handsomely for it, lead to a number of perceptions about traders. First, traders are perceived to be motivated by money, and second, they are *expected* to act calmly and quickly under pressure, and failure to do so results in condemnation. But greed for money, and fear of loss, as well as the misreading of situations, can lead them to act irrationally, so money is lost—not made. Hence, restraint is called for, and the rogues I discuss here lack this characteristic.

P.I.G.—Panic, Ignorance and Greed

According to the *Economist* (15 Apr. 1995, p. 29), the ten years since the stock market crash in 1987 had been 'a decade of greed and glory'. Greed more than any other motivation surfaces as a prominent concern about traders. In October 1996, for example, the *Wall Street Journal* published findings of a survey conducted about perceptions of the (metaphorical) Street. It found that 61 percent of respondents believe that rapaciousness and egocentrism drive Wall Street, and that money making above any other concern dominates (*Wall Street Journal* 18 Oct. 1996, p. A7A). A month later, a second survey reaffirmed this perception, diagnosing it as a problem (*Wall Street Journal* 8 Nov. 1996, p. B5A). Greed has two contradictory effects: it can either cultivate an appetite for money making, or it can become a dominant trait, overcoming others such as restraint. Nevertheless, in the main, greed persists as an undesirable trait, and when it is combined with selfish individualism it gives money's mythologies a powerful moral.

According to Fay's text, *The Collapse of Barings*, panic, ignorance, and greed are 'the three base motives that drive the financial markets' (1996, p. 44). This perception is a fairly common one (Smith 1968, p. 79; Ridpath 1995, p. 72; Bronson 1995, p. 19). The perception is that traders, like foxes, live by their wits, and they must be money hungry.[2]

The combination of fear and greed is also found in most popular (financial) novels. In *Bombardiers,* for example, Coyote Jack, the sales manager, keeps his traders motivated by playing on their primitive instincts of fear and greed (Bronson 1995, p. 57). From this perspective, traders are unevolved creatures, reacting instinctively rather than rationally to market circumstances. In addition, competing for glory but having little money is necessary to maintain trading hunger: if you are already rich you cannot have greedy instincts.

The Takeover features the greed of the 1980s as a central theme. ' "The late eighties really were incredible there was so much money thrown around. We made huge fees. Whatever happened to all of that?" "A few people got a little too greedy" ' (Frey 1995, p. 63). The novel develops through playoffs between the government and a secret society of investment bankers who murder the Federal Reserve chairman in order to avoid taxation. Its theme is structured around a conflict between government protectionism and rampant capitalism, and the threat to stability comes from the latter quarter: money–hungry investors who '[try to derail] a socialist devil and [restore] capitalism' (Frey 1995, p. 381). These characters' excesses push the boundaries of the financial system; they destroy all regulatory bodies. The narrator of *The Takeover* is often very explicit, forcing moral perspectives on the reader: 'he's worth millions, and all he cares about in the world is turning that into millions more. The greed factor is written all over him. And he doesn't care about anyone who isn't like him' (Frey 1995, p. 85). It seems that the age–old dislike of greed serves as a persistent trait for disagreeable characters.

Because traders depend upon yearly bonuses, which are usually calculated as a percentage of their achieved sales, they are hungry to sell, and money constitutes an enticement. The first line of *Bombardiers* explains that 'it was a filthy profession, but the money was addicting, and one addiction led to another, and they were all going to hell' (Bronson 1995, p. 3). Thus, a number of central problems are thrown out at the beginning of the text: identity, fall from grace, constraint, and the centrality of money. Significantly this line is repeated at the beginning of the final chapter, so that the degeneration involved in trading is viewed as inescapable.[3]

The inference that trading and money are addictions gives them a cyclical quality. Addictions, like cycles, are difficult to escape from, but the final payoff seems to promise release (recall Frey's first line: 'Life was good. Andrew Falcon was about to come into a tremendous amount of money—he hoped [1995, p. 1]). But, money is 'a game without end' (Ridpath 1998, p. 91). Effectively traders are trapped in a temporal cycle from within and playing the game gives an illusion of possible ends.

Like Buffett, the traders are not necessarily 'in it' euphemistically for the money; they just love winning. 'Traders remain people of vast and insatiable ego, however; their reward comes far more from the instant gratification of the successful trade than from the money they make' (Mayer 1993, p. 68). So it seems that the quest, or the fight, depending upon the operative metaphor, could be privileged over monetary gain.

But according to Partnoy, yearly bonuses are never sufficient:

By the time bonuses are paid, most salesmen and traders are so infused with greedy, revolutionary fervor that no matter what amount the firm actually pays them, they automatically think they have been screwed. Even the lowest–paid employees received a significant multiple of the average income of the American family. But perspective is not one of Wall Street's qualities, and the firm's employees were mad as hell.

'Man, I got fucked. They fucked me again. Can you believe it?' (1997, pp. 40–41)

Frequently characterised as unreservedly greedy, self–interested, and ruthless, the rogue attempts to mimic the lifestyle and status of the financial hero, but his behaviour is more erratic, a factor that can cause him substantial losses—in both reputation and money. In *Bombardiers* and *The Marketmaker*, traders' characters are reconstructed when they leave their firm. In *The Marketmaker*, for example, Dave Dunne is sacked for speaking to the press, but 'the market will be told that he made large trading losses, and that he covered them up....Dave's character was rewritten', explains the principal focaliser

(Ridpath 1998, pp. 133–4). According to Rowe, 'most people regard money as essential for the survival of the person', and this idea is pertinent here in terms of character assassination (1998, p. 36).

In some respects, the rogue of financial novels belongs to melodrama, because 'the melodramatist tries to make us feel that we have penetrated what shows on the surface to the inside story; he offers what appears to be the dirt beneath the rug, the secret power behind the scenes' (Cawelti 1976, p. 262). Thus, some novels reinforce and represent perceptions about traders as morally deviant and rarely satisfied.

The Hunter and the Hunted

Noses and the sense of smell play a significant part in the making of money: Buffett has an 'otherworldly nose for stocks' (*New York Times* 9 May 1997, p. B1), and Gekko, like Winnie the Pooh has 'stuck his nose in the honey pot once too often' (*Wall Street* [motion picture] 1987). Leeson's description of his arrival at SIMEX (The Singapore Stock Exchange) also focuses on the olfactory: 'When I first stepped out on to the trading floor, I could smell and see the money. Throughout my time at Barings I was inching closer and closer to it' (1996, p. 33). This representation conflicts sharply with the statement in West's *Vanishing Point*: '*pecunia non olet*, money carries no smell' (1996, p. 218). I wondered whether anyone could smell 'the millions and millions which had gone up in smoke' in a single day at Barings in Singapore in 1995 (Leeson 1996, p. 7)?

Traders are trackers and hunters, people who can sniff out money–making deals. Andrew Falcon, the central character of *The Takeover*, could '[sniff] the five million he was trying to track down the origin of the billion dollars' (Frey 1995, p. 202). The same sense is referred to a few pages on: 'the smell of a quick profit was in the air, a scent which hadn't pervaded the Big Board in some time. Those on the floor of the exchange seemed almost intoxicated, as though under the influence of a drug. It was a drug called euphoria, and they were all on it' (Frey 1995, p. 208). To readers passages such as these contribute to a sense of money's appeal, as well as its sensory, naturalised aspects.

Yet, from some traders' perspectives, the metaphors of war and the hunt apparently define their actions. According to the trader, Faulkner, the metaphors a trader uses to describe the market determine his or her actions (in Schwager 1994, p. 432). Thus, the metaphors Gordon Gekko adopts in *Wall Street* of war ('it's trench warfare out there, Pal') define his attitude to the markets: 'every battle is won before it's ever fought'.

The narrator of *Bombardiers* consistently attempts to conceptualise financial practices as being warlike. But this analogy, like others in the text, is usually undermined later by the same narrator: 'it wasn't war at all, not really'

(Bronson 1995, p. 124). Therefore the text makes its position clear unlike some others: the metaphor of war should ultimately be rejected by the reader.

Often money rogues are attributed with aggression as well as greed. In *The Vulture Fund*, all the characters are 'heartless', 'they have no feeling' (Frey 1996, pp. 260, 317). Compassion, loyalty, and a sense of duty to other people are conspicuously absent in the characterisations of traders in financial novels. They '[relax their] morals a bit to get money' (Frey 1996, p. 136). As trackers and hunters, their predatory activities always imply primitive violence.

Gekko's speech and actions highlight the perception of monetary aggression: he asks people to 'rip their fucking throats out', and resorts to physical violence when a deal goes against him by smashing china or assaulting people. Aggression and physicality are frequently referred to in texts about traders as if they have an innate compulsion to express their money anxiety through their bodies. Ranieri of Salomon's mortgage department has had almost a complete book devoted to him: Lewis's (1989) *Liar's Poker*. He is an infamous trading character, described by Mayer as a 'fat, Italian, uneducated [graduate] of the mailroom [who] established a raucous "culture" of practical jokes and enormous fast–food eating frenzies' (1993, p. 159). Lowenstein maintains that Ranieri often '[winged] slices of tomato across the trading room' (1996, p. 373). Ranieri's excess relates not just to money, but to food as well, thereby completing the hungry trait.

In *F.I.A.S.C.O.*, Partnoy emphasises the more violent aspects of trading culture, claiming that according to his experience at Morgan Stanley traders are positively encouraged to cultivate a warlike instinct. The title refers to an annual event held by the firm—The Fixed Income Annual Sporting Clays Outing. Partnoy claims that 'shooting doves or clay pigeons was excellent training for the even more exhilarating real–life kill, when the shrapnel of a complex financial instrument tore through a wealthy, unsuspecting human pigeon' (1997, p. 104). Conning a commission out of a client was apparently known as 'ripping his face off' at Morgan Stanley in the early 1990s: 'you grabbed the client under the neck, pinched a fold of skin, and yanked hard, tearing as much flesh [commission] as you could' (Partnoy 1997, p. 61). Effectively, Partnoy concludes, 'You have to be a criminal to be good at this business' (1997, p. 179), and a murderous one at that.

Rogues fail to make a killing if they do not act decisively when there is money to be made. Thus in terms of outcomes the rogue suffers from a fall from grace: he (and rogues are disproportionately male, like the heroes) makes an error of judgment and is forced to pay the price, in terms of character assassination. Furthermore, it only takes seconds for changes to occur in volatile markets. In the novel *Free to Trade,* for example, Tommy Masterson 'had gone from successful [junk bond] salesman to failure in five minutes' (Ridpath 1995, p. 174). In a milieu such as the markets, acting quickly and with restraint is necessary to be a hero. According to Monroe Trout, a CTA (commodity trading advisor), 'A successful trader is rational, analytical, able to control emotions, practical, and profit oriented' (in Schwager 1994, p. 171), and these qualities are not generally handed out to typical traders, so in some respects traders undermine the supposed inherent rationality of the market.

The New Market Wizards (1994) is the second volume of interviews Schwager has published about traders, and is marketed to both the expert and the curious amateur investor. The book contains hot tips for the way to success as a trader, such as the following: 'It all comes down to: Do your own thing (independence); and do the right thing (discipline)' (Blake in Schwager 1994, p. 248) and 'The key to trading success is emotional discipline' (Sperandeo in Schwager 1994, p. 265). Schwager found that '*discipline* was probably the most frequent word used by the exceptional traders that [he] interviewed' (1994, p. 466). Ironically, however, Schwager himself no longer trades, because he cannot bear the emotional turmoil, he becomes nervous and agitated. Therefore by his own admission, Schwager is a failure.

Some characters mentioned so far are actual people who have played the markets unsuccessfully and their stories are repeatedly fictionalised as we have seen with Ranieri; others begin as fictional constructs. The boundary between fiction and reality is always blurred in the money myth. As we have seen with the Bill Gates construct, Gates's real existence has become fictionalised, while other fictitious characters simultaneously become real. While Bill Gates is generally perceived to be a monetary hero, with positive characteristics, many rogues (real or otherwise) are set up ambiguously, such as Gekko from *Wall Street*. He is also associated with greed and could therefore be deemed to be morally bereft, but he is also a wealth creator. In some respects the character shifted the meaning of greed in the 1980s, so that it became a positive attribute, which arguably led to the deregulation and the dismantling of restraint in our current financial system.

'Greed Is Good, For Lack of a Better Word'

Known as the proponent of the 1980s 'greed is good' creed, Gordon Gekko has come to symbolise the villainous market manipulator for some readers. He is attributed with a range of traits that together constitute a greedy character. Gekko's central motivation is the acquisition of money through the markets, and this determination is pursued at any cost.

Westbrook makes the following observation, which is pertinent in terms of Gekko's moral status:

Give the American writer a story about the stock market or high finance, and he turns it into an allegory. Wall Street is a type of paradise filled with enough fruits of the tree to satisfy all man's needs. Yet there is a knowledge forbidden to men in this world, knowledge not of good and evil but of speculation and high finance. Against a Puritan background long suspicious of money and commerce. Wall Street becomes the battlefield in which a man's soul is lost. The stock market, not woman, is the agent of his fall. (in Light 1981, p. 557)

Wall Street, the movie, can be read in precisely this manner. Significantly, too, Gekko's view that Wall Street is a battleground and that women are commodities ultimately leads to his downfall.

Released in 1987, *Wall Street* has become perhaps the model generic text about traders, the twentieth-century markets, and moral dilemmas. The video cover explains that the movie is 'a modern day morality tale of greed and corruption. *Wall Street* is set in the quick–moneyed, ultra–slick world of stock-broking in Manhattan' (1987). For Lewis, a cynical commentator of the markets, morality and the markets are a mismatched pair: 'Wall Street and its people simply do not belong in conventional morality tales. The only moral on Wall Street is that there is no moral' (1991, p. 19). This perception is represented in *The Marketmaker*: trading is not 'immoral, just amoral' (Ridpath 1998, p. 92).

Gekko's character is a particularly powerful example of the crossing between fiction and actuality. He could be a timeless character, one who will always exist in different physical guises, but will remain representative of an amoral and unrestrained quest for money. Wark contributes to this representation (and hence mythologisation) by taking Gekko from a fictional context in order to describe a range of real–life behaviours. For example, we find phrases such as 'the aggressive gung–ho individualism of the Gekko ethos' (Wark 1994, p. 174), and 'Gekko personifies capital lost to itself' (Wark 1994, pp. 175–76). Wark even reads Gekko into Marx by suggesting that 'when Marx said that "capital is man completely lost to himself", he might have been describing Gordon Gekko' (1994, p. 175).

In a similar vein, Jackson writes, 'Sir Issac Newton—who besides his work in physics, alchemy and Biblical commentary was also briefly possessed by the spirit of Gordon Gekko' (1994, pp. 78–79). The Gekko character seems to be a monetary mutation, intertextualised to extremes, but representative of a type of behaviour that seems to demand cultural condemnation. So powerful is Gekko to the popular imagination that he creeps up in numerous texts as proof that the 'greed is good' principle ultimately fails. In this context greed is undesirable, because it encourages a ruthless pursuit of money.

Wall Street characters Bud Fox and Gordon Gekko seem to represent two different sides of the coin in terms of their relationship to money, and the moviegoer is goaded into sympathising with either Fox or Gekko. Fox is intended to be a moral check on Gekko, and the moviegoer follows him through a picaresque journey into Wall Street, and a flirtation with corrupt financial practices. At the beginning of the movie, he wants to be a hero like Gekko, telling traders when to buy and sell. But he gradually discovers that sacrificing his family and dispensing with the codes of trade is reprehensible. Effectively his life is torn between loyalties to Gekko, his family, and money. In the final analysis, Fox is not a hero as defined in my previous chapter, rather he is a crusader for nonmonetary values, such as love, the family, and loyalty.

As Fox gets richer, unlike Gekko, he finds his individuality dissolving. He questions his own identity, later realising that he has become 'the invisible man'. He is very offended when another character snubs him, so he strives harder 'to be a giant, a mover, a shaker', to emulate his chosen monied and monetary hero. But the potential of money to corrupt enlightens him, and prevents him from being absorbed by Gekko's persona. In their final confrontation, Fox tells Gekko: 'Much as I always wanted to be Gordon Gekko I'll always be Bud Fox'. Thus, both Gekko and Fox represent the two sides of money's irresolvable play: creation and loss.

The viewer's moral sympathies are pushed towards Fox, who is '[played] like a grand piano' by Gekko whose only interest is getting Fox to trade for him. Unlike Fox and Wildman (another wealthy investor), who consider the 'lives and jobs' of other people, such as the workers at Blue Star, Gekko has no concern for them, implying simply that 'what is worth doing is worth doing for money' alone. Concerns about people only surface in the movie when monetary climaxes are imminent and they present moral dilemmas for Fox. When his father has a second heart attack, for example, he decides to make a deal with Wildman and break Gekko, which he successfully accomplishes. So, Fox's journey ends with a realisation about the futility of never–ending money making. He asks Gekko, 'Tell me, Gordon, when does it all end? How many yachts can you ski behind?', effectively undermining Smith's idea about satisfaction being endlessly deferred, as well as the cyclical nature of trading addictions.

Gekko's speech to Teldar's stockholders' AGM is at the centre of the movie, and is potentially appealing to the moviegoer, depending upon the perspective he or she brings to the movie. To some Gekko can win appeal at this stage of the movie, provided that his ideology is taken to be inventive, creative, and hence heroic. In this sense, Gekko embodies the appealing idea that 'individualism [can rise] above the limiting structures of society' (Hourihan 1997, p. 150). But Gekko has a particular view of reality, and he measures worth in terms of political, national, and economic bottom lines. In fact, his speech is nothing more than a reiteration of the rhetoric of the 1980s neoclassical economists. He begins his speech, 'Well, ladies and gentlemen, we are not here to indulge in fantasy but in political and economic reality. America has become a second rate power. Its trade deficit and its fiscal deficit are at nightmare proportions' (*Wall Street* [motion picture] 1987). He sets up his argument in terms of destroyed dreams, but these dreams constitute the illusion that countries have an economic reality that can be undermined, which is fictitious. Furthermore, the nightmare resides in deficit, that is, in the absence of money. In these respects, Gekko's speech keeps the economic idea of money alive.

He then draws viewers and the story's shareholders into a critique of the bureaucratic (rather than the entrepreneurial) system and its squandering: 'You are all being royally screwed by these bureaucrats, with their steak lunches, their hunting and fishing trips, their corporate jets and golden parachutes' (*Wall Street* [motion picture] 1987). In addition, his description of the United States as a 'malfunctioning corporation', run along bureaucratic lines, is effectively a mourning for the demise of old–fashioned accountability and personal financial interests in companies. But the movie shows Gekko up as a hypocrite, for free and deregulated markets preclude the kind of accountability Gekko advocates.

The most frequently cited phrase from this speech in all manner of texts is 'greed is good'. But Gekko actually says, 'Greed, *for lack of a better word*, is good [my italics]'. Gekko is challenging the adequacy of language to express monetary concepts, and rejects any received moral signifieds in the term 'greed'. He practically pushes for additional signifieds for the term, which do not neatly tally with some perceptions of money's alliance with greed. In this respect, Gekko foregrounds his creative (monetary) role:

In the last 7 deals I have been involved with there were 2.5 million stockholders who have made a pre–tax profit of 12 billion dollars. [applause] Thank you. I am not a destroyer of companies, I am a liberator of them. The point is ladies and gentlemen, that greed, for lack of a better word, is good. Greed is right, greed works, greed clarifies, cuts through and captures the essence of the evolutionary spirit. Greed in all of its forms: greed for life, for money, for love, for knowledge has marked the upward surge of mankind and greed, you mark my words, will not only save Teldar paper, but that other malfunctioning corporation called the USA. (*Wall Street* [motion picture] 1987)

Gekko liberates greed from the concept of money, and forces it to signify striving. His speech defines greed as the motive for progress, and as a factor in clear thinking. Greed, as Gekko's argument would have it, initiates a range of creative enterprises.

Moviegoers are torn between two positions, admiring or disliking Gekko as an embodiment of the capitalist ideal. As a market player (still successful at this stage in the movie), Gekko represents as vast a sum of money as is imaginable; after all, he has made $12 billion. But his principles are questionable: greed as a positive attribute does not ring true to many from the (Christian) Western world, and thus ignores other values that could be taken as admirable, such as selflessness or charity. For some, the best things in life are free, including love, life, and knowledge. Gekko's $12 billion constitutes the appeal of the market, but his philosophy could present a discordant idea of progress for moviegoers, because it is framed around money as the prime motivator.

Gekko's words to Fox could be applied to the movie's general public: 'The illusion has become real and the more real it becomes the more desperately they want it' (*Wall Street* [motion picture] 1987). The movie presents the problem of money's elusiveness in a number of ways, many of them contradictory: the nightmare is absence, but the reality is financial. In this respect, I concur with Wark's diagnosis that 'the *Wall Street* movie is framed between the fear and the desire for the becoming abstract of finance capital' (1994, p. 175).

While there is little cash in evidence, visual signs of money proliferate in the text: cheques, and numbers on screens, and in the metaphorical form of capital assets such as houses and paintings. Money's ability to be exchanged into anything is illusory. On the other hand, being 'practical', as Gekko expresses it, involves collecting material objects: the rarest pistol in the world, paintings, and women. His utterances define money as abstract, but his character is defined for the moviegoer by visual icons (such as his dress and the setting), which contradict his speech. The moviegoer realises that Gekko can afford to be philosophical about money, because he has money to burn, and this particular realisation is prompted by the larger–than–life painting in his outer office that depicts a huge hand holding a burning $20 note. Gekko wears braces, tie pins, chunky gold rings, and bracelets, all icons or symbols of wealth, which contradict the immaterial aspects of money the movie plays with. Williamson explains this contradiction in *Deadline at Dawn*:

the tension between plot and image is what gives film an enormous capacity for containing contradictions popular films re–work conflicts and contradictions within a wider cultural field they must be quick to address new experiences in their audiences (markets) while at the same time, no matter how frightening or disturbing those experiences, they must deal with them in a way that is bearable, even enjoyable in other words marketable. (1993, p. 28)

Wall Street was released in 1987, the year of a significant stock market crash, and in this sense, Williamson's point about new experiences is pertinent. Gekko, appealing, on one hand, for his success and creativity, is also a character who represents corrupt monetary practices, made easier by money's abstraction. Ultimately the movie is a commentary on the contradictions inherent in the economic view of the money markets.

Gekko is a distinctive character for money's mythologies: his name, his physical aspect, and his money are constantly recalled in other texts. He has become a type, a character associated in the popular perception of the greedy, noncreative person: 'not only would [he] sell his mother to make a deal, [he'd] send her C.O.D.!' Fox's position in the movie assists in this respect; his father tells him: 'stop going for the easy buck and produce something with your life, create'.

Ultimately, I would argue that money in this movie is perceived to amount to very little, in terms of its creative aspects.

When Gekko argues, 'I create nothing, I own', he is not only defining himself as a monied hero (as distinct from a monetary hero), he is also denying his ability to be creative, and there is an implicit tension here. Making money is a creative exercise, but it can only occur from within its own referential system, because, as Kurtzman observes, 'money is mostly involved in nothing more than making money' (1993, p. 149).

This idea is supported by Gekko's assertion that 'money itself isn't lost or made, it's simply transferred from one perception to another, like magic'. The significance of this remark is threefold. First (in monetarist terms), Gekko is implying that there is only a *finite* amount of money in circulation, and that it is limited so that he cannot actually 'make' more money. This idea is contradicted by the above remarks about money as a self–multiplying system. Second, by equating money with pure conceptual exchange, Gekko challenges his own equation of money with reality. Third, Gekko refers to a magical element of money; its ability to appear as well as dematerialise. The idea that money is magic, illusory, and evasive is persistent in popular texts, adding to its mystery and its mythologisation.

Describing himself as a 'liberator', Gekko creates an intimate affiliation between himself and money, because he alone (like the monetary hero) is in a position to liberate money from its material fetters. A shot of the Statue of Liberty supports this allusion to freedom when it appears after Gekko has instructed Fox to manage his funds. Images on the screen frequently contribute to Gekko's idea that 'the illusion has become real', and this is the core source of tension in the movie. This is 'capitalism at its finest', Gekko maintains. But what does he mean? Material goods (which are in effect 'capital') refer to the illusion of the power of money. But they also represent money as a more concrete, observable phenomenon, which contradicts the idea of money being magically transferred from one perception to the other. Or does it? At the party where Fox meets Darian, she explains the value of some of Gekko's paintings in terms of their exchange value, so that hypothetically the value of one painting could be represented as two penthouses or one luxurious beach house.

In terms of its title and milieu—Wall Street—the movie clearly points towards the problematic dichotomy between abstract money and real needs. The Gekko character is rich in money, rhetoric, and contradictions. For some readers he could represent the triumph of money culture, or neoclassical economics. For others, his traits and belief in greed represent the amoral aspects of money and power.

Gekko's momentous loss on Blue Star is accompanied by a screen blackout, and is followed by the comment 'did somebody die?' I would argue that for most of the population in our culture, the movie's closure is a fitting one: Gekko's unbridled greed and corrupt monetary practices deserve retribution.

CAPITAL LOST TO ITSELF

Some characters (including Leeson, whom I shall turn to shortly) behave like money: they are elusive and slip through your fingers. Like digital money, they are also often highly charged, both emotionally and physically. When Lucas (the supertrader from West's *Vanishing Point*) is described as 'a brilliant man in a manic flight from reality' (1996, p. 45), we could read a parallel story about money as digital bits escaping our grasp. In an interview with Phillip Adams on the Australian Broadcasting Commission's 'Late Night Live' on 18 August 1997, West said that 'everything in the world is a part of the same thing'. The corollary of this position for my argument is that money and characters can be read as one and the same thing in his text.

A similar reciprocity is created by the short phrase 'Cash will look like a hero' from *Free to Trade* (Ridpath 1995, p. 76). The reader knows that Cash is a character who courts investors, but the sign assaults the eye because of its money reference. Often money is traited like a human, but on other occasions people are traited by money; and to me this interchangeability provides evidence of the unquestioned assumption that people are dependent upon money for their identity.

Vanishing Point is about money trails and disappearing traders. Carl Strassberger's brother–in–law (Larry Lucas) has recently disappeared after completing a $5 billion deal. Strassberger is sent to find him, and he goes to the Paris office to track down some clues. He eventually discovers that Lucas had gone through an agency called Simonetta Travel, which specialises in 'disappearances'—an action that could be likened to money–laundering activities. Strassberger changes his identity and embarks on a journey to find Lucas and to convince him to return; he locates Lucas in a mental hospital at the end of the text. Lucas's character does not come into the novel until the end, thereby maintaining a distance, like the money in the text: money is implicit in *Vanishing Point*, but it leaves a trail. The whole story could be considered as a kind of allegory about money. If we were to consider the following quote to be about money rather than clients, the parallel would be quite clear: 'Presumably the clients are satisfied, because they've got exactly what they paid for—they've dropped out of circulation, disappeared completely, stepped off the sidewalks of their home place into a special nowhere, discovered, recommended and tailored to their personal needs' (West 1996, p. 63).

This extract concerns representation outside the bounds of discernible institutions. Interestingly, the rogue in this text is Simonetta Travel, and my reading is that the text points towards a cultural need for outward, or manifest, phenomena.

So ideologically, money laundering could be an apt parallel, as could money's digitalisation, or the tailoring of forms of money in the financial markets.

Characters and money are also noted for their ability to disappear without a trace in *Bombardiers*. No trace is left of Eggs (Mark Igino) when he leaves the company, even his signature is missing from all found documents. This absence causes the other characters to question whether he really ever did exist. This gesture suggests an inherent connection between paper, money, and character. Ironically perhaps, before his departure, Eggs was the only trader to have wanted to see a real bond (Bronson 1995, p. 169). His boss is incredulous: 'it's just a piece of fucking paper with a bunch of colors and words printed on it' (Bronson 1995, p. 169). The paper brought back to show him is a substitute, 'a receipt, stamped with the embossed seal of the Fed' (Bronson 1995, p. 170); it is like 'monopoly money' (Bronson 1995, p. 171). Money in this text is rarely represented in paper form, because new money is no longer like this—it has no fixed form (Bronson 1995, p. 10), and so the text points towards the idea that money only exists conceptually, and that it is the concept that is exchanged.

In many texts, money is, to use Gekko's words, transferred from one perception to another. Partnoy relays a conversation he reportedly had with a lawyer about a particular trade he was involved in at Morgan Stanley in the early 1990s:

'First of all', she said, 'how do we know the Pre4 bonds even exist'?

There was a long pause. That seemed like a pretty basic question, even for a novice lawyer. Should I laugh at her? Or should I scream? Her question was not only naive and irrelevant, it was absurd. Ontology? At this hour? Somehow I held back. I waited patiently for the Cravath lawyer's response. It was perfect.

'As a matter of fact, they don't exist', he said. 'There are no physical bonds'. (1997, p. 151)

An old adage reads: 'Money speaks. Mine keeps saying "Goodbye" ', and this concern is implicit in many texts, seemingly referring to money's dematerialisation and its elusiveness. Money is persistently constructed as either disappearing or invisible, even though it does not exist per se. It is important to bear this in mind for my discussion of the Leeson character. Money forms traded in the market bear little resemblance to the cash–money our cultural senses are accustomed to. It can therefore easily be taken as immaterial, in the sense both of insignificance and abstraction. The perception of abstract money as dispensable frequently surfaces in texts written about behaviours endorsed by particular investment houses (such as Mayer's *Nightmare on Wall Street*).

Where are reader's sympathies directed in terms of real-life characters who resemble Gekko as far as traits and monetary loss go? Can we empathise with Nick Leeson (the trader who brought down Barings Bank)? Or do we, like the *Economist* (15 Apr. 1995), take the fall of Barings as a signal that the markets are becoming increasingly precarious (p.30)? Buchan's diagnosis seems correct: 'Dr. Johnson's formulation—that money–making keeps men out of mischief seems to have no place for Mr. Nick Leeson, 28' (1995, p. 24). Leeson has been jailed, scorned, and pitied for his monetary and ethical losses. I will consider a range of constructions of his character before explaining how our continued construction of money systems could itself be responsible for money's elusiveness. Leeson's story can only be told within the framework of the money market, and so they are both called into question.

FROM HERO TO VICTIM

Since his arrest on 2 March 1995, there have been at least four books written about the Barings collapse, one co-written by Leeson himself (*Rogue Trader*), which was Blackwell's May 1996 book of the month.[4] According to Gapper and Denton, the 1990s was the "decade of the 'rogue trader" in financial markets and characters such as Leeson have become commodities themselves' (1996, p. 340).[5] Indeed, after his arrest Leeson's old business cards are said to have sold for £130 each and a rush of jokes proliferated in various financial districts.[6] Board games were formulated around his escape, and apparently a song and an opera were composed about the incident (Hunt and Heinrich 1996, pp. 173, 246, 248). A full–length movie of the story was released in 1999, with Ewan McGregor playing the part of Leeson. Surprisingly, the movie was not a box office success, despite our earlier fascination with the character.

There is a great deal of speculation about Leeson's character and his motivations. Fay notes that David Frost's description of the Barings story as ' "a modern morality tale" [is questionable]. Since morality tales deal with the triumph of good over evil, there ought to be some good guys involved. It is hard to find any heroes in this story' (1996, p. 270). What was Nick Leeson's crime? How did he come to see himself as a sacrificial lamb? In brief, in March 1992 Leeson was sent to the Singapore International Monetary Exchange (SIMEX) to trade derivatives on behalf of Barings Bank. This prestigious but small merchant bank was London's oldest, apparently holding £40 million of the Queen's money, and a total share capital base of £470 million (Leeson 1996, pp. 12, 197). Despite its label as a 'blue–blooded' bank, its capital base was very small compared with the sums of money that Bill Gates, for example, possesses.

Martin, the man who hired Leeson says, 'he worked hard; he also had an intellectual ability and good lateral thinking. He was a cut above the rest. He had no experience as a trader, but it was a matter of learning on the job' (in Fay 1996, p. 77). A novice to both management and trading, Leeson found himself in a relatively autonomous position at SIMEX for two reasons: first, no rigid reporting structure had been established, and second, according to Leeson, 'the world of futures and options was expanding rapidly, and few people really understood how they worked' (1996, p. 18). Therefore, when errors were made by his staff (often caused by an over–indulgence in alcohol), Leeson was forced to cover his position and hide the extent of the losses from Barings in London. He claims that the first error amounted to (a mere) £20,000 and was caused by a trading error: one of his recruits had '*sold* rather than bought twenty contracts' (1996, p. 40). To cut a long story short, Leeson gambled on the markets to cover his losses, but by December 1994 he 'had lost almost £160 million' because of his speculations: almost one–third of the bank's entire share capital base (Leeson 1996, p. 145).[7] He hid the losses in an account infamously known as 'The Five Eights Account'— which had somehow escaped the auditors' notice. By the middle of February 1995, the account had 'absorbed something like £300 million of funding' (Leeson 1996, p. 197). By the time his birthday came around at the end of February 1995, Leeson was forced to make an escape and was on the run from losses that Gapper and Denton estimate to have been £600 million (1996, p. 48).

Leeson's losses took a relatively short time to occur. Moments of glory can be reversed abruptly, almost at the toss of a dice. The contrast between the hero and the rogue surfaces at precisely those moments when the balance is waiting to be tipped between success and failure. These can be literally fractions of seconds where a glance into the market abyss provokes either fortitude or weakness. Compare Soros's remark quoted previously, 'going to the brink serves a purpose. There is nothing like danger to focus the mind, and I do need the excitement connected with taking risks in order to think clearly' (1995, pp. 15–16) with Leeson's confrontation with the monetary brink:

I felt like a ghost on the edge of the pit. I seemed to be fading away from it. I went off to find the Gents and ducked over the filthy lavatory, my stomach retching and my mouth full of slimy green regurgitated fruit pastille. In forty five minutes time the trading floor would be deserted and I'd have nowhere to hide. I hunched over a desk and looked at the screens. To the outsider I looked like Nick Leeson, the trading superstar. What a joke! I had lost hundreds of millions of pounds and had run out of rope. (1996, p. 217)

On 2 December 1995 Leeson was sentenced to six and a half years in a Singapore jail: six months for deceit (forgery), and six years for cheating SIMEX (Gapper and Denton 1996, pp. 39–40).[8] According to Gapper and Denton (1996), his crime was creative avoidance: he failed to accept responsibility for the losses he incurred, but for the Singaporean courts his crime was that he had deceived the Singapore Exchange. Barings incidentally did not press any charges against him.[9]

There are three versions of the cause of this enormous loss. Gapper and Denton (both journalists on the *Financial Times*) maintain that Leeson 'squandered millions' (1996, p. 241), 'spun a web of deceit' (1996, p. 339), and 'had apparently brought down Barings unaided' (1996, p. 340). But according to Leeson, the money he dealt with was not real, so he could treat it as if it were literally immaterial, because it bore no relationship to reality. The markets are often seen to encourage an enterprising separation from the everyday. Kurtzman's *The Death of Money* (1993) pursues this dichotomy as his central thesis. He highlights the disparity between what he terms the 'real' and the 'financial' economies, by suggesting that globalisation, and its incumbent volatility, is detrimental to real (i.e., local and fundamental) needs. The ' "global landscape" is an abstract land, a land of description rather than reality, where the real and the financial economies barely touch' (1993, pp. 164–65). In other words, small investors at Barings could have lost all their savings because of Leeson's trading position in Singapore, but neither Leeson nor the investor would know of each other.

Leeson acknowledges the autonomy of the markets. He maintains that 'it was widespread practice to conjure up fictitious deals if an error took place' (Leeson 1996, p. 44). But this is where some tension lies: readers recognise that their money is not fictitious, and that an error in the markets has reverberations in real life. But Leeson maintains that 'all the money we dealt with was unreal: abstract numbers which flashed across screens or jumped across the trading pit with a flurry of hands' (1996, p. 56). In this respect, money's fictionalisation seems to be conducive to dishonest financial practices. The conventions that maintain that money has a reality determine correct behaviour, but when Leeson undermines these conventions he calls into question the foundations upon which this monetary reality is built. Castells takes a somewhat extreme position in relation to the bank's collapse by suggesting that 'Puritanism [was] buried in Singapore in 1995 along with the venerable Barings Bank' (1996, p. 436). Castells seems to imply that money was previously part of a system of restraint.

Hunt and Heinrich present a slightly different perspective by maintaining that 'the rhythms of capitalism's purest forum, the financial markets, had eaten away at Leeson's integrity' (1996, p. xv). Leeson also resorts to finger pointing when he refers to the market's capacity to distort a character's integrity: 'Like the light bending in the strange world of plate glass, my morals had bent in the unreal world of the trading I was doing. I had become crooked' (1996, p. 79). In effect, Leeson's actions can be perceived to be caused *either* by his own character traits, or by the monetary system itself.

Leeson's character is impossible to pin down because he has pushed out the borderlines of monetary conventions. The (British) *Daily Telegraph* describes Leeson as 'neither a victim nor a hero' whereas Leeson thinks otherwise (Hunt and Heinrich 1996, p. 252). According to *The Sun* (newspaper), Leeson said: 'I have taken a risk and it has gone wrong. If it had worked out I would have been a superstar, a hero set up for life—if not, a villain' (in Hunt and Heinrich 1996,

p. 186). Leeson's comment is directed at the fickleness of cultural constructions, and in particular the transitoriness of money's characterising hierarchy.

Gapper and Denton provide the most comprehensive character construction of Leeson. He was 'a typical trader: loud and boastful' (1996, p. 16), 'bright and hard–working a determined fighter [with] plenty of drive and determination' (1996, p. 186). Not only does he have drive like the heroes in the previous chapter, but he also has a penchant for junk food, claiming to be able to 'excel at a blind tasting of Big Macs around the world' (Leeson 1996, p. 10). Most importantly perhaps for this story, 'Leeson was an exceptionally fluent liar' (Gapper and Denton 1996, p. 249). Nevertheless, Leeson's actions partially unveil the truth about the markets: that they are founded on inexact principles, yet any attempt to expose them as such is deceitful and destructive.

Initially the perception was that Leeson 'had imagination, could think on his feet and did not just rely on instructions' (Gapper and Denton 1996, p. 187). He had 'physical presence [and was] quick thinking', with a 'low boredom threshold' (Gapper and Denton 1996, pp. 190, 191). His 'natural authority' (Gapper and Denton 1996, p. 194) meant that '"money people" looked up to him' (Hunt and Heinrich 1996, p. 82), he was a 'cock–sure Maestro' (Hunt and Heinrich 1996, p. 93). Rawnsley includes the following descriptions of Leeson from his colleagues: 'He was the Michael Jordan of the trading floor the king he changed the password for his electronic mail to Superman. He had some sort of Midas touch' (1996, p. 152). In the beginning, it seems Leeson conformed to established configurations of a promising, even heroic trader.

Many traders are not 'movers and shakers' or 'market makers' like our monetary heroes (Hunt and Heinrich 1996, p. 84). Instead they are perceived to be 'agents of creative destruction' (Millman 1995, p. xviii) or 'Bank [Breakers]' (Hunt and Heinrich 1996, p. 267). All traders have the capacity to be 'bank killer[s]' (Partnoy 1997, p. 207). The power traders are perceived to have is momentary, derived from a gung–ho or cock–sure attitude—they are what Fay calls 'Big, Swinging Dicks' (1996, p. 36). Nevertheless, their jobs involve making money, so they can be regarded as controllers, or 'Masters of the Universe' (Wolfe 1988, p. 17).[10] The trader is attributed with autonomy from this perspective, and in many ways the freedom that traders are given is proportionate to money's current emancipation.

Hunt and Heinrich maintain that Leeson is 'some sort of working class hero, abandoned to his fate by the establishment' (1996, p. 190). But as we have seen in the last chapter, monied heroes are those characters that have accumulated and held on to money. Therefore, because Leeson is said to have made no money himself out of the collapse, he cannot be described as a monied hero. Millman believes that Leeson is 'undistinguished except for his youth and his losses', but the losses make him distinctive (1995, p. xiii). So *distinctive* in fact that he is used in *The Marketmaker*: 'You'd think I was Nick Leeson, the way they treated me' (Ridpath 1998, p. 217).

Initially, Leeson was a 'godsend' for the Singapore branch of Barings because he was the only one who claimed to know anything about futures (Gapper and Denton 1996, p. 193). But his fall was hard, because he relied upon shaky foundations. He claims that 'it was impossible to see where the market was heading: by its very nature it was like trying to drive using only the rear–view mirror' (Leeson 1996, p. 71). Accordingly, 'He was forced to begin rethinking his strategy and widen the parameters to account for an act of God. Leeson may have prayed for divine intervention but the omens were not good' (Hunt and Heinrich 1996, p. 125). In any case, there was no one to listen—neither boss nor god.

For Saul, the money markets are the subject of 'tragicomedy' (1997, p. 153). After all, if we cannot control losses then we may as well laugh to ease the pain, and joking about Leeson's losses is one such strategy. *Bombardiers* is a text that plays on helplessness by laughing at no–win situations. The explicit concern of the text as a whole is to expose the hypocrisy of the financial market, and on the front cover of the 1995 edition is written Mario Puzo's recommendation: 'you will never invest again', which supports the critique. Bronson's text presents the markets as a *tableau mort*: a milieu trapped in a hell–like structure that is inhabited by hyped–up stereotypes. In some respects this is scarcely surprising, according to Rawnsley, because 'the trading system is dominated by a simple value system: win or be damned' (1996, p. 143).

But the money markets are certainly not risible when they collapse in real life, because there is nothing but a spider's web of interlocking mythologies of money holding the structure together. In 1998, for example, Russia (as an 'emerging market') found its people bartering food for education, because their monetary system had failed.

F.I.A.S.C.O.—THE DERIVATIVE FINANCIAL MARKETS

The real villain of the piece, according to Leeson, is the system which takes a fictional concept—money—expands it, and embellishes it until it eventually trades what are (not surprisingly perhaps) called derivatives. The deregulation of the markets from government accountability and national boundaries, as well as the invention of a vast range of new financial instruments by traders in recent years has given the financial system excessive autonomy, with few ethical, geographical, or monetary (in short, conceptual) demarcations.

The financial system of the last two decades or so has given traders the leverage to create financial instruments at will, and they often use their financial knowledge to create (fraudulent) instruments (which is the subject of Partnoy's *F.I.A.S.C.O.*). These are fanciful reconstructions of the fictional premise that money is simply a 'medium of exchange'. In this way money can be anything that is traded, regardless of its intrinsic value. The threat to readers as real people is actual: instruments such as derivatives (futures) are creative beyond the call of trading duty, and are actually seriously threatening the stability of many readers' financial lives.

Nick Leeson traded futures. Also known as derivatives, there are many variations of them, which it is impossible to list here. Futures have been traded for a long time, centuries in fact, as 'a means to take out *protection* against vagaries in the prices of commodities over which [traders] had not control but which dramatically affected their income [my emphasis]' (Carew 1988, p. 107). In other words, these financial instruments protected against monetary loss caused by, say, crop failure or disease, rather like an insurance policy. Financial futures, however, are relatively new; they 'offer the chance to hedge or protect against movements in interest rates and currencies. They have been a boom industry in the past [two decades] as investors, traders and speculators seized on a new method to protect themselves against, or make money out of, increasingly volatile interest rates and exchange rates' (Carew 1988, p. 107). The references to which financial futures are gauged then are interest and exchange rates. They are sophisticated third–order monetary instruments designed to assist with the control of the money supply and spending.[11] Traders watch interest rates with the same rigour as they do the Dow Jones index. Unlike soybean futures, which protect real commodity prices, financial futures are traded *despite* their lack of real reference.

For Lowenstein, buying futures amounts to nothing more than a very risky gamble (1996, p. 319). In a letter to the *Washington Post* some time ago, Buffett expressed his view that 'the new esoteric instruments were not "investments", they served no social agenda; they did the work not of the Invisible Hand but of "an invisible foot kicking society in the shins" ' (in Lowenstein 1996, p. 320). Mayer concurs: 'The value of these pieces of paper was increasingly a function of the price of other pieces of paper, not of real production and consumption' (1993, p. 45).

The gap is widening because real production is not matched by the exponential growth in the markets, and hence value is disproportionate in the latter. In addition, if West is correct that everything in the world is part of the same thing, then it is finite. Therefore financial instruments should be restricted to some sort of reference (even if its value is variable). 'The problem with [futures] markets always is that anybody can create contracts to sell a commodity, but only God can make a tree or a wheat crop, and there's a limit to how much copper the miners can take out of the hills in a year' (Mayer 1993, p. 192).

Furthermore, 'As the derivatives market has grown, it has become more volatile and dangerous current proposals before Congress are for *less*, not more, regulation' (Partnoy 1997, p. 252). This is true conceptually, mythologically, and politically: the systems of money have been overtaken by an excess of creativity that affects trading practices. Partnoy admits that when he was trading, he found it difficult to assess the value of his trades because they had become so slippery (1997, p. 154).

The quotation from Nietzsche cited at the beginning of this chapter contained an intentional ellipsis: I omitted the words 'metaphor' and 'metonymy'. The full sentence reads: 'What then is truth? A movable host of metaphors, metonymies, and anthropomorphisms' (Nietzsche 1992 [1873], p. 84). Our truths, and hence our systems, begin in language, which as I constantly maintain have no referential base. 'Man [is] a mighty genius of construction, who succeeds in piling up an infinitely complicated dome of concepts upon an unstable foundation' (Nietzsche 1992 [1873], p. 85). This creativity can be celebrated, but not at the expense of starvation.

In the final analysis, the construction of heroes and villains as I have shown them reveal a cultural duplicity. The belief that greed is a vice makes Leeson and Gekko villains, whereas Buffett and Soros are *not* greedy. But conversely, they are not altruistic either. Heroes possess unnerving conviction, rationality, and vision, thereby supporting money's mythological structures, such as the idea of a self-regulating market. Rogues, on the other hand, are erratic, careless, and dishonest, ultimately sharing more features with money and the market, but as a culture we seem to prefer to condemn the visible characters, rather than the institutions of money.

In the next chapter I will focus on money's metaphors, teasing out a selection of transferences that are foundational to our money culture. The metaphors range from those found in Smith, Marx, and Simmel to the metaphors which circulate in late twentieth–century texts. My aim is to attempt an unearthing of some of the steps that have taken our culture from the word 'money' to a financial instrument—Brazilian discount bonds—known as 'discos' (Ridpath 1998, p. 30).

NOTES

1. I will use the term 'traders' as a short–hand convenience to include all these different jobs in the market. Despite their differences in terms of the 'division of labour', they all deal with other people's money.

2. All of these perceptions conflict quite substantially with the idea of the rational economic man. He does not 'act capriciously [he compares] the expected costs and benefits of available opportunities before [he acts] and [he learns] from and therefore [does] not repeat [his] mistakes' (Heyne 1994, p. 9).

3. There are numerous references to Christian values in relation to money. They seem to be used currently for the purposes of irony, to indicate a shift in values from the past to the present: money is no longer necessarily bad.

4. The others are: *Barings Lost, All That Glitters, The Collapse of Barings*, and *Going for Broke: Nick Leeson and the Collapse of Barings Bank*.

5. According to Fay's analysis, 'the bankruptcy of Barings was the biggest cock–up in the history of British banking, and it enabled Nick Leeson to become the biggest trading disaster in the history of financial markets. In fifth place is Joseph Jett, who created phantom profits that cost Kidder Peabody $350 million. Fourth is Howard Rubin, who ignored instructions and lost $700 million. Two Japanese share second place. Toshiihide Iguchi lost $1.1 billion, as did lesser–known Yukihusu Fujita with losses of $1.4 billion, Leeson is streets ahead of his rivals' (1996, pp. 266–67).

6. One example will suffice: 'What is the difference between Nick Leeson and Elvis Presley? Nick Leeson is definitely dead'.

7. It should be noted that the figures involved differ quite dramatically from text to text, and many of these vary because of exchange rate differences, thus confounding the *value* of the money itself. Obviously Leeson would not wish to over estimate the losses he incurred, if they could be established accurately anyway. For my purposes the exact sums are immaterial, it is the perceived magnitude of Leeson's error that is of greater significance.

8. Leeson was released in 1999 before he completed his prison term. The fall was certainly hard: before being released he contracted colon cancer, and his wife left him for another broker. Upon his release he returned to London and set up his own public relations company. His assets had been frozen, and he had a £100 million court order against him.

9. The bank did, however, issue a writ 'to preserve their position', and 'to prevent [Leeson] from benefiting financially from the collapse' (*Australian Financial Review* 21 Sept. 1995, p. 28).

10. *Bonfire of the Vanities*, like the motion picture *Wall Street*, came out in 1987. Wolfe explains in his Introduction that it 'reached bookstores a week before the Wall Street crash'. He 'began to read with increasing frequency that [the text] was "prophetic" ' (1998, pp. xxv–xxvi).

11. By 'third–order', I mean that they are extensions, twice removed from the money concept: money is a thing, its value is expressed in exchange rate terms that fluctuate, and financial futures can be bought that speculate on that fluctuation.

5

Money Is No Object

Money is dirt, time is money, money is art, money is a cushion, money is a tool; these metaphors are the foundations upon which particular money mythologies are built. Jackson identifies a whole range of metaphors of money: a cushion, a bridge, a vehicle, liberty, happiness, ritual, art, thought, and time (Jackson 1994, pp. 69–70).[1] The time is money metaphor, for example, enables Marx to equate money with work and the productive process, whereas the cushion, liberty, and happiness metaphors are all invested with expectation. Every metaphor attributed to money can reveal certain ideological perspectives in relation to the object itself. So, as Rowe maintains, 'money binds us together and splits us apart' (1998, p. 11).

Ricoeur proposes that metaphor '[reorganises] our perception of things' by mapping 'entire realms' onto the primary domain (1986 [1978], p. 236), so that words such as 'capital' have become mythological constructs that shift meaning from what is believed to be their referents. All metaphors are distortions, or accretions, and function as systematically as the narratives, histories, and characters that I have discussed thus far. Money has been developed along a series of metaphorical trajectories, and in this chapter I present some prevalent concepts of money which are located in the metaphor, and that repeatedly resurface. Three key perceptions are identified from a range of ideological positions: namely, money is an economic tool (and is regarded as such by Soros, for example), an agent of transformation (which transforms the character of people), and finally a bridge (so that it holds a promise or a future orientation).

Money and its metaphors are evaluative tools that modify the understanding we have of the world we currently live in, and more importantly of ourselves. They are taken as truths, when in fact they are simply cultural evaluations that have become ingrained. My argument follows Nietzsche's, which stresses the idea that metaphors become entrenched concepts over time, because as concepts they become separated not only from the object itself, but the metaphor even takes on a life of its own (apart from its original innovation) (1992 [1873], pp. 79–97).

The body of this chapter identifies the evolution of some monetary concepts, such as 'money is a tool', from Adam Smith (1776) onwards. Discussion touches on the ways in which money both *creates* (monetary characters and relationships) and *destroys* the particularity of forms and ideas. I shall also show (after Lane) how money can encourage goal–oriented thinking that focuses on the ends and not the means, and in this sense money is a bridge to the future. Some of my discussion will return to previous chapters—on narrative and character, for example—partly because metaphor, as I explain it, is one facet of a larger semiological system, but also because the thread of money is so intricately entangled in our culture that cross–references are inevitable. It should also be noted that occasionally discussion may seem to slip between metaphors of money and money as a metaphor, but this slippage is purely an operative—it is constitutive of money's mythological system, or the game of 'hide–and–seek' as Barthes calls it (1989 [1957], p. 128).

That money itself is a metaphor is not a new idea: intrinsic to both money and metaphor is the easily recognised mechanism of exchange, be it in the form of translation or correspondence. In the twentieth century there was a dominant view that money is the archetypal metaphor, which mimics our cultural systems. According to the poet Gioia, for example, '[Money] is the one true metaphor, the one *commodity* that can be translated into all else [my emphasis]' (in Jackson 1994, p. 70). Saussure and Jackson both solidify this idea by emphasising the concept of exchange value, which is shared by both money and language (both critics, like myself, approach money from the perspective of language). Jackson explains that 'money and literature are both conventional systems for representing things beyond themselves, of saying that X is Y. A poem asks us to believe that it represents a nightingale or a raven; a coin asks us to believe that it represents a bushel of wheat or a number of hours of labour' (1995, p. xiii). Key words of note here are 'represent' and 'believe'. Some of our monetary representations that partially derive from metaphor are believed to the extent that they become dogma. Take, too, Saussure's monetary explanation of linguistic exchange: 'To determine what a five–franc piece is worth one must therefore know: (1) that it can be exchanged that it can be compared with a similar value of the same system. In the same way a word can be exchanged for something dissimilar, an idea. Its value is therefore not fixed so long as one simply states that it can be "exchanged" for a given concept' (in Sieburth 1987, p. 157).

The commodification of money (as well as language in this case), and the privileging of exchange as a purely monetary exercise, is relatively new to human thinking and reveals a functionalist economic bias, which has the tendency to become a mythology of commodification.

A further relationship can be inferred with language. Stevens's phrase that 'money is a kind of poetry' makes some sense because both artefacts share a number of creative facets—we make, or produce them, and they have a value (in Jackson 1995, p. xiv). But poetry itself is becoming devalued. In the last two hundred years or so, the function of money has assumed more importance in education than poetry, as well as in policy decisions. Education departments are opening business or commerce schools often at the expense of arts schools, a gesture indicative of a disregard for nonpecuniary thought. Nevertheless, their use of money metaphors means that their discourse remains to a certain extent poetic.

The commodification of money and thinking was initiated, I suggest, by the economics discipline. It is of no importance to the totalising economist what the 'material' of money is composed of, so managing money is more important than interrogating its material or cognitive status. As we shall see, generalised concepts of money as appropriated by economists to signify *function* are resisted in metaphor by the very writers who write economic treatises. The exchange function itself becomes either re–metaphorised, or characterised, in its turn.

FROM METAPHOR TO CONCEPT, AND BACK AGAIN

I am now going to trace some aspects of both money and metaphor that have contributed to our current economic thinking. It would be possible to argue that a world without words would be a world without metaphors, and correlatively without concepts. Furthermore, without language, the concepts of money would simply not exist. But for *economic* thinking, the reverse is argued—namely, that the concept of money arose prior to language.

According to Vico's argument, pictorial language was humankind's first metaphorical gesture. Glaser's summary of Vico's work uncovers the primary supposition that 'metaphor belongs to pictorial expression and the personification of nature through metaphor' (20 Mar. 1997). The anthropomorphic quality of early language cannot be overemphasised, because it is an aspect of language that has stayed with us. Labels such as the 'leg' of the table and the 'mouth' of a river illustrate this point. Initially, as Glaser's reading has it, people were known simply as 'heads' because of the spontaneous focus on another's visage in times of contact. Some natural elements such as the sea and thunder were named gods, and other nonhuman objects were similarly 'spiritualised by metaphor' (Glaser 20 Mar. 1997).

Metaphor has its origins in human experience, and according to Vico, the personification of things is an explanatory gesture:

When men wish to create ideas of things of which they are ignorant they are naturally led to conceive them by means of resemblances with things which they know. And when there is not an abundance of the latter they judge things of which they are ignorant in accordance with their own nature. And since the nature which we know best consists of our own characteristics, men ascribe to brutish things and insensible things, movement, sense and reason, producing the most luminous works of poetry. (1982, p. 141)[2]

Over many centuries, Glaser continues, 'pictorial expressions [came to be] ousted by abstract concepts' so that 'head' was eventually replaced by the word 'man' with all its attendant conceptual connotations (20 Mar. 1997). Glaser concludes that 'poetry was the original language of mankind', and that its pictorial aspects in particular were nonrational (or, if you prefer, nonreasoning), whereas concepts are entirely rationalised and hence obscure and indefinite.

Despite the speculative aspects of this genealogical account of concept formation, it is one that has been taken up by a number of subsequent thinkers. Johnson's *The Body in the Mind,* for example, argues that there is much evidence to support the notion that meaning has progressively shifted from the 'more concrete and physical towards the more abstract and non–physical' (1987, pp. 107-108). In his [1873] essay on metaphor entitled (in translation) 'On Truth and Lie in a Nonmoral Sense', Nietzsche outlines a chain of events leading to the configuration of concepts. The formation of a concept begins with a sensory provocation or 'nerve stimulus' that is represented in terms of an 'image'. Hence feelings and perceptions are given an appearance that resembles aspects of the sensory in limited respects. Thereafter the image is rationalised into a concept—a process Nietzsche equates to evanescence:

The creator [of language] only designates the relations of things to men, and for expressing these relations he lays hold of the boldest metaphors. To begin with, a nerve stimulus is transferred into an image: first metaphor. The image in turn, is imitated in a sound: second metaphor. Every word [or sound] instantly becomes a concept precisely insofar as it is not supposed to serve as a reminder of the unique and entirely original experience to which it owes its origin; but rather every concept arises from the equation of unequal things. We obtain the concept, as we do the form, by overlooking what is individual and actual. Everything which distinguishes man from the animals depends upon this ability to volatilize perceptual metaphors in a schema, and thus to dissolve an image into a concept. (Nietzsche 1992 [1873], pp. 82–84)

Nietzsche shifts the anthropomorphic quality of metaphor slightly by emphasising the *relation* of people to things. His view seems to be that metaphor is not an explanatory gesture, but a homogenising one. This view of metaphor is eminently applicable to Marx's metaphor, 'capital', as I shall discuss below. Not only does capital define relations, but it is also a pure concept, without a referent, so it always refers to 'unequal things'. Nietzsche's overwhelming conclusion, like Vico's, is that 'as a *"rational"* being, he [the creator of language] now places his behavior under the control of abstractions' (1992 [1873], p. 84).

It is my contention that our present use of the word 'money' in economics causes a reversal of the historical development of metaphorical language as Vico and Nietzsche explain it, perhaps because of money's status as pure concept. With the economic concept of money, concept precedes 'poeticisation'. According to the reasoning and historicisations of this discipline, money is a purposeful invention facilitating exchange and trade. As a corollary of this—still within economic thinking—the concept of money is prior to language, which is a formulation I categorically reject. In a sense economics formulates new metaphors of money from the experiential world, working backwards, as it were, along Vico's evolutionary trajectory, so that metaphors such as 'money is a cushion' throw up sensory and pictorial structures through which we are able to 'understand' money's current status. Concretisations are an essential feature of economic abstractions.

Because money is not an object, and did not exist prior to language, there is an implicit tension between abstract and concrete in metaphor, which opens up in this chapter. The tension is never resolved, however, because the tendency for money to become abstracted is countered by its concretisation—which once again becomes abstracted—and so on. As I perceive it, the problem of representation is caused by money's metaphoricity, because on a simple basis it always 'stands for' some*thing*, or some *idea* other than itself. Jackson's quote, 'money is art', expresses a metaphor (money) in terms of another (art). Whilst the impulse in this metaphorical statement is to clarify, we find that 'art' as the secondary domain is borrowed from a paradigm that is in itself highly metaphorical, and hence the metaphor's clarifying function is precluded: a concept is exchanged for another concept thereby pushing money towards the abstract. Nevertheless, as Barthes says, we have a need to possess fixated objects, not simply elusive ideas (1989 [1957], p. 169), and so the numismatist may think of money as coin, whereas Alan Greenspan (the chairman of the U.S. Federal Reserve Bank) may think of money as a circulating medium.

Money's mythological histories share evolutionary features with metaphorical language, because money is perceived to have historically evolved from the nonrational (or sacred) to a highly evaluative abstract position in our perception. For many, money did not begin its 'life' as an economic instrument to facilitate trade. Bloom, like many noneconomists, believes for example that money emerged from ritual: *'to facilitate relationships'* with the sacred, the spiritual, the familial, and the seasons (1996, p. 12). However, Buchan's perception is that money's increasing abstraction, enabled by the underscoring of its newfangled functional aspects, has wrenched it from what Buchan calls its 'natural habitat' so that we have come to view money purely as an instrument of commerce, and the subject of greed (1997, p. 192).

CONVERTING MONEY THROUGH METAPHOR

In its simplest form, metaphor is either about 'translation' or 'correspondence'. In the first instance metaphor involves a conceptual *modification* of the primary term. In the second manoeuvre, that is 'correspondence', *similarity* of concepts dominates. I have found that very few (if any) monetary metaphors are correspondences; they are all re–presentations of value systems. Therefore, most money metaphors are translations, clarifying in unexpected ways—such as money is dirt—so that the pairing of concepts is partially discordant and causes semantic irritation. Nevertheless some metaphors are more dominant than others.

Taking the 'money is a cushion' example, we realise that 'money' is modified by the term 'cushion', and the connotations associated with cushions such as comfort, protection, and insulation. This metaphor insinuates that money has purely favourable characteristics. Thus the metaphor characterises money at the expense of what it is not. Each time metaphors are employed then, they modify or transform the 'target' (or primary) domain by projecting a particular insight onto it (which is money in this case), by ignoring what it is not.

It should be noted that this process is not reciprocated by the first term. Forceville explains that 'the transfer or mapping of features is from a secondary subject (on)to a primary subject and not vice versa' (1996, p. 65). In this regard, to take an example of Marx's, 'money may be dirt, although dirt is not money', and so the secondary term is the one that imposes concepts onto the first, thereby providing the dominant meaning (1990 [1867], p. 204).

Lakoff's work in the field of metaphor focuses on the identification of a series of 'general mappings across conceptual domains' in everyday conventional language (1993, p. 203). In his view, metaphor is not simply a question of poetic language, it is an evolved conceptual framework. The idea is a fascinating one for metaphors of money. If 'mapping is conventional [it] is a fixed part of our conceptual system', and so money should have conventional mappings particular to it (Lakoff 1993, p. 208). Lakoff and Johnson's (1980) *Metaphors We Live By* tags money onto the end of the text with little consideration of its conceptual ramifications. Its importance as a *modifying* term is peculiarly 'discounted' in the following example: 'If a new metaphor enters the conceptual system that we base our actions on, it will alter the conceptual system and the perceptions and actions that the system gives rise to Westernization of culture throughout the world is partly a matter of introducing the TIME IS

MONEY metaphor into those cultures' (Lakoff and Johnson 1980, p. 145). *Partly* indeed, for money provides the deviation in this metaphor and is the vehicle of conversion. Nevertheless, Lakoff's general point is clear–cut: as new metaphors are introduced, our cultural systems change.

Everyday language is modified by prevailing expert discourses that at the current time are largely economic. It is only very recently, for example, that financial market reports (and hence their discursive metaphors) have become as much a part of the news on television as the weather.[3] Likewise, our textual culture is bombarded by money metaphors and concepts, but they sneak in, often unheeded. A component of McCloskey's work draws attention to the metaphors used by economists as part of their rhetoric—a vital exercise in my view. As an economist, she maintains that metaphors in economics are the models that illustrate the story being told. 'The market for apartments in New York', says the economist, 'is "just like" a curve on a blackboard. No one has so far seen a literal demand curve floating in the sky above Manhattan. It's a metaphor' (McCloskey 1990, p. 1). True, but more importantly, the demand curve is a highly abstract mathematical concept. Economists use many conceptual metaphors, as another (exaggerated) example from McCloskey demonstrates:

[Some metaphors in economics] eventually become silent or unmarked [for example] 'children are durable goods'. But of course [this] is a metaphor. Children in some ways are like refrigerators, they are expensive to produce, they have a long service life, they have a very bad second hand market. Of course this metaphor shows some strengths as well as failures. Children are not ordinarily enamelled [and] they haven't got handles. ('Metaphor in the Dismal Science' Jul. 1996)

McCloskey is making the point that many monetary metaphors are unmarked; they have performed their translation, and it is only the secondary term that is retained in common parlance (in the above example it is the concept that anything can be 'goods'). It is absurd to conceive of children as durable goods, because they are not traded (except in some morally depraved blackmarkets). Nonetheless McCloskey's illustrations amplify a tendency towards monetary quantification and commodification, which alerts us to a transformation in our evaluative yardsticks.

Frequently tropes silence the assumptions inherent in the secondary–term mapping that become unrecognisable because of their worn or clichéd quality. An awareness of metaphorical play can be useful, because as a rhetorical device, an apt metaphor 'is one thing that makes people believe the truth in your story' (Aristotle 1984, p. 178), and forgetfulness enables the rhetorical strategy to be perpetuated. In fact, we often overlook the metaphorical nature of our language, so that the distinctiveness of clarifying metaphors that so impresses Aristotle is often forgotten, particularly in the monetary metaphor.

Money is becoming naturalised in two respects. First, as has already been suggested, many monetary metaphors have become 'worn out and drained of sensuous force' (Nietzsche 1992 [1873], pp. 84).[4] In other words, the original (creative) translation between metaphor and thing is forgotten, and this is nowhere more evident than in the metaphors used in the (economics) financial press. Furthermore, 'the wearing away of metaphor is dissimulated in the "raising" of the concept', which in the cases above could be said to refer to money as the measure of all things (Ricoeur 1986 [1978], pp. 285–86).

Second, some money metaphors do not (in the Aristotelian sense) naturally belong to the concept; they merely account for money's perceived behaviour. This gesture marks a reversal of the Vico genealogy and signifies a resistance to excessively abstract monetary concepts. For example, blood and the body become significant homologies for the circulation of money in the seventeenth and eighteenth centuries. According to Millman, 'the language of finance and economics has always borrowed from the physical sciences. We speak of the circulation of capital by analogy to the circulation of blood, of equilibrium by analogy to Newtonian physics, and so forth' (1995, p. 27). De Bolla's observations about metaphors of the body and circulation in eighteenth–century financial discourse verify this tendency, and he concludes that 'the figure of chiasmus around the body demands that we make a series of analogic substitutions, from blood and body to money and nation, bullion and world' (1989, p. 113). Money in this sense defines the individual's relationship to the nation. On the other hand, Buchan's recent reading that 'money [was seen to vivify] each social organ and limb' attributes money with a curative dimension (1997, p. 106). Bodily metaphors such as these in turn pave the way for the acceptance of economic 'prescriptions' for 'ailing' nations, and the like.

That these metaphors are used in reference to money's circulating properties also indicates a cultural desire to construct a natural foundation from which money could have come. The metaphor of the body, for example, recalls the anthropomorphic aspects of metaphor, so the conceptual movement here is from the abstract (or conceptual) towards the actual (or the concrete). The phrase 'money grows on trees again' from Bronson's *Bombardiers* signals a similar return, whilst also disguising a story about the financial markets (1995, p. 43). Bronson refers to the perception that in recent years the financial markets seem to be able to propagate and harvest money easily.

Setting the Wheel in Motion

Adam Smith's most–quoted metaphor is the 'invisible hand', which concretises and vaporises simultaneously. It is 'a metaphor that belongs more in a thriller than in a work of philosophy' because it infers a hide–and–seek plot (Buchan 1997, p. 176). But, as McCloskey points out, the metaphor is over–valued: 'Smith used the phrase "the invisible hand" only once in each of the two books published in his lifetime' (1994, p. 135).[5] The scarcely mentioned metaphor has come to dominate many secondary texts on Smith's work and is commonly used in debates about government intervention. A recent example can be found in the *Economist* where its cover story has the title 'The Visible Hand: Big Government Is Still in Charge' (20 Sept. 1997, p. 17). The opportunities for punning and creating new semiological chains derived from metaphors such as this are endless.

Buchan's comments on the invisible hand are also worth noting in passing: 'In Smith's first use of the phrase it is the supernatural agency to which primitive peoples attribute irregular or alarming natural phenomena', whereas nowadays the invisible hand is a conduit for avarice (1997, pp. 176–77). Once again Buchan suggests that money and its metaphors have departed from their natural habitat.

I now turn to Smith's work, *An Inquiry into the Nature and Causes of the Wealth of Nations* (1776); it is a search for a system of meaning with which to correct the uncoordinated eighteenth–century economy. It seems to me that Smith's choice of title sets the scene. *An Inquiry into the Nature and Causes of the Wealth of Nations* is just that; nevertheless only the mythological tag *The Wealth of Nations* has been kept.

As a study of disparate monetary networks, *The Wealth of Nations* has become perhaps the economic concept manual. Smith has 'provided the foundation of a great edifice, which has been extended rather than destroyed by those who followed' (Skinner 1979, p. 13). The text itself is laden with metaphors that usher in a range of perceptual problems because they confuse rather than clarify. It is surprising then that the reverberative consequences of his metaphors have proved monumental in terms of our thinking about money and monetary relationships. Nevertheless, Smith's concepts constitute a part of money's mythological system.

In keeping with the intellectual fervour of his time, Smith sets about to schematise a seemingly disordered, or poorly understood, economy. But Smith's attempts to come to grips with money's form and the pecuniary problems he perceives to exist results not only in metaphorical confusion, but also in a very bewildering schematisation of capital so that money features very little. Some aspects of Smith's work are later challenged, but also elevated, by Marx.

Smith's concern to schematise aspects of the economy was, I suggest, caused by several factors. First, there was an unprecedented widespread issue and distribution of paper currencies in Great Britain at the time, thanks perhaps to John Law, the monetary hero. Numerous banks were issuing their own paper currencies and there was no central regulatory body to control them. Most of these issues were promissory notes backed by material deposits such as gold and silver. Customers could reclaim their treasure at any time, hence the phrase 'on demand'. Not only was paper money a relative novelty, but for the first time it exceeded metallic money: 'By the middle of the [eighteenth] century, paper money considerably exceeded specie money in [England, Wales,] and Scotland' (Davies 1995, p. 278). Despite his overall lack of concern about monetary form, Smith represents the distinction between paper and gold as a definite rupture, and this can be gleaned from his language, rather than his reasoning: 'The commerce and industry of the country, however, it must be acknowledged, though they may be somewhat augmented, cannot altogether be so secure when they are thus, as it were, suspended upon the Daedalian wings of paper money as when they travel about on the solid ground of gold and silver' (1986 [1776], p. 420).[6]

Second, changes to England's fiscal system between 1688 and 1756 were momentous and have been labelled a "Financial Revolution" (Dickson in Davies 1995, p. 280).[7] Why? Because 'when paper money began to exceed metallic money the power of the royal purse became thereafter permanently, irreversibly and progressively diluted. For the first time in history money was being substantially created, not ostentatiously and visibly by the sovereign power, but mundanely by market forces' (Davies 1995, pp. 280-81). So, when *The Wealth of Nations* was published, two trailblazing changes had occurred to the economy: the quantity of paper money exceeded metallic money, and 'ordinary people almost any Tom, Dick or Harry' could now create money (Davies 1995, p. 281).

Smith's most prolifically used metaphor is the 'wheel', selected from the wide–ranging concept of mechanical inventions or tools. The concept of money as a tool enables Smith to metaphorise money both as 'the great wheel of circulation, [and] the great instrument of commerce' in his *The Wealth of Nations* (Smith 1986 [1776], p. 388). Smith's mapping of 'tool' onto money enables him to draw prodigiously from an industrial paradigm—which is hardly surprising since economics began as a response to industrial and metropolitan expansion. With tool as the secondary domain, money has a whole series of connotations: it becomes mechanical, functional, useful, and productive, echoing the surge of technological expansion in the eighteenth century. The wheel metaphor enables Smith to map the industrial paradigm as well as the concept of circulation onto money. Indeed, the wheel metaphor yields many paradigmatic associations, so that the economy, too, is subject to a host of mechanical metaphors: 'oiling' the wheels of industry, 'lubricating' the economy, and the like. Production then is conceived to be wheel–like, a concept Henry Ford arguably used as a foundational concept for his assembly lines.[8] If this pairing is accepted, then it is a very small conceptual leap to comprehend (postindustrial) financial *instruments* such as futures, whereby money can be made out of fancied future production, because what goes around, comes around.

Smith's use of the 'wheel' metaphor is decidedly uneconomical; it is excessive and confusing, cohering perhaps with the unregulated British economy of his time. However, he does have the courtesy and foresight to address his reader about his obscurity: 'I must very earnestly entreat both the patience and the attention of the reader: in order to understand what may, perhaps, after the fullest explication which I am capable of giving of it, appear still in some degree obscure' (1986 [1776], p. 132). He has touched on a vital point here: however much his metaphors are designed to clarify in an Aristotelian sense, they are doomed to failure. Let me now turn to the 'wheel' metaphor.

As Smith uses it, the 'great wheel of circulation' is a metaphor for the entirety of economic transactions, not just money. Within this great wheel we find two types of stock [or forms of capital]: one fixed and one circulating. It is at this point that the wheel metaphor turns back on itself and demands a new schema. The stocks, as he divides them, are respectively fixed capital (machines, buildings, land, and work skills) and circulating capital (stock, material, and completed work).[9] The first, fixed capital, 'affords a revenue or profit without circulating or changing masters'; therefore, it is concrete and immovable, i.e., nonliquid (Smith 1986 [1776], p. 377).

The second type of stock is money, a wheel within a wheel. It is 'the only part of the circulating capital of a society' (Smith 1986 [1776], p. 385). It is constantly moving, it is 'the great wheel of circulation, the great instrument of commerce' (Smith 1986 [1776], p. 388). Where eight pages earlier material and completed work were circulating, we now find money is the only part of circulating capital. Despite the existence of differing monetary forms (or 'stock'), Smith reduces them all to one. He considers circulating and fixed capital to 'bear a very great resemblance to one another' (Smith 1986 [1776], p. 385), and their similarity is to be found in their instrumental or functional aspects. Therefore, Smith considers the functions of money to override its form in many ways.

Fixed capital and circulating capital are also similar because they entail maintenance costs (Smith 1986 [1776], p. 385). The consequence of this is that coins (circulating capital presumably) wear out so they are 'like' machines, buildings, and land. So money becomes the bridge (not the wheel) between the various types of capital, both entailing and discharging expenses at its own cost: money costs money. Fortunately, however, 'the substitution of paper in the room of gold and silver money, replaces a very expensive instrument of commerce with one much less costly, and sometimes equally convenient. Circulation comes to be carried on by a new wheel, which it costs less both to erect and to maintain than the old one' (Smith 1986 [1776], p. 388).

Smith does not acknowledge the privileged status of money per se in his own analysis, despite the common–sense fact that fixed capital is always derived from and dependent upon circulating capital (i.e., money). The wheel unites all forms of money in one metaphor, so that machines are money, land is money, and buildings are money because they can all be converted into currency (liquid cash). But this use of the metaphor seems perceptually incoherent: there is no physical similarity between a machine and a money note. We have the beginnings of an abstraction here. Smith defines money as *part of* the great wheel, because in itself it has no value. Therefore, value is derived from circulation alone: 'it is only by means of circulation, or successive exchanges, that [money] can yield [the merchant] any profit' (Smith 1986 [1776], p. 374).

Smith continues with his line of reasoning: 'The great wheel of circulation is altogether different from the goods which are circulated by means of it. The revenue of the society consists altogether in those goods, and not in the wheel which circulates them' (Smith 1986 [1776], p. 385). I have read this phrase from *The Wealth of Nations* countless times and have found its tenets extremely difficult to grasp; it makes little obvious sense to the reader uninitiated into economics. Thankfully Smith again acknowledges a degree of obscurity: 'It is the ambiguity of language only which can make this proposition appear either doubtful or paradoxical' (Smith 1986 [1776], p. 385). Does this mean that without language, individual and social net revenue would be self–evident as Smith suggests? Is the economic conceptual framework prior to language? So how effective is the wheel metaphor as an explanatory device?

Precisely because of the slippage inherent in the wheel metaphor, Smith resorts to directional metaphors that delimit the wheel's paradoxes. Barthes's observation is apt here: 'the concept is much poorer than the signifier, it often does nothing but re–present itself' (1989 [1957], p. 129). Once again Smith apologises for his style: 'The gold and silver money which circulates in any country may very properly be compared to a highway, if I may be allowed so violent a metaphor' (1986 [1776], p. 420). He defines the highway as a 'sort of waggon-way through the air' that facilitates the conversion of gold and silver into 'good pastures and cornfields' (Smith 1986 [1776], p. 420). This is how money 'changes shape' (in Smith's terms [1986 (1776), p. 374])—it is represented as a metaphor corresponding rarely with his concept. The layering of metaphor upon metaphor is excessive in this case: circulation becomes a highway that is finally sent sky-high. Money does not change shape then, metaphor re–presents money, and in turn, distortions are constitutive of mythology (Barthes 1989 [1957], p. 131).

Another metaphor Smith uses is the channel, but this time it is for the purposes of delimitation: 'The channel of circulation, if I may be allowed such an

expression, will remain precisely as before. One million we have supposed sufficient to fill that channel. Whatever, therefore, is poured into it beyond this sum
cannot run in it, but must overflow' (Smith 1986 [1776], p. 390). Smith's argument here is that even if the banks only hold £200,000 in gold and silver, but
issue £1,000,000 in notes, then there is only £800,000 in circulation. Therefore
any sum above £1,000,000 will 'overflow' abroad 'because it cannot be
employed at home' (1986 [1776], p. 390). The puzzling question of why it would
not be used within the nation's boundaries arises here. Smith answers by referring to character: 'Though some men may sometimes increase their expense very
considerably though their revenue does not increase at all, we may be assured
that no class or order of men ever does so, because the principles of common prudence [influence every individual]' (Smith 1986 [1776], pp. 391–92).[10] The highway and the channel tame the excessively–destabilising wheel metaphor, albeit
'violently': the highway sets up a direction for money to flow that is *both* ethe-
real and earth bound, while the channel limits the size of circulating capital
(which is unsurprisingly liquid) with reference to frugality. In Lakoff and
Johnson's (1980) terms, the wheel metaphor exemplifies both the 'orientational'
and 'container' metaphors. The former designates movement alone, and explains
the functional aspects of money both metaphorically and literally (i.e., circulation). The container metaphor, on the other hand, limits the movement spatially
(in terms of money supply within national boundaries).

The great wheel represents money in abstract, functional terms, under the
rubric 'capital'. Money is only a portion of capital, and hence it is distanced from
its form—as if its material does not matter. According to Simmel, the division
between form and function is the very aspect that constitutes money's character.
He writes, 'The dual nature of money, as a concrete and valued substance and, at
the same time, as something that owes its significance to the complete dissolu-
tion of substance into motion and function, derives from the fact that money is
the reification of exchange among people, the embodiment of a pure function'
(Simmel 1990 [1900], p. 176).

The phrase 'money is a tool' is taken up by many economists to signify function, but there is often resistance to the rigidity of this concept. For example,
despite Maestro's decidedly economic inclination—which enables her to smug-
gle in terms such as 'medium of exchange' and 'surplus' into a children's book—
it is surprising that her *Story of Money* is structured around a chronology of
money's developing form (1993, pp. 14, 8). She makes the puzzling remark,
'Money is a tool that has changed as the world has changed. Now it is changing
again' (Maestro 1993, p. 43). Many questions are left unresolved in this text, but
here the question is how the 'world' and 'money' share a dependency in terms of
transition. It appears on the surface that they share natural rhythms, but of course
this is a conceptual imposition.

The primary metaphor 'money is a tool' is now a decidedly conventional concept; money is merely an instrument of exchange. However, this particular tool is a semantic concept in the sense that it can take any shape. But Maestro needs to shape the tool for illustrative purposes, so she resorts to concretisation. Maestro's analysis seems to suggest that money has changed its form in keeping with nature's rhythms. Money appears to have accompanied our progress from land to virtuality, it is represented chronologically from shells to salt to gold to paper and lately to digital bits. Perhaps the text deviates from strict economic schematas, because it has contradictory sets of concepts to draw from. On the other hand, the economic picture is incomplete and demands to be filled with additional meanings.

The tool metaphor is entirely dependent upon its concept becoming conventional, and Dodd makes the powerful claim that 'ideas and perceptions of money do not merely inform how it is used. They are essential to the possibility of its being used at all' (1994, p. 154). Thus, the continuing existence of money as a cultural instrument is dependent on its conceptual, and hence its metaphorical, representation. The point is that by unpacking metaphor we can '[put] more of what persuades serious people under the scrutiny of reason' (McCloskey 1990, p. 6). We could also entertain the (perhaps frivolous) idea that if our perceptions of money were different, we might eliminate its 'currency' as a concept and therefore not use it at all.

The idea of money as a tool has been unconditionally accepted by policy makers so now money is traded as a commodity in its own right: it is made to *make* money. Therefore a distinction between money and commodities is no longer tenable. Smith is insistent that 'money is neither a material to work upon, nor a tool to work with' (1986 [1776], p. 392). But, as Saul observes

Those devoted to market forces tend not to mention Smith on the subject of money. The reason is very simple. The Chicago economists and their friends are in total self–contradiction on this very large subject. In fact, they have gone over to Smith's enemies—the mercantilists—an economic movement which believed, among other things, that money was a value in itself. (1997, p. 154)

The 'money markets' do use money as a tool to make money. The prominence of hedge funds, futures, and foreign exchange in our current financial markets is evidence of this. And, 'we must be alert; money values change more rapidly than do physical things, and require monitoring' (Lane 1991, p. 81).

Currently, money appears in a myriad of forms, but its newest transmogrification is into digital bits. To the noneconomist, money could potentially break with conventional mappings, and any resulting new metaphors could assist us in the formulation of new conceptual systems. However, forms of (actual) money can rarely be mimicked in metaphor, the circular coin being an exception.[11] Until now new global financial systems (such as the foreign exchange markets and technology–driven monetary networks) have been metaphorised as amplified versions of old mappings rather than throwing up new correspondences.[12] This metaphorical inflation is also indicative of semiotic confusion, and to some extent parallels the instability of current financial systems. Just as Smith's concerns about paper money surfaced in his metaphors, we are now experiencing a similar angst, occasioned by money's protean aspects.

Marx considers Smith to have the whole thing 'jumbled up' and to have committed a blunder (1992 [1885], pp. 272, 292). He writes: '[Smith] confuses fluid capital, as opposed to fixed, with the forms of capital pertaining to the circulation sphere, with circulation capital; a confusion which has been uncritically taken over by his successors' (Marx 1992 [1885], p. 290). Marx's three–volume work *Capital* has also been frequently taken over, and because it is a lengthy exercise in definition, it should also be analysed for its metaphors of money.

Marx's Metaphors of Transformation

Smith's metaphor for money is the wheel, and the wheel in turn refers to all types of capital, so Smith makes a metaphor of a metaphor. In his early writing, Marx recognises that money is an exemplary metaphor, with a capacity to represent itself. In his *Economical and Philosophical Manuscripts* (1844) he writes: '*Money* is the external, universal means and power to change *representation* into *reality* and *reality* into *mere representation*. It transforms *real human and natural faculties* into mere abstract representations, i.e. *imperfections*' (in Jackson 1995, p. 8). Ideas about representation are central to Marx's view of the world, and they inform his discussions of money. Marx's *Capital* is essentially a reflexive mythological exercise.

For Marx, money and people have reciprocal effects. Individuals make money, and money makes the individual in the sense that it defines their social position. 'Individuals are the personifications of economic categories', Marx explains in his Preface to the first edition of *Capital* (1990 [1867], p. 92). A later footnote by Engels explains his translation: 'the concept of an object (person) as the receptacle, repository [or] bearer of some thing or tendency quite different from it appears repeatedly in *Capital*' (1990 [1867], p. 179). Where originally they shared no attributes, objects and persons are all infected by money, and so ultimately individuals are defined by economic tendencies. There is an implicit determinism in Marx's argument that is easily satirised: 'Because money has no qualities, few financiers have any character at all' (Buchan 1997, p. 234).

Money not only transfigures itself and people, but also its related commodity. Marx illustrates this in his C–M–C (commodity–money–commodity) formula:

The two inverted phases of the movement which makes up the metamorphosis of a commodity constitute a circuit: commodity–form, stripping off of this form, and return to it. Of course, the commodity itself here is subject to contradictory determinations. At the starting–point it is a non–use–value to its owner; at the end it is a use value. So too the money appears in the first phase as a solid crystal of value into which the commodity has been transformed, but afterwards it dissolves into the mere equivalent–form of the commodity. (1990 [1867], p. 206)

The exchange mechanism is explained here as a process in which forms simultaneously dissolve and solidify. In this section of *Capital,* money is at first solid crystal and then dissolves so that circulation always entails a change in material. Just as in the financial market cycle the ascent is characterised by a demand for financial 'paper', such as shareholdings, and the descent is for a different demand: for liquidity (or cash). Marx's circuit metaphor implies a structural transformation of the material of money itself. From this perspective, money alone has circulation intrinsic to it: the capitalist 'circuit' is an endless inauguration of metamorphoses.

Marx maintains that commodity exchange instigates a whole range of transformative effects. At the beginning money is 'over there in someone's pocket in all its hard, material reality' (Marx 1990 [1867], p. 206). At this stage money has a real, albeit temporary, concrete materiality. Then money 'comes face to face' (Marx 1990 [1867], p. 206) with a commodity and mutates when the commodity is exchanged for money (this is Marx's material transformation). Meanwhile, 'by taking part in the act of sale, the commodity-owner becomes a seller; in the act of purchase, he becomes a buyer its two forms exist simultaneously but at opposite poles. Being a seller and being a buyer are not fixed roles' (Marx 1990 [1867], p. 206). Thus, 'money, the final stage of the first transformation, is at the same time the starting–point for the second' (Marx 1990 [1867], p. 206). All things and people are constantly at the point of being transformed into their monetary antithesis by the most compelling 'dramatis persona' of them all, money (Marx 1990 [1867], p. 206).

Aristotle suggests that metaphors are devised because they illuminate or clarify in *unexpected* ways that are 'surprising' (1984, p. 192). He even goes so far as to say that 'opposites are in the same class' (Aristotle 1984, p. 169). The result of this is that 'unlike' things come to form a synthetic relationship after the metaphor is coined, so that dissimilar concepts take on shared meanings. Thus, while a good metaphor may take time in coming in Aristotle's terms, it will eventually solidify into a fixed relationship. Similarly for Marx, money and people come to share functional characteristics that are determined by their economic actions.

Marx's metaphors always fulfil the Aristotelian postulate of '[representing] things in a state of activity' (1984, p. 190). But Marx uses metaphor in two ways: first, to prohibit his readers from being deceived by notions of historical permanence, and second, as a tool to express the paradoxes inherent in money/people relations. His metaphors are irreducible, they evade grounding and are in a sense synecdochal, mimicking his system of representation. Nevertheless, Marx takes up the metaphor 'capital' and develops it into a system, rather than a distinctive thing.

By highlighting the transformative aspects of economies, Marx appears to be favouring a cyclical pattern above one that privileges linear progress in money economies. He attacks the economists' (metaphorical) trinity of 'capital–profit land–ground–rent, labour–wages', saying that 'their mutual relationship is like that of lawyer's fees, beetroot and music' (Marx 1991 [1894], p. 953). The argument for Marx is that connections between objects are illusory. Furthermore, relations between people and money objects (or capital) should be defined by labour alone because 'value is labour' (Marx 1991 [1894], p. 954). All profit derives from the labour put into it, whether it be from a crop, machinery, or housing. Thus, Marx privileges labour value and maintains that forms of things are illusory because they disguise the production process. In other words, money's appearance is a deceptive representation of labour that is accepted as real. Marx decries the fetishisation of form as unoriginal, creating 'current and usual modes of thought' (1990 [1867], p. 682).

Marx has given us two central concepts in his work: first, that labour is a commodity; second, that money and labour are inextricably linked so that labour (a term that implies back–breaking sacrifice) conveys virtuosity. In the main, however, money is not Marx's preoccupation because it is merely a disguise for contradictory processes and is always converted to capital: 'Money and commodities need to be transformed into capital' (1990 [1867], p. 874). His overarching concept—capital—seems to provide him with more scope, precisely because it has no form.

A Capital Idea: The Tension between 'Thing' and 'Relation'

Marx's capital metaphor stands for money's relativising power: 'Capital is not a thing, it is a definite social relation' that is historically determined (1991 [1894], p. 953). Characterised by metamorphoses and cyclical change, 'present society is no solid crystal, but an organism capable of change, and constantly engaged in a process of change' (1990 [1867], p. 93). There is little solidity because 'in the reproduction process of capital, the money form is an evanescent moment, a moment of mere transition' (Marx 1991 [1894], p. 517). Reflecting upon a single sentence from volume 3, we observe a reflexive impasse: 'Capital is now a thing, but the thing is capital. The money's body is now by love possessed' (Marx 1991 [1894], p. 517). In the brief moment when capital encounters its money form, a potential marriage between form and concept occurs. But, as always, it cannot last beyond the 'now'. The notion of change or reversal surfaces repeatedly in Marx's language, but he can often only explain this process by reference to living entities.

Marx's 'capital' metaphorises individuals, money, and history, because we are all the bearers of economic categories and determined by capital. 'Capital, as self–valorizing value, does not just comprise class relations, a definite social character that depends on the existence of labour. It is a movement, a circulatory process through different stages, which itself in turn includes three different forms of the circulatory process. Hence it can only be grasped as a movement, and not as a static thing' (1992 [1885], p. 185).

The label 'capital' has become over used, worn out, and unspecific—a mythology itself of the 'Left'. The word 'capital' does not capture a single referent, because it applies to a range of phenomena. It does however conjure up a specific abstract concept: relational determinism. As Marx explains it, 'The name of a thing is quite external to its nature. I know nothing of a man if I merely know his name is Jacob. In the same way, every trace of the money relation disappears in the money–names pound, thaler, franc, ducat, etc.' (1990 [1867], p. 195). Correspondingly for Marx the hidden signification in the price of commodities is the labour process, whereas to me this is just one part of the Marxist mythology of capital.

Marx's metaphor of the capitalist as a butterfly is a prolific one in terms of monetary thinking, yielding many interpretations including notions of metamorphosis, antagonism of form, imminent emergence, and flight. The predominant reading of the metaphor is transfiguration, and this is developed in Marx's narratives. He writes, for example, 'The money–owner, who as yet is only a capitalist in larval form, must buy commodities at their value, and yet at the end of the process withdraw more value from circulation than he threw into it at the beginning. His emergence as a butterfly must, and yet must not, take place in the sphere of circulation' (Marx 1990 [1867], p. 269). Similarly, the 'chrysalis state' refers to the gestation period of monetary concepts (Marx 1900 [1867], p. 207). The cashed-up money maker takes flight (like Smith's wagon), but he has to return again to reinvest his profit, and once again take from the land. The butterfly metaphor stands for money's imminent getaway from terrestrial bonds, as well as the evolution of capitalism.

The *Courier Mail* took up the pairing of the capitalist (hero) with the flight metaphor in an article about the October 1997 stock market debacle. 'The world's richest man Microsoft founder Bill Gates lost $2.57 billion yesterday. But Mr. Gates is not penniless. The lifestyles of the world's rich and famous are unlikely to be greatly affected. They will still fly first class, just with lighter pockets' (29 Oct. 1997, p. 41). The perception that money has a weight and exists in 'all hard reality in the pocket' is tenacious, but it conflicts with the metaphor of capital in flight.

The metaphors Marx uses in support of his philosophy tend to reverse the concepts he is attacking. He criticises 'the bewitched, distorted and upside–down world haunted by Monsieur le Capital and Madame la Terre, who are at the same time social characters and mere things' (Marx 1991 [1894], p. 969). The assertion is a fascinating one, rife with concepts that surface in a range of contemporary texts. If I could paraphrase this sentence adequately then it might read something like this: concepts such as capital and land provide the basis for magical, perverted and erroneous thinking, so that these two instruments of profit are enabled to take on lives of their own. Deceptive images always return to haunt us, because 'capital is trapped in a world of illusion' (Marx 1991 [1894], p. 969). As a figment of our imagination, money is both a character and a thing, because of the relative power we perceive it to confer on us. 'Capital confronts society as a thing, and as the power that the capitalist has through this thing' (Marx 1991 [1894], p. 393). Therefore, according to Marx's reasoning, we frequently idealise the power of things by personifying them because we are confused by money's (capital's) appearance. Furthermore, the things we idolise change in time: 'Capital is a definite social relation of production pertaining to a particular historical social formation, which simply takes the form of a thing and gives this thing a specific social character' (Marx 1991 [1894], p. 953).

The concept of capital, which Marx defines partially in response to Smith, makes little reference to money—even though the concept of capital and capitalism is ultimately dependent on money. Like Smith's 'wheel', Marx's 'capital' metaphor adds conceptual layers onto the concept of money. Therefore Marx's metaphors, like Smith's, are highly abstract in the sense that they render form redundant.

The Ruination of True Value

Simmel critiques Marx's principle that privileges labour as a source of value. He explains that 'if labour is the ultimate authority to which all value determinations of the object must be referred, then it is inappropriate and a diversion to measure it in terms of an alien object such as money' (Simmel 1990 [1900], p. 409). Ultimately everything, according to Simmel, is renumerated in money payments. These payments, in turn, encourage what I call 'bottom–line thinking', that is, in Simmel's terms, evaluation by a single monetary criterion. But according to Simmel, money has numerous symbolic dimensions that cannot be expressed simply with reference to a sole common denominator.

Simmel struggles to develop a theory of money's philosophical value with which to partially dismantle the concept of *economic* value. 'The money economy enforces the necessity of continuous mathematical operations in our daily transactions. The lives of many people are absorbed by evaluating, weighing, calculating and reducing of qualitative values to quantitative ones' (Simmel 1990 [1900], p. 444). Simmel is alluding to the fact that the peculiarity of objects is ignored in money cultures, and the corollary of this is that our understanding of things becomes more rough and approximate: rounded off in fact (1990 [1900], p. 507). This is a form of economic rationalism, whereby values such as beauty are replaced by monetary worth.

Simmel asserts that 'money is the most terrible destroyer of form', because it reduces 'qualitative determinations to quantitative ones' (1990 [1900], pp. 272, 277).[13] In other words, all objects are converted to a neutral value yardstick so that the concept of money becomes the catalyst between unlike objects. He puts forward a good example of this now–naturalised cultural conceptualisation: 'Foolish parents attempt to hold their children back from wilful destruction by asserting that the things they wish to destroy cost money! Instead of explaining to children the value of the object itself, they immediately react economically only to the idea of money spent' (Simmel 1990 [1900], pp. 268–69). His point is that evaluation is no longer possible without money. In addition, by referring to familial relationships, Simmel partially explains the handing–down of monetary concepts.

Simmel's observations about his new money economy cause him to conclude that money should not be a true measure of value, because quantification merely converts particular essences into gross aggregates. He writes: 'Money as abstract value expresses nothing but the relativity of things that constitute value; and, at the same time, that money, as a stable pole, contrasts with the eternal movements, fluctuations, and equations of the objects' (Simmel 1990 [1900], p. 121). As an abstract (rather than an inexorable) measure of value, money fixes an equivalence between, say, skulls and pig jaws.[14] Simmel suggests that as a 'stable pole' or neutral quantifier, money has caused the numerous ideas about objects to be ousted in favour of a single immutable value.

Both Marx and Simmel were students of Hegel's philosophy and so part of their work focuses on the historical development of human relations (Frankel 1977, p. 22). Both stress a finality, too: Marx in the demise of capitalism and Simmel in the destruction of real value. Simmel's tracing of the steps that led to a money economy begins with so–called primitive money. This was 'entirely concrete in value, such as cattle or cotton cloth' (Simmel 1990 [1900], pp. 150–51). Gold and silver were the first incarnations of money as a symbol, which both caused and occasioned 'a greatly enhanced intellectuality' and a 'growth [in] abstract thought' (Simmel 1990 [1900], pp. 151–52). Simmel then participates in the construction of money's mythological history, but his emphasis is on particularity of form, which is threatened by the openness of represented concepts, such as capital.

Marx's, Smith's and Simmel's metaphors of money embellish it, and transform it, but they never define it. Marx and Smith use metaphors to support their conceptual systems, whereas Simmel attempts to dismantle the concepts inherent in money as a metaphor. So far we have seen several ideas about money recur. For example, as a form money is not significant, but as function it is. Money is also perceived to define our culture and our relations. The most important metaphor perhaps that Simmel identifies is that money is a bridge, providing us with a path to the future, and it is this metaphor that arguably makes us retain money as a system. Unlike Marx's capital or Smith's wheel, the metaphor of the bridge gives money a progressive temporal element, because it encourages goal–oriented thinking.

MONEY IS A BRIDGE

The symbolic aspects of money are metaphorised by Simmel both as a 'tool' and a 'bridge' as we can see from this extract: 'Money is perhaps the clearest expression and demonstration of the fact that man is a "tool–making" animal, which, however, is itself connected with the fact that man is a "purposive" animal' (Simmel 1990 [1900], p. 211). Our actions are a 'bridge' to the realisation of a final purpose. But in a money economy we prefer money to objects:

This is how matters stand in the relation between money and concrete objects of value; a choice between the objects as a whole and money as a whole would immediately reveal the intrinsic valuelessness of the latter, which provides us only with means, not with an end. Yet when a given sum of money is set against a given quantity of commodities, the exchange of the latter for the former is usually demanded much more strongly than vice–versa. (Simmel 1990 [1900], p. 216)

As a bridge, money is the means to obtaining what we desire, and the destination generally resides in some idea about the future. From this perspective money has an inherent potentiality. Money is 'congealed desire', it is invested with an 'imaginary potential' (Buchan 1997, p. 108). Part of the reason that money is the subject of so many of our desires is the result of our perception that money itself can better our condition. Money then provides us with conceptual and temporal bait, to coin a metaphor of my own. But, *There is no limit to human desire* [Buchan's emphasis]' (1997, p. 30), and hence money's bridge has no end. Nevertheless, according to Buchan, the illusion of a better future promised by money remains, but in terms of security, it is as useful as 'the drunken guard on the Moscow subway' (1997, p. 274).

Simmel's bridge metaphor, and Smith's wheel are partially constructed from their observations about their cultural milieux. Toffler's *Third Wave* examines the impact of 'modernisation' (or industrialisation) on our thinking about space and time, making an important point about new concepts of progress and futurity: 'Linear time was a precondition for the indust-real views of evolution and progress [it] made evolution and progress plausible. For if time were circular instead of line–like, if events doubled back on themselves instead of moving in a single direction, it would mean that history repeated itself and that evolution and progress were no more than illusions' (1980, p. 121). Toffler is implying that prior to modernisation, people perceived themselves to be trapped in states of recurrence, and that they had no concept of alternative orientation or purpose. While this state corresponds with Buchan's idea about natural rhythms—whereby people's lives were formed around the seasons and faith—it also corresponds with Marx's capitalist circuit. The wheel and circle metaphors are both traps, connoting temporal recurrence. In addition, they appear from certain perspectives, such as the evolutionary one, to be outdated.

Because money has tended towards the abstract, it has encouraged thinking about 'how things might be otherwise' (Lane 1991, p. 80). Thus, as a metaphor, money undoubtedly refers to 'a perspective or frame, a way of looking at things' as well as to 'a certain kind of process', and that process is end oriented (Schon 1993, p. 137). Simmel remarks that as a simple tool, money '[adds] a new link to the chain of purposive action, thus showing that the straight road is not always the shortest' (Simmel 1990 [1900], p. 209). As a linking device, money is a concept that has been newly added to our chain of needs (if we evolved from barter), but has subsequently become a goal in itself. In basic terms, money is perceived to be the necessary link, the bridge, between people and a loaf of bread: we need to acquire money in order to get bread.

As we have seen in relation to character and quest, money is often conceived as a lack or resolvable omission. Many of our fairy tales and myths are similarly oriented towards the future acquisition of money, as Bloom points out. He identifies a number of 'unearned unlimited wealth myths': the pot of gold at the end of the rainbow, the golden–egg–laying goose, the quest for hidden treasure, and the genie's lamp (Bloom 1996, p. 161). What these stories do is promote the idea that once we have secured infinite amounts of money we are able to resolve all problems. In this sense money is a bridge, connecting the means with the ends and the present with the future so that 'instead of thinking of deprivation as lack of sufficient food and clothing and shelter and other things, a person using money schemata may conceive of deprivation as the lack of funds to buy these things' (Lane 1991, p. 80). The new link in purposive action is to acquire money, and the idea is being increasingly adopted (successfully and unsuccessfully) throughout the world. The monetary metaphors quoted earlier, such as 'thought', 'time', and 'happiness', similarly emphasise money's ability to resolve difficulties.

Money is not simply a metaphor, as we have seen, it actually facilitates conceptual development. Three studies from different disciplines can be used to demonstrate the idea that money can be a 'tool for thinking'. Lane's (1991) *The Market Experience* contains two chapters specifically devoted to both the symbolic and the cognitive aspects of money in market [or money] economies. Drawing heavily upon psychology and social theory, Lane comes up with a number of conclusions about the cognitive effects of money schemata (signs and symbols). As a sign, money has both positive and negative effects on our thinking. It can be an 'instrument of cognitive facilitation, a tool for thinking' (Lane 1991, p. 79). Lane argues that money is useful as a representative or mediator between things and time, and that it also encourages a sense of potentiality (1991, p. 80). But money can also be 'a fetter that constrains clear thinking' (Lane 1991, p. 79) because 'when the single monetary criterion obstructs others, it may be fairly said to constrain thought' (Lane 1991, p. 90). In many ways, Lane argues, 'money payments serve as an instrument of control that shortcuts education and eliminates cognition' (1991, p. 93).

A metaphor such as money can clarify abstract thought by making connections appear self–evident—that money is a cushion is self–evident to a miser (even though he or she may not want to purchase one). But, 'money hampers and fetters [just as much] as it facilitates, for the very qualities that facilitate the thinking process invite overuse' (Lane 1991, p. 95). According to Smith, it is not the money we want, but rather various objects that are only obtainable with money. Smith perceives the pursuit of self–interest to be geared towards the pursuit of luxury. He writes, 'The desire of food is limited in every man by the narrow capacity of the human stomach; but the desire of the conveniences and ornaments of building, dress, equipage, and household furniture, seems to have no limit or certain boundary' (Smith 1986 [1776], p. 269). This desire is insatiable: complete satisfaction can never be achieved.

Money has changed significantly since Smith, Marx, and Simmel considered their economies. The financial markets have taken over from Marx's smokestack economy, and are responsible for significantly more income generation than manufactured products.[15] Money itself has become a commodity to be traded despite Smith's assertion that 'money is neither a material to work upon, nor a tool to work with' (1986 [1776], p. 392). Both these financial developments have been made possible by the belief that money has endless abstract potential.

We have encountered the tenacious ideas that money is a tool, as well as a bridge, that enables people to accomplish objectives that would not be possible without it. I have also pointed out that the means is often overridden by the ends, so that a preoccupation with money alone and the possibilities it engenders can ultimately obstruct thinking. In effect notions of money's ability to convert and transform states and people are replicated by metaphor itself. Thus, money as a metaphor (a mechanism of exchange, transformation, and conversion) has no one literal signified. Its indefinite metaphorical nature allows it to be appropriated by a range of disciplines. At this moment in time, it appears that economics and the free marketeers have an unquestioned monopoly on monetary wisdom.

If Marx's claim that coin and circulation are intricately linked is correct, what will happen when we no longer have cash? Which metaphors will we use? For Marx and Smith, coins, wheels, and circuits are metaphorical expressions enabling the material of money and its behaviour to be explained in concrete terms. But money has lost a lot of its material dependency: plastic and electronic cash are coming forward as new monetary materials, bearing little resemblance to our much–loved cash.

New spatial metaphors, appearing particularly in popular fiction, are often diametrically opposed to our worn metaphors, and they reveal an anxiety about the future of money. As yet these are incomplete metaphors and ideas, but angst about money seems to be a feature of late twentieth–century texts. The shift from coin to paper was not painless, but the shift to plastic and technology–driven e–cash may be. Lash and Urry adopt an apprehensive tone, believing that '[objects are being] progressively emptied of material content. What is increasingly produced are not material objects, but *signs*' (1994, p. 4). If digital money is adopted by governments as well as banks, 'one could suggest,' as Lash and Urry do, 'that money has become a kind of free-floating signifier detached from the real processes to which it once referred' (1994, p. 292).[16] Observing the lack of a material signified, Lash and Urry construct their own metaphor of money: 'Money is the world going round faster and faster', so the world and money are one, and they are pure speed (1994, p. 292).

The preceding discussion has revealed a plethora of distortions and contradictions in metaphors of money. Money is certainly not perceived simply as either a function *or* a thing, it is endlessly represented. 'If money were only a sign, or a neutral quantity like measures of weights,' Lane explains, 'it would be merely a tool for the normal processes of rational inference' (1991, p. 108). As we have seen, it is not simply a tool, it is constitutive of a whole mythological system: a series of semiological chains with which we position ourselves ideologically.

If we consider the real economy (the one that you and I are involved in every day) and the financial economy, we see that they have two separate metaphorical spheres. But where do these spheres actually meet? Boundaries between national economic centres have been dismantled by technology, so that in a sense we are all a part of the global monetary landscape. Millman asserts that 'financial innovations, especially the development of financial derivatives, have dissolved the barriers of geography, regulation, and custom that once divided the world's financial system into separate markets. The financial world has changed and that means the whole world has changed', and this is an assertion I do not buy (1995, p. xxii). Changes to money management affect us all, both conceptually and in terms of the cash in our back pocket, and many commentators maintain that unprecedented changes must be monitored.

The financial markets participate in an illusion of separation: they use metaphors of the circle to distance themselves, believing that theirs is an intensely fast centre of transactions, subject to 'vicious boom/bust cycles'. The press and market players thereby support their own mythologies and defy regulation. Their lack of accountability is exacerbated by the circumlocutory language of the financial markets, which some popular fiction sends up. A trader in *Bombardiers* asserts that when trading 'it [is] better to talk in circles than to talk straight' (Bronson 1995, p. 26). Furthermore, 'even though it [makes] no sense it [is] what everyone [wants] to hear' (Bronson 1995, p. 69).

In the next chapter I will turn my attention to the financial markets: the centres of our monetary culture. The chapter takes up two aspects of the market. First, I consider market metaphors, and second, I explore some inconsistent representations of the market as a character. As we have seen in relation to Marx's Monsieur le Capital and Madame la Terre in this chapter, personification seems to provide clarification where metaphors fail. While it will be noted that metaphors and characterisations of the market are prolific, I will also show how their confusing aspects mimic the perceived chaos of financial market economies.

NOTES

1. Casual readers will find a fascinating range of perceptions of money in Jackson's (1995) *The Oxford Book of Money*, which is organised around headings such as 'Opening Accounts', 'Getting and Spending', and 'Prices and Values'. I say 'casual' because his bibliographical details are often incomplete.

2. As previously noted, we continue to attribute money with human characteristics.

3. Early in 1997 I contacted all five Australian national television stations with regard to their programming of money matters. I wanted to find out if financial programming was intentionally on the increase. I only received a reply from four. The letters explained that they do not compile statistics in relation to the proportion of airtime devoted to finance, but one station mentioned that these programmes do increase their ratings. The only conclusion to be made from these responses is that television stations, while not conscious of their participation in the mythology of money, are nevertheless active in it.

4. Significantly his analogy is that metaphors are like 'coins which have lost their embossing and are now considered as metal and no longer as coins' (Nietzsche 1992 [1873], p. 84).

5. And for critics of the invisible hand: '[You will believe in] the supreme majesty of Adam Smith's misunderstood *invisible hand*—until one dark night some other invisible hand drags you by the throat down the stairs and out the door into the reality you've been ignoring' (Perlman 1998, p. 142).

6. With the widescale sell–off of gold from reserve banks around the world in 1997, to guarantee the money in circulation, gold has seemingly become a thing of the past, causing the 'value' of gold to drop and its appeal for investors to wane. One stock-broking company asked in its March quarterly report: 'whether gold will respond to economic and political events in the future, [because] central banks [are] questioning the need to hold [it]' (J. B. Were and Son March Quarter 1998, p. 62). Apparently we are now more than ever in danger of getting our wings burned.

7. It is not insignificant that the financial revolution that has taken place in the Western world in the last two or so decades 'has generated over 500 new accessions with "money" in their title in the last few years alone' (Jackson 1995, p. vii).

8. Evidence of Ford's view can be ascertained by the following: 'Money, after all, is extremely simple. It is part of our transportation system. It is a simple and direct method of conveying goods from one person to another. Money is in itself most admirable. It is essential. It is one of the most useful devices in social life' (in Jackson 1995, pp. 14–15).

9. Like the wheel, stock is a part of the entirety as well as *being* the entirety. The confusion surrounding the term 'stock' for the reader, derives from Smith's obscure use of the word. We retain the term 'stock' today, and it is according to Carew 'interchangeable with equities, shares and bonds. It can also mean a company's inventory of goods' (1988, pp. 230–31).

10. The lack of prudence seems to characterise many monetary myths, metaphors, and characters: we only have to think of Midas, or even Leeson, as a blueprint for *im*prudence.

11. When Marx says, 'Money takes the shape of coin because of its function as the circulating medium', he is attributing the coin with a form particular only to its function (Marx 1990 [1867], p. 221).

12. The bodily disease metaphor, for example, is used frequently in the financial press. Two extreme examples that were used in relation to the 1997 Asian market collapse will suffice here: 'Blue–chip stocks, thought to be bullet-proof, were also bleeding' (*Weekend Australian*, 18 Oct. 1997, p. 1) and 'Asian flu continued to spread on Wall Street' (*Eleven AM* [video recording], 28 Oct. 1997).

13. An admirer of Simmel, Buchan lifts this idea directly: 'Money, far from being the harmless arena of human emulation as its apologists hold, is a great destroyer' (1997, p. 278).

14. This is an example selected by *Millionaire* magazine, designed presumably to be as far–fetched as possible (Smith 1997, p. 14).

15. 'Every day the currency traders [alone] move $1 trillion around the world at the speed of light. Add up all of the Saudi oil, Japanese cars, American wheat, and European aircraft, and throw in the rest of the things that countries buy and sell from

each other, and you will get only a small fraction of the $1 trillion' (Millman 1995, p. xxi).

16. For Lash and Urry, as I read it, money originally referred to the production *process,* not a specific referent.

6

The Discordant Market

To market, to market to buy 1,000 index rate futures and a loaf of bread. But where is the market? To buy bread one goes to a bakery, but if one wants futures then the market is everywhere and nowhere, it is a digital market with a global spread. Traditionally the markets were places where buyers and sellers met face to face to exchange goods or services; they were congregational centres and meeting places. Produce was laid out and handled. Maestro emphasises the centrality of those first markets in her *Story of Money*, maintaining that such physical gatherings were vital social, as well as trading, hubs (1993, pp. 8–9). In effect, merchants traded tangible goods with identifiable people.

But now the market has a global spread, and therefore it is simply a web like network of transactions that generally does not involve tangible exchange. As Wark explains it the market has 'broken loose from the sites that once preserved its image and customs [T]he market is everywhere' (1994, p. 172). The market is now merely a metaphor for the economy of transactions. The financial or money market extends beyond nations, banks, and direct exchanges; it is amorphous and shaped only by the numerous digital networks through which it runs.

In this chapter I take up two textual indices that structure and naturalise the increasingly abstract financial market: metaphor and character. The metaphors for the market are abundant, particularly in the financial press as I discuss below. As second–order signs, these metaphors mythologise the financial market simply because they are persistently reiterated, and like metaphors of money, they do not expose a market nature, they simply borrow from other conceptual frameworks. The financial market is removed from its original spatial centre, free of government intervention in most cases, and deals in 'products' that frequently have no tangibility—at inconceivably high speeds. The twentieth–century financial market is represented in metaphors that are generally borrowed from types of activity such as the temporal cycle, musical rhythms, and play, which recall the activities of early communal markets.

Often, as we have seen, actual and physical (sensory) experience is mapped onto a complex and increasingly abstract monetary system that is a reversal of Vico's account of metaphor creation. The financial market's uncertain status, combined with its aura of mystique, encourages metaphorisation. Without the stabilising effect of language, the market would retain its obscurity in popular perception. But understanding is never completed by metaphor; rather, a mythical essence, a 'market–ness', is formed, which is merely repeated rather than interrogated.

The second section of this chapter involves a brief discussion of the characterisation of the financial market: as a female and a male. This section will demonstrate that the traits attributed to the market conflict just as metaphors do. Characters are an important part of money's mythology, as I have shown in chapters 2 (money as a character), 3 (heroes), and 4 (rogues). Characterisation, like metaphor, shapes incomplete concepts by making reference to familiar or comprehensible phenomena.

MARKET METAPHORS

Metaphors of the market correspond with the active, dynamic aspects of the markets themselves. Accelerated growth and the speed of structural change are mimicked in a deranged cocktail of metaphors. In a sense market metaphors demonstrate what de Bolla calls 'discursive excess', occasioned by a perceived parallel excess in the market (1989, p. 109). A recent statement from a market analyst, cited in the *New York Times* (28 Feb. 1998), provides evidence of such metaphorical excess: 'There are all kinds of warning flags flying around this market, and bears like me are getting tired of waiting for the other shoe to drop' (p.D3). Mixing metaphors is characteristic of the financial press, and examples are plentiful. On 3 October 1998 the *Courier Mail*'s business headline, for example, read: 'Stockmarket melt down in wave of selling' (p.61). *Time* magazine's cover (14 Sept. 1998) mixes metaphors on its front cover: the illustration depicts a graph with a downward jagged line (rather like a slide), and has four people tumbling down it into empty space, which supports the metaphor of the market being in 'free fall' (Ridpath 1998, p. 240). The headline reads: 'IS THE BOOM OVER?' The boom metaphor, which is one of sound, is generally equated with upward movement, whereas bust infers a downward freefall. But the relationship between sound and space is accepted by readers and commentators alike, regardless of its spuriousness. Rowe maintains that ideas about money and financial products 'take on a kind of "reality" only when a number of people hold the same ideas' (1998, p. 66). This reality is simply a linguistic cacophony in relation to the financial market. A profusion of metaphors, such as waves, booms, flags, falls, and bears, have all been appropriated by financial discourse, and they appear to be natural in their monetary context.

The *Economist*'s Review of Wall Street

Before I move onto specific metaphors such as the cycle, I would like to discuss an article about Wall Street, published in the *Economist* in early 1995, that attempts to assess changes that have impacted on the Street as a consequence of the 1970s deregulation. I have chosen this article because it is a particularly good example of how market metaphors are nonsensical, but they are accepted in toto. It begins, 'Today [Wall Street] is arguably the most important market anywhere. In recent decades, both innovations and excesses have spread from Wall Street to change the way finance is conducted around the world' (*Economist* 15 Apr. 1995, p. 3). The twenty–seven–page report initially claims to be able to 'outline the shape of [Wall Street's] new role' (*Economist* 15 Apr. 1995, p. 3), but it is a comprehensive failure in explanatory terms.[1] The metaphors and images the article draws upon are mixed and conflicting, but they might not be questioned by the general reader, because many of them have become conventional signifiers of the market, and so they appear common–sensical.

To begin with, the article is peppered with illustrations; almost every page has a graph ('illustrating' profits, risks, and growth), but each page also has a cartoon. One of these cartoons is of a figure sitting cross–legged on a straight–sided high–rise building. He is wearing an overly large stetson and pointed boots (minus spurs), and is throwing (what look like) paper notes down onto the smaller buildings below. On one of these buildings is his mount, an emaciated equine that hunches, seemingly dejected. The illustrations recall Wall Street's origins: it was a barrier to keep the native Americans out of New York in 1624 (p. 3). Derived from a defensive wall constructed *by the Dutch* out of 'mere brush', the 'wall which gave the Street its name is no longer an appropriate image for what is now perhaps the world's most open and efficient market [my emphasis]' (p. 3). So why the cowboy? Clearly the image recalls the frontier myth, but in doing so it distorts, or rather shifts, the market from its origins.

Wall Street is the discursive centre of the financial markets—it is the most famous and most discussed market in the world; in fact, it has become the reference point for all other markets. A whole cultural mythology has been built up around the idea of Wall Street and its people, but it is a mythology constructed by 'inflexion' (Barthes 1989 [1957], p. 140), or distortion, whereby metaphors mapped onto it reshape it. In an attempt to delineate Wall Street in the 1990s, the *Economist* article presents a confusing array of metaphors for the market: health, shopping, games, Darwinism, and war (to name but a few). The implication to be drawn from this is that the current U.S. market is less comprehensible than it was before: deregulation of the markets in the 1970s seems to have been accompanied by a parallel deregulation of tropes. Financial journalism of this sort simply recycles metaphors taken from its own mythology (such as 'trading places' (15 Apr 1995, p. 26), taken from the movie of that name), and clarity is not achieved; rather the mystique of the markets is retained. Identifying key metaphors in the article will elucidate my point.

The notion that the markets are all racing to the winning post is a prominent one. When firms 'jockey for position' (p. 25), there have to be 'surefire [winners] in the race' (p. 15). In the stands, the 'risk game' (p. 5) is 'a worldwide gamble' (p. 24)—which horse should we back? There are winning streaks and losing streaks: 'swings and roundabouts' (p. 13), and 'ups and downs' (p. 23). Occasionally a horse may take 'a wrong turn' (p. 30) and end up in 'the graveyards of Wall Street', metaphorically speaking, of course (p. 29). Other horses hurdle over the '[trickles and floods] of money' (p. 6), and watch out for the fifth hurdle: the 'interest rate cycle' (p. 13).

On other occasions in the same article, the market is a vast game: the 'lure of a quick buck' (p. 19) means anything 'for a deal' (p. 13). The market is compared to a game of two–up: 'heads I win, tails you lose' (p. 26). So the worldwide gamble is metaphorised as a one–on–one flip of a coin.

Admittedly this reworking of key metaphors from a single article is a little frivolous. But gravity is hard to maintain when we realise that this is one of many articles that consistently fails to fulfil its explanatory function for its readers. It is evidently a war out there, and the 'shock troops of capitalism' (p. 30) are merely perpetuating the 'spiralling of imperfectly understood financial techniques' (p. 30) by using volatile language. The article has outlined the shape of the market by representing the market in a series of metaphors that distort it in multifarious ways.

Metaphorical excess in relation to the market could also be read as a problem-solving initiative, whereby, to take up Schon's argument, metaphor is 'central to the task of accounting for our perspectives on the world: how we think about things, make sense of reality, *and set the problems we later try to solve* [my emphasis]' (1993, p. 137). In a later section of this chapter I will be showing how one particular popular fiction novel (*Bombardiers*) explains some problematic aspects of the market through metaphor. For the general reader of this particular novel, the metaphors are directly problematised. One could say that the difference between the *Economist* and generic popular novels in their use of metaphor is that the former constructs a mythology from within its own discourse whereas the latter enables, in Radway's terms, 'reformulation' (1983, p. 68). In this respect, language, if attentively observed, does provide avenues for interrogation.

The Financial Revolution: A Mystery and a Threat

Changes to the financial markets have, as many writers emphasise, occurred in a remarkably short space of time. According to a recent article in the *New York Times Book Review*, a slow revolution has been taking place—rather like the gradual revolution that brought widespread industrialisation—but this time the shift is one of power: from governments to financial markets. As the sub-heading explains, 'the shift in power from government to markets is reshaping the contemporary world' (Garten 1998, p. 7), and our language is active in this reconstruction.

The free market system that Smith advocated in 1776 was beginning to tri-umph in many ways at least a century ago. Effects of changes to the stock mar-ket in only thirty years were noticed by Engels not long before his death. He writes: 'Since 1865, when [*Capital*, vol. 3] was written, a change has occurred the stock exchange [has become] the most pre–eminent representative of capital-ist production as such. In 1865 the stock exchange was still a secondary element in the capitalist system' (Engels in Marx 1991 [1894], p. 1045). Six years later, Simmel too observed a change to the monetary system, whereby money was becoming concentrated in centres, a feature of money as a magnetic attraction perhaps. 'In so far as the economy of a country is increasingly based on money, financial activities become concentrated in large centres of money transactions' (Simmel 1990 [1900], p. 504). He continues, 'the same interrelationship operates in the opposite direction: the convergence of large numbers of people brings about a particularly strong need for money' (Simmel 1990 [1900], p. 504). Simmel's observations are somewhat prophetic, because like Marx he anticipates the effects of money on thinking, as evidenced in the following remarks:

[The] condensation of values into the money form and of monetary transactions into the form of the stock exchange makes it possible for values to be rushed through the greatest number of hands in the shortest possible time [the stock exchange is] the geometrical focal point of all these changes in valuation, and at the same time the place of greatest excitement in economic life. Its *sanguine–choleric* oscillations between optimism and pessimism, its nervous reaction to ponderable and imponderable matters, the swiftness with which every factor affecting the situation is grasped and forgotten again—all this represents an extreme acceleration in the pace of life, a *feverish* commotion and compression of its fluctuations, in which the specific influence of money upon the course of *psychological life* becomes most clearly discernible [my emphasis]. (1990 [1900], p. 506)

In the hundred years or so since Simmel wrote this passage, almost all his observations have become both actualised and amplified. For example, in rela-tion to psychological life, as Lane's research reveals, 'people do use "rich" and "poor" as default values for assessing the desirable personality qualities a person has' (1991, p. 90). In some ways then, values are becoming increasingly related to the money form and the stock exchange is the centre of this value system. Technological change has also contributed significantly to a 'feverish' acceleration in our financial lives and our metaphors. Furthermore, Simmel's metaphors of (mental) health are pervasive, and they counter the concept of economic rationality.[2]

Amongst commentators of the financial markets, it is now widely accepted that 'money itself has moved onto the exchange as a commodity to be traded' (Kurtzman 1993, p. 155). In our news bulletins the commodities markets regularly update currency movements, whilst the 'old–fashioned' pork bellies and soya beans remain unreported. Hamilton echoes the idea: 'money is ceasing to be a medium of exchange, the direct link between saver and borrower. It has become a commodity in its own right, to be traded across the world over the green screens of dealers as currency, as bonds and as equity' (1986, p. 9). As a result, 'about 800 billion worth of dollars, marks and yen changes hands every day in the cash and futures markets of the world. That money is mostly involved in nothing more than making money' (Kurtzman 1993, p. 149).[3] The idea that money can be exchanged for money rather than goods and services is quite absurd in some ways. And Marx's material transformation of money (C–M–C) no longer occurs, because the 'C' (commodity) is now 'M' (money).

Metaphors of flight are frequently used to describe the contemporary market, as well as capital. Free markets and floating rates do not have material or regulated bonds, they are fleeting and impermanent. A cursory glance into any edition of the *Economist* reveals numerous metaphors of descent: landings, crashes, and freefalls. What goes up as we saw with Marx's butterfly, must come down. Metaphor is becoming worn out, and it is enforced by the financial press, as part of its descriptive mythology, rather than by distanced observers.

'Freeing money from government control would allow individuals to make their own decisions on where to invest or borrow, so the invisible hand could guide international affairs to the best possible economic result' (Millman 1995, p. 101). The belief in global self-regulation has been contested by the current prime minister of Malaysia, Mahathir, according to *Time* magazine (14 Sept. 1998):

When [Malaysia's] currency and stock market came crashing down of its own weight, Mahathir blamed outsiders—a cabal of speculators [including Soros], Jews and enemies of the developing world. To replenish the treasury, he asked the rich to pawn their jewelry overseas and bring the money back to Malaysia. To cut a huge foreign bill for food, he asked people to plant vegetables in their front yards. Last week Mahathir took the bold step *backward* of withdrawing Malaysia from the global economy, sealing off its currency from outside trade and sacking the pro-market Finance Minister [my emphasis]. (p. 48)

Steps forward relate to second-order mythology—those creative accretions of money concepts that form the financial market. Mahathir wanted to dismantle the effects of a variable currency market by re-establishing closed national boundaries.

We have retained the word 'market' as a metaphor to refer to a range of trading spaces, from telephone networks to town squares. The market signifier is thus partially emptied of its experiential dimensions. '[It] is clearly not a place, though it may sometimes be closely identified with a particular place. Nor is it anything one can observe in the usual sense of observation. It is not a 'market*place*' in the proper sense of the word, the market 'is a place for matching buyers and sellers, not necessarily a physical location' (Bennetts 1995, p. 59). It is generally agreed that the new financial markets are not observable or physical, and hence they are free.

Currently the biggest and most powerful market in the world is undoubtedly the financial market (and within this FOREX—the foreign exchange market). Like many branches of the financial markets it has no centre, 'there is no marketplace. Traders meet only socially, never to transact business, which is all done through banks of telephones or, increasingly, through computerized systems on the pervasive screens' (Roberts 1995, p. 156). Wark emphasises the dislocated aspect in his analysis: 'the term "market" [has become] a metaphor for an abstract space in the form of a network, not necessarily located anywhere' (1994, p. 187), perhaps making it a postmodern phenomenon as Lowenstein suggests (1996, p. 304). 'A stock market has no setting. It occurs in people's minds, a collective will that determines what is valuable and what is worthless, from day to day, minute to minute. To understand finance has nothing to do with economics or accounting. Instead it is a philosophical discipline, of the mind determining reality, the natural territory of Plato and Kant and the rest' (McManamy 1988, p. 3).

The perception that continues is that the financial market is independent, free of material and legislative boundaries. Furthermore, the global reach of the markets is sometimes understood to be cyberspace, or virtual space. A story entitled 'The Virtual Flight of the Cyber Trader' published in *Euromoney* (Jun. 1994), introduces some of the tensions inherent in the digital market. In this tongue–in–cheek short story set on 'Saturday, June 1 2019, 3.30 GTT [Global Trading Time], we find Callum (the cybertrader) entering a computer program that could reverse currency positions he had taken (as far back as 1994):

He entered the anti–trade program. In his hands was a virtual joystick. The tetranomial landscape spread out before him, above him and behind him, contoured with peaks and troughs of volatility and probability. It seemed ridiculously simple to [fire] at trades to reverse or neutralize them, dodging crisis points and squalls of extreme market behaviour' (Kimsey 1994, p. 46).

In a story such as this the intangible is countered by the tangible: the joystick controls the landscape and volatility is shaped by metaphors borrowed from the landscape. Significantly, while it is possible to manipulate time and currency as well as to produce 'virtual tobacco', technology is unable to replace '*Alpine* snow or *Caribbean* surf [my emphasis]' (Kimsey 1994, p. 45). The implication is that time and currency are open to re–presentation, but the sites of sensory experience cannot be imitated.

Virtual aspects of the market are similarly taken up in Ridpath's *Trading Reality*. Once again technology is used to fashion a landscape for the market. The central character, Mark Fairfax, is a bond dealer, trying to make 'financial sense' of the market that caused him to lose £2.4 million in ten minutes (Ridpath 1996, pp. 106, 196). The plot is centered on a murderous corporate battle for virtual reality technology—a system called 'Bondscape'. Introduced at the beginning of the text, this technology reshapes the bond market into a landscape of tall buildings and hills: 'the hillside was made up of a series of ridges. Each ridge represented a bond market; the higher the ridge, the higher the yield. The plains in the foreground represented the Japanese market. By looking at the landscape [through a headset], it was possible to see immediately how yields in the different markets related to each other' (Ridpath 1996, p. 5). Bondscape enables Fairfax 'to visualise the whole bond market, to get right inside it, to see and feel it moving' (Ridpath 1996, p. 13), in short to make the bond market more 'life-like' (Ridpath 1996, p. 26). In effect, the machine reorders abstract networks into understandable spatial forms, such as ridges, plains and hillsides.

Technology is cited as one of the key agents of change in our society (Castells 1998, p. 336), but deregulation has played a crucial part too. According to an analysis in the *Economist* (19 Sept. 1992, p. 5), the three key forces of change in the 1980s were 'innovation, technology and deregulation (in that order)'. Park backs this idea up in his paper on the 1998 East Asian Economic Crisis. He maintains that the three changes to have occurred in the last quarter century are 'the birth of large scale offshore funds', 'the demise of Bretton Woods', and 'the rapid development of communication and electronic technologies' (4 Mar. 1998).

A brief recapitulation of some of the key legislative changes to the financial markets in the last thirty years will elucidate the course of financial change. In the late 1960s, the United States continued to be subject to tight fiscal regulation following its experience of the 'depression' in the 1930s. However, high inflation in the early 1970s, a large U.S. balance of payment deficit, a zero–growth economy (which together are termed 'stagflation'), as well as two dollar devaluations meant that the United States was forced to abolish the fixed exchange rate system in 1973. Investors were no longer interested in buying the U.S. dollar. Consequently, the Bretton Woods agreement, which tied most currencies to the

U.S. dollar in order to maintain stable exchange rates, was dissolved. Many other countries followed by 'floating' their currencies on the world market.

The 'Euromarket', as it is known, deals in currency loans and deposits, and this market began as a market that traded in U.S. dollars *outside* the United States. According to Carew's *The Language of Money*, the Euromarket is a market for 'currencies and securities held in Europe and outside their country of origin (euro–is equivalent to external in this context)' (1988, p. 85). In other words, this market deals in de–nationalised money.

Moffitt explains the effects of the 1973 deregulation a decade later: 'The move to floating exchange rates was initially viewed as a temporary expedient until order could be restored in the money markets. Yet speculation continued and quickly ended any hopes of returning to fixed exchange rates' (1983, p. 75). Floating currencies have had far–reaching consequences for the *world's* financial markets as well as perceptions of those markets. Moffitt's forewarning has passed unheeded by the advocates of free markets. Nevertheless his diagnosis is that the Euromarket 'has rapidly become the headquarters of the global financial systems. Today, the Euromarket is a huge pool of "stateless money" [it] has become a 24–hour–a–day financial supermarket which provides banks and other customers with instant access to all the world's major currencies and money markets' (Moffitt 1983, p. 65). Here we find words such as 'headquarters' and 'supermarket', which indicate a confusion about 'statelessness', and an impulse to reposition the market in a specific site.

Moffitt is clearly disturbed by global currency speculation and uses a range of metaphors (most of which I have identified earlier), but which I again highlight here to illustrate their recurrence:

the *stakes* riding on global currency speculation escalated tremendously in the 1970s. Today, currency speculation is far more than just a *game* to play against governments to make money. It has transformed the nature of international monetary relations. In the face of the massive *flight* out of the dollar in 1973, Western governments were pushed into a *floating* exchange–rate system. Since then, we have been living with the consequences of that fateful decision. Global currency speculation has increased markedly [and] currency fluctuations have been more erratic (1983, pp. 91–92).

The 1970s deregulation could certainly be said to mark the beginning of the end for government control and stable currency values, and instability was merely helped by technological innovation, and a plethora of mixed metaphors.

The size of the currency markets is also cause for alarm. For readers outside the market, it may be difficult to fathom uncontrolled and spiralling growth. In fact, market mythologies themselves are often the cause of actual irrational behaviour. George Soros is depicted in the press as a mover of markets, because of his intervention in currency movements. Often characterised as controllers, currency traders like Soros are seen to be in control of whole countries, as well as currencies, and this perception leads to muddled (sometimes ritual) behaviour. In October 1997, for example, an effigy of Soros was burned in Malaysia's capital, because he was seen to be directly responsible for South East Asia's financial difficulties (*Australian Financial Review* 28 Oct. 1997, p. 12). For those outside Western markets, or in so–called emerging markets, Soros is not a hero then; he is a destroyer.

Growth in proportions as large as the market's does not occur on a daily basis in most people's lives, and it is perceived as excessive: 'The last two decades have seen the flowering of the Eurodollar banking system. In consequence an incalculable proportion of all currency in circulation is now beyond the control of the states who issue the money. The total volume of money sales is now vastly in excess of the amount needed to finance international trade' (Hart 1986, pp. 639–40). Hart presents an interesting metaphor here for market dominance. 'Flowering' is used to explain uncontrollability and excess, but it is a 'natural' metaphor, again implying contingency. On 25 February 1995, the *Economist* published a feature entitled 'Let the Digital Age Bloom'. The article argues that governments should not interfere in technological developments, they should let the Internet technologies 'evolve' (*Economist* 25 Feb. 1995, p. 14). They should 'water' the technology (i.e., promote competition) and do 'a little weeding' (i.e., monitor lawlessness) (*Economist* 25 Feb. 1995, p. 14). This language shift is 'the very principle of myth: it transforms history into nature' (Barthes 1989 [1957], p. 140). Hart's reference to trade is to the tangible, and to the historical market that Maestro first describes. The global financial market is becoming naturalised by metaphorical descriptions like Hart's and the *Economist*'s.

Real, tangible forms of money such as cash, or exchangeable items such as food, are being replaced in the financial markets by abstract financial instruments. And Park blames the Asian crisis on this global abstraction. The 'vast majority of financial transactions became "pure financial transactions" not involving real imports and exports. Like the cyber space, a new "financial space" is created and the actors in this space acted entirely according to their own dynamics independent of the real economies' (4 Mar. 1998). Kurtzman's *The Death of Money* (1993) pursues a similar real/abstract dichotomy as one of his central arguments, highlighting the disparity between what he terms the 'real' and the 'financial' economies, and I quote it again in this context: the 'global landscape is an abstract land, a land of description rather than reality, where the real and the financial economies barely touch. It is from this remote station in life, a kind of financial Tibet, that the mathematicians of Wall Street dream' (1993, pp. 164–65). But as we shall see, the dream is only shattered with a crash, and the abstraction becomes real when people cannot afford to eat unless, like Mahathir suggests, they plant food in their own gardens.

The financial markets are now dedicated towards making money out of money (currency). This conflicts dramatically with Smith's notion of trade, as Saul again points out:

The money markets [are] the most successful area of economic activity—the most successful in a very long time. Every day, currency traders move $1 trillion around the world. There are, unfortunately, two impediments. This money is not available for taxation. And more importantly, it doesn't really exist. Money that bears no relationship to reality is imaginary. It is pure inflation. In the matter of money markets, it is Smith and Hume who are right. The explosion in these markets does not finance growth because money markets unrelated to financing real activity are pure inflation. And for that matter, they are a very esoteric, pure form of ideology. (1997, pp. 153–54)

In other words, free markets have rapidly become free of taxation, and indeed reality in the reader's terms. The mythology of the market is made possible by an absence of anchored activity; money is no longer purely a measure of value. This is a vital point in terms of the consequences of abstraction in the financial markets; we only have a finite amount of resources on the planet, and these have to be tied to money as value. Creating new forms of money with no material base makes the value of money totally arbitrary, and some would argue, destructive.

Strange considers that 'changes leading to the present mess have happened very fast, in the short space of about 15 years' (1989 [1986], p. 4). The rapidity of change is widely acknowledged. For the *Economist* (19 Sept. 1992, pp. 6; 15 Apr. 1995, p. 29), the markets have changed perhaps too rapidly. In 1995, the *Australian Financial Review* explains that compared with twelve years previously, the temporal aspects of the market have changed too: trading used to be carried out before lunch, but now it occurs twenty four hours a day (7 Sept. 1995, p. 32).

Undoubtedly the markets are getting bigger and bigger as more and more nonexperts are jumping on the market bandwagon and investing. But the higher it rises, so the argument goes, the harder it will fall. Fifteen November 1972 marks the anniversary of the Dow Jones Industrial Average's 'first ever finish above 1,000', according to the *Wall Street Journal* (15 Nov. 1996, p. C2). On 15 November 1996 the Industrial Average stood at 6313 (*Wall Street Journal*, 15 Nov. 1996, p. C2). At the start of the new millennium, the Dow Jones passed the 11,000 mark—an *eleven fold* increase in less than thirty years. Of course I am not in a position to predict (nor would I want to) the future movements of the Dow Jones. Numbers such as these are merely metaphors of value, market activity, and growth, but they do have a powerful effect on our behaviour.

According to a psychological study that Baker cites (1995, pp. 246–47), traders experience a reluctance to push financial indices over certain numerical barriers, particularly those ending in double zero. In other words, the Dow Jones index demonstrates a close relationship between people and numbers.

The idea about breakthroughs in numerical boundaries is backed up by metaphor. For example, while the headline of a *New York Times* article reads: 'What Goes Up May Keep Going Up', the article repeatedly uses the term 'barrier' (5 Apr. 1998, p. 3). Of course, what goes up must come down, according to the market's own mythological cliché, and metaphors simply highlight the notions of ascent and descent.

In addition to the new Euro and foreign exchange markets, financial futures (in various forms) were also introduced in the 1970s and 1980s, thanks to Melamed. 'The USA's greatest export of a financial technique in the 1980s is undoubtedly financial futures and options' (Hamilton 1986, p. 72). Previously, the majority of futures traded were directly related to farming so that in Chicago (the home of futures trading since the nineteenth century) futures in grain, butter, and eggs were traded as protective measures.

Gambling on the future is one of the ways in which the markets have sought to protect themselves in situations of uncertainty. Therefore futures themselves are based on uncertainty: they were invented to hedge risk. 'In the 1980s, futures trading in commodities has been completely overtaken by trading in financial futures. This is a direct result of the increase in financial uncertainty' (Strange 1989 [1986], p. 113). Furthermore as soon as these instruments are invented, they are ferociously traded. 'Stock–index futures were introduced in 1982. Yet by 1983 the dollar value of the trading in futures on the stock index actually exceeded the dollar value of trading on the New York Stock Exchange' (Hamilton 1986, p. 73). Despite their protective function, futures are uneconomic as the story of Nick Leeson has demonstrated.

Floating Rates and the Foreign Exchange Market

I would like to focus now on one particular market—the Foreign Exchange Market. It is *the largest* market in the world, in the sense that it moves more money in a single day than any other: 'The main card room in [the] electronic casino is the currency market' (Castells 1996, pp. 434-45). Exact figures for the exchange vary. The Bank for International Settlements (BIS) has shown in a survey that 'foreign exchange dealing is more than twenty times the level of world trade' (Roberts 1995, p. 106). Castells estimates that 'in 1995, US $1.2 trillion were exchanged every day in the currency market' (1996, p. 435). According to Baker, 'The actual size of foreign exchanges is unknowable. If in doubt about the size of the market, guess on the large side, and then add a zero (1995, pp. 18–19).

A trillion dollars is currently the generally accepted figure for each day's currency trades—an enormous sum. More to the point, because the foreign exchange market deals with unfathomably large sums of money, it has become a menacing yet unknown quantity (*Economist* 19 Sept. 1992, p. 6). The FOREX market is a floating one (that is, unstable), and will remain so unless the market is re–regulated. Floating currencies are undependable and speculative, they bear no relation to real value. This market is a threat to countries like Malaysia, because the value of national currencies is purely subject to speculative demand. According to Roberts, because 'foreign exchange dealing is many times the volume of international trade and investment, [most] of it can have no underlying purpose other than speculation' (1995, p. 257).

The 1997/98 East Asian Economic Crisis is the result of this speculation, as Park recently explained:

While it is entirely correct to blame the East Asians for mismanagements of their economies, it will take a height of naivette [sic] to believe that this crisis was a creation of East Asians by themselves alone. It needs two hands to make the sound of clapping. [The other side is] 'hot money terrorism' [which] is a kind of unplanned and unintended, nevertheless devastating reality. (4 Mar. 1998)

For Park, reality has been reshaped by the currency markets, whereas for Kurtzman the two areas are quite distinct: the market is abstract and hence unreal, whereas everyday experience is real. In addition, for Kurtzman, the abstract (intangible) has effects on the concrete.

FOREX is a threat because no body is monitoring its effects, but also because real harm can occur. The market is limit*ed* and limit*less*: limited by our metaphors and limitless in terms of understanding. There are infinite possible constructions of the market, and an overall structure is impossible to glean from these structures.

Whilst the Foreign Exchange Market is the biggest market in the world, it is also the least regulated. It is little wonder that observers of this market are alarmed about its speculative aspects. 'When banks take huge daily positions in foreign–exchange markets, they are gambling: they cannot know whether the price is going to rise or fall' (Fay 1996, p. 296). Value of currencies in this market are effectively decided only by the buyers and sellers in the market, because floating currencies have no material foundation, and are not controlled by government. As Mayer puts it, 'Wall Street [has] had a purely instrumental view of government. Government helped or hindered traders in their pursuit of government' (1993, p. 234). As a consequence, values (and national economies) are always insecure, there is no stable pole with which to measure a currency, and so 'in a world of shifting benchmarks and changing "spots", value is not intrinsic but ephemeral' (Lowenstein 1996, p. 418).[4]

The inability of governments to control the financial markets is new to the history of money as Williams (1997) and others have found. Strange adopts an alarmist tone, justified perhaps because of decreasing government control of the markets. Her book *Casino Capitalism* has provided a gambling metaphor that has been taken up by sceptical commentators, such as Park (4 Mar. 1998) and Castells (1996). A whole genre of books about the market threat seems to be emerging. Like many observers, such as Millman, Roberts, and Castells, Strange demands some form of governmental intervention or control before the domino effect of a market crash could effect more 'real' people's lives as it already has done in Asia recently. Wolfson calls for a 'new system of financial regulation' (1994, p. 232). Perhaps more interrogation of the myth would help too.

Despite a degree of optimism about some aspects of the emerging 'network society', as he calls it, Castells's tone changes markedly when he discusses what he calls 'the Global Casino': 'for the first time in history, a unified global capital market, *working in real time,* has emerged' (1996, p. 434). By this Castells seems to mean that the consequences of ill–considered actions can have an immediate effect. But Castells does not cast blame on any individual, preferring like Marx to construct a 'faceless collective capitalist' (1996 p. 474). In a single sentence we see the following terms used by Castells to describe 'these markets': 'crises, economic instability, wrecking, unforeseen changes, increasing gap, gambling, risks, dependence of entire economies, subjective perception, and speculative turbulence, destruction, "quick buck" common ideology, damage' (1996, p. 436).[5] For Castells, then, the market is a destroyer.

There is undoubtedly a sense of angst about developments in the money market from outside observers. Some of the monetary instruments that are currently traded in the markets have simply not been around long enough for their effects to be ascertained. More importantly perhaps, the possible consequences to all of us if they fail to perform is unknown: we might, according to the metaphors, crash, fall, or burn. Metaphors give shape to the financial market, as well as voicing concern about its unknown factors. The next section will consider spatial metaphors in *Bombardiers* that question the notion of the market's self-containment.

Profiting from 'Up' and 'Down'

The money markets are caught in a metaphorical deadlock. There is a contradictory impulse in financial metaphors: on the one hand, metaphors assert money's liberation from measured material, and on the other, they seem to check money's march towards growth and abstraction. This section focuses on two diametrically opposed metaphors that could be termed 'orientation' and 'containment'; the first signifies movement and the second, restraint. My focus here is on one text's struggle with market transformation. To a certain extent the disappearance of traditional forms of money has encouraged increased metaphorisation, but the coining of new financial metaphors does not accurately account for developments in market practices.

Bronson's *Bombardiers,* published in 1995, is a lively, comic novel set in Wall Street, New York, in 1993.[6] The narrative follows several bond traders through three trade deals, each surpassing the previous one in ludicrousness. The final deal, for example, is a buy–out of the entire assets of the Dominican Republic.

The publication date of this novel is crucial for my study. Since the 1970s and 1980s the financial markets have been largely self-regulating, operating with little government intervention, so that they have been given free rein to trade numerous forms of money. *Bombardiers* could not have been written before the 1987 crash, a fact made explicit by the text itself: 'the 1987 stock market crash was the Bomb, and time was measured Before the Bomb/After the Bomb' (p. 124). The text then is grounded on the notion of monetary crisis. There is a persistent fear of a recurrence of the 1987 crash, combined with a sense of no return in this text (p. 247).

The market is the central feature of *Bombardiers,* providing both the setting and the impetus for the plot. Metaphorical links between money and the markets in this text undergo a series of unresolved struggles between mutual constraint and liberation. However, the relationship between the two becomes increasingly problematic and the text struggles with this dependency. Our language seems to be grappling with acquired metaphors and questioning their continued applicability.

Two prominent metaphors of the market are repeatedly played off against each other in this text. I have found that the types of spatial metaphor that Lakoff and Johnson describe as complementary in fact conflict in relation to the market in *Bombardiers.* The first is the 'orientational' metaphor, which describes market movements, and the second is the 'container' metaphor, which describes the market itself. Confusion about the nature and role of the financial markets in *Bombardiers* can be inferred by considering the play–off between these two metaphorical types. Neither the container nor the orientation metaphor could be considered to be the authoritative metaphor for the financial markets.

I shall turn first to the orientation metaphor. Signalled by words such as 'up' and 'down' and 'in' and 'out', this type of metaphor designates movement. Fluctuations in financial markets are typically referred to in terms of spatial orientation: inflation rises, indices drop. In *Bombardiers* we find numerous sentences burdened by unrestrained metaphorical orientation: '[the traders] were dropping like flies, and [they] were told to start dumping their positions in other bonds in order to free up capital' (p. 299). Phrases such as these characteristically pull the reader in many directions.

When applied to money the orientation metaphor attributes money with fluidity, thereby resisting notions of terra firma. A repeated line is that 'as long as there were markets, money would always have a direction, and a speed, and an acceleration, all of which could be sold' (pp. 10, 67). Thus even movement itself has a price. After the final deal, the following line summarises some of the text's orientations: 'when the dust cleared, only Sidney Geeder was left standing. Only those who can defy gravity and those who were made of steel' survived (p. 306). Metaphors of storms and weightlessness conflict with stability. Moreover, unpredictability and threat are in direct opposition to the composure of market men of steel. Orientation metaphors defy stasis, and this is because the market needs money to continue to circulate. Sidney Geeder, the principle character, explains his trading practices: 'You have to stop thinking about up *or* down. It's going to do both. You have to think of how to profit from up *and* down. You have to profit from the volatility' (p. 42). The procurement of profit from orientation alone is markedly asserted in this text.

The market is 'gargantuan' (pp. 21, 22) and has a significant impact on monetary movements. This intensified situation can be noted in an instance of metonymic gesturing that occurs towards the end of the novel when the final deal is being completed: 'every investor and dealer and broker in the world watched the market on his screens and prayed that the whole goddamn system wouldn't come tumbling down' (p. 299).

Once again metaphors are deployed extravagantly to illustrate monetary excess. *Every* male involved in finance in the world watches the market (a series of numbers flashing across a computer screen) and prays (appeals to an outside force) that the whole goddamn (they have been abandoned) system would not go down. Distressing questions arise from this intensified account: How can an ill-defined system go down? Where does it go? Where was it in the first place? Why does it 'tumble' when money is 'liquid'? Is this the same as a 'crash'? In this particular case the passage merely reinforces popular myths of the market. And by reinforcing them, they are further enforced, so that to some extent even traders become a part of their own mythologies.

So far I have only considered the notion of money's direction. Perhaps if I could capture money for a second, I could explain how it behaves within the market. Unfortunately money's material referent is unstable in *Bombardiers,* and its forms too are limitless. But it does jostle towards positions of definability. Traces of its physical form remain, residues of organic or earthly metaphors are retained in *Bombardiers,* but they are backgrounded. Characters trade pastries (p. 14), and mortgages are likened to zucchinis: 'coming out of the ears' in summer (p. 228).

My second metaphor, the container metaphor, typically describes the market in *Bombardiers.* Narratorial assertions, such as 'they're in this for the money' (p. 118) and 'money stays in the system' (p. 144), set firm boundaries around the characters and monetary materials that form the substance of the market. As I perceive it, the feeling one gets from considering the market in this way is that it is a controllable space, because it is perceived as *containable.* Thus the container metaphor stands for that part of the market that is controlled, finite, and real, that maintains money's predictability. The container metaphor stands in direct opposition to the orientation metaphor.

The container metaphor defines space, but also implies incarceration. The traders are 'locked in' with money in a twenty four–hour trading circle (p. 187). Promised final payoffs keep characters confined but release is always frustratingly imminent. It seems to be impossible for either money or people to be released from this container. Money is locked into the markets, because 'you can't put eight million dollars in a mattress' (pp. 144–45). Interminable restlessness prevents the market from becoming dormant.

The container metaphor works as it marks the coordinates of the market's internal structure. But containers are only useful if they do not leak or the bottom does not drop out leaving us in a void. It is significant that money is frequently characterised as liquid, in *Bombardiers* as well as in economic terminology. The market contains a brew of floating notes and liquid assets: a veritable slush fund. Liquid is a natural substance subject to physical laws, liquid always takes on the shape of the space in which it is contained. And so, to function successfully in the market, financial instruments need to be malleable: to be converted into cash quickly and without loss.

The concept of a container also implies a finite amount of container space. Does this mean that there is a finite amount of money available, at the disposal of the markets? Can the market be topped up? Does it overflow? As long as money remains inside the markets, it can be described as gullible. The inference to be made from this metaphorical gesture is that money is infinitely malleable, it is liquid so it can adapt to all spaces, it yields to persuasion and interest. By constructing conflicting metaphor types, the text both questions and reinforces some popular myths of the changing financial markets.

'What is at issue is not the truth or falsity of a metaphor but the perceptions and inferences that follow from it and the actions that are sanctioned by it' (Lakoff and Johnson 1980, p. 158). In the main, readers are not familiar with new financial instruments as they are being formulated almost every week.[7] So these developments are left open to the reader. But money is contained in a market characterised as a multifunctional machine. These unsettled delineations disrupt the readers' assumptions about the stability of the financial system. By reading texts such as *Bombardiers,* readers are able to reformulate their perceptions about the mechanisms of money and question these 'sanctioned actions'. In *Bombardiers* they are greatly assisted by narratorial comment as well as the distancing effect of the past tense. The narrator aims several comments about the market at readers that cause them to question their assumptions. One such example amongst many follows: 'What drives the market is what people think is true' (p. 244).

Many of the financial metaphors in *Bombardiers* are liberating ones, money has a 'speed' and an 'acceleration' but no resting place (pp. 10, 67). It is liquid, it is addicting, it can be eaten, and it seems to be moving ceaselessly. These metaphors are disorienting, causing the reader to recognise crisis. Notions of directionless and groundless money proliferate through this novel, and can be sharply contrasted with economic conceptions of control, balance, and equilibrium, as expressed in the container metaphor.

Metaphors in popular fiction texts seem to be picking up on the worldwide trend towards financial market deregulation. Siding with the pessimistic view, popular fiction generally upholds the idea that we live in a 'chaotic world victimized by market spikes and unforeseeable global crises' (p. 134). The passive voice in some instances adds to the suggestion that money is controlling us. *Bombardiers* is a novel that jostles with metaphors of money and the market, suggesting that the market is in fact more erratic and more dominant than most of our balanced models seem to suggest.

Money's appeal in popular fiction can be said to derive from the exciting play-off between predictability and uncertainty. As readers we are empowered to either resist innovation or embrace its evolving abstraction. The mystery of the markets encourages speculation about its nature, but as complete knowledge about its activities is untenable, there is an inherent conflict between differing metaphors of the market.

Shaping the Market with Metaphor

The apparently uncontrollable market is both naturalised and mythologised. In this section I will discuss metaphors that attribute the market with familiar types of activity that may have been found in traditional community markets, such as gambling, the cycle, and sound. These metaphors distort the financial market, and some of them make it a contingency. But the game that I turn to first is one metaphor that enables readers to question monetary and ethical values in the market, because it brings with it a suggestion of winners and losers. The game metaphor essentially implies risk management, but it also enables the haphazard and least–enduring facets of the market to be accented. The game contrasts in many respects with the metaphors I discuss afterwards—the cycle and (briefly) sound, which attribute predictability to the market.

One of the most enduring metaphors for the space of the financial market is the gambling casino, which highlights the irrationality and uncontrollability of the markets. Strange's *Casino Capitalism* (1989 [1986]) emphasises this perspective:

the Western financial system is rapidly coming to resemble nothing as much as a vast casino. Every day games are played in this casino that involve sums of money so large they cannot be imagined. At night the games go on at the other side of the world. In the towering office blocks that dominate all the great cities of the world, rooms are full of chain–smoking young men all playing these games. They are just like the gamblers in casinos watching the clicking spin of a silver ball on a roulette wheel. (pp. 1–2)

Strange's point about unimaginable sums of money is a pertinent one: she considers only the imaginable to be 'real', whereas the imaginary is fictitious. The metaphor of the casino positions the market at a distance from its ideal function as economic regulator, and causes concern because it is not the individual gamblers' money at stake.

In addition, it is not the money these chain–smoking men want, it is the game they thrive on, an idea I have previously highlighted. Smith explains that the money is inconsequential in this game: 'The irony is that it is a money game and money is the way we keep score. But the real object of the Game is not money, it is the playing of the Game itself' (Smith 1968, p. 14). Mayer expresses a similar opinion, 'Traders remain people of vast and insatiable ego, however; their reward comes far more from the instant gratification of the successful trade than the money they make' (1993, p. 68). Therefore, the game takes precedence over money in the financial markets, so that making a killing reflects the traders' moral characters. Many texts that I have read that comment on the markets enforce the perception of the markets as arenas of self–interest, an idea that coincides with Smith's universal characterisation of humans as rational pursuers of gain.

The casino is, of course, a place where games are played, and they are generally amusing, but potentially compulsive and injurious. Casinos also factor in a large percentage of gain, so that winners are always in the minority. Therefore, with the casino metaphor the 'down' side is always implied: 'If you want to play the game, sometimes somebody is going to get assassinated' (Lipschutz in Schwager 1994, p. 49). Ten days before the October 1997 stock market debacle, the *Weekend Australian* argued that only those people who can afford to lose should play the market, otherwise they will get 'hurt' (18 Oct. 1997, p. 20). Saul explains that the markets can be fun but only 'for those who can afford to have a sense of humour' (1997, p. 122)—or for those who are gambling with *other people's* money.

The Money Game and *A Fool and His Money* make light of the markets. Their tone is sardonic and whimsical. The author of the former text uses the Adam Smith pseudonym specifically to ridicule economic stoicism. Baker adopts a similar tone, describing his book as 'an agnostic's bible' because it challenges current market wisdom (1995, p. xiii). He explains that we are living 'closer to the edge of the precipice than ever before [and] this provides good reasons to be cheerful. There is another legacy of the twentieth century that is even more terrible, and consequently hilarity–provoking. It is the notion that the market is perfect' (Baker 1995, p. xii).

Rhinehart satirises market ethics in his most recent novel. He has revived the subject of his 1970s *The Dice Man* for the 1990s: *The Search for the Dice Man* takes up where the first book left off, but with a new slant. Now the focus is on the son, Larry, who is a conservative Wall Street analyst, the antithesis of his anarchic dice–throwing father. The humour in this text derives from the play-off between differing notions of the arbitrary and the random: markets and dice vie with each other in terms of predictability. Initially Larry supports the logic of the markets, as the narrator explains: 'At Wharton Business School Larry had determined to prove the value of reason and research over his father's bastard deity, Chance' (Rhinehart 1994, p. 15). Having made a lot of money in the 1987 crash, Larry has since found himself on a consistently bad streak in the markets. Following an unexpected visit by the FBI, he is goaded into searching for his father in Lukedom: an anarchic community devoted to die–ing. Upon arrival in the community he is given an instructor, who tells him 'the dice are nothing special just a gimmick to dramatize the arbitrariness of decision–making' (Rhinehart 1994, p. 153). After some cultlike brainwashing, Larry returns to work, deciding to use the dice to make his decisions. 'Larry hoped the die would say "sell" [his position on futures]. With odd meaning buy and even sell, the die fell a three: buy [so] he picked up the phone [and bought]. The BB&P Futures Fund made money that day. Larry's personal account made even more, since the stock market, for reasons of its own, went up, as the dice had said, and not down, as Larry's scientific indicators had said' (Rhinehart 1994, pp. 279–82). Dice and markets apparently have 'reasons' of their own, independent of human intervention. 'Larry kept computerized records of his dice decisions and their results. He theorized that by introducing chance into his trading he was enabling himself to eliminate the usual human emotions that sway a trader's decisions and lead to losing streaks' (Rhinehart 1994, pp. 316–17).

One day towards the end of the text, when Larry throws the die, he finds that it has chosen that he should be 'complete saint' for the whole day (Rhinehart 1994, p. 322). He recalls what happened:

In preparing the morning trades I knew I had to let moral principles be uppermost in my mind, and I'm afraid I probably overdid it. I ordered my men to buy wheat because it was the source of the staff of life, to sell cattle and pork bellies because they were being cruelly butchered for mere money, to sell the D–mark to punish the Germans for the Second World War. I had to sell them oil futures to cut down pollution, but buy bond futures to support the Government's effort to clean up the pollution. As for the stock market I saw that most of the companies owned in the various BB&P–managed accounts were definitely sources of evil and would have to be sold. The word spread Larry Rhinehart was selling. I, one of the most creative traders to come along in years, was selling. The stock market opened lower and headed south. (Rhinehart 1994, pp. 324–25)

The text throws up two central ideas about the market to its readers. First, that playing the markets is a random exercise, much like dice throwing. Second, it suggests that the market is independent of, and stronger than, its participants: 'the stock market, for reasons of its own, went up'. But the humour in the text is created by discordant characterisation; it plays with the perception that there are no saints in the market, so 'ethical' trading is a misnomer.

Rhinehart's text questions the tenacious idea that the market is predictable. The 'cycle' is the main metaphor used to describe predictability, and clichés formed around the metaphor abound in the press. The cycle is used to suggest seasonal, as well as diurnal/nocturnal, repetitions in the market. The general concept is that 'As sure as night follows day', 'markets will always move up and down' (*Courier Mail* 29 Oct. 1997, p. 42; and *Australian Financial Review* 30 Oct. 1997, p. 20). The cycle metaphor conflicts conceptually with the artificiality of the financial markets; therefore it distorts the market, but does not allow its artificiality to dissipate. The main function of this metaphor is to naturalise the market by giving it an identifiable pattern based on historical precedent, the implication being that if the market follows regular patterns then it is implicitly controllable. The *Economist* continually takes up this naturalisation, drawing out additional connotations such as growth: 'As *night* follows *day*, so each *upswing* carries the *seed* of the next *recession* [my emphasis]' (18 Mar. 1995, p. 14). Here we find the myth of the diurnal/nocturnal, combined with the metaphor of the flowering economy—both bound within the cycle metaphor, and each of these metaphors functions as a naturaliser.

For market players, an ability to predict upswings and downturns is a prerequisite. The cycle metaphor implies a type of preordination or market itinerary that, if uncovered, earns one the status of expert. For those of an economic bent, the market is the Ideal in many respects:

From within [the market, economists] see the purest application of abstract theory, extremely complex, requiring specialist skills. Even public officials are seduced by the intricate interior logic represented by the burgeoning financial speculative markets. Our belief in salvation through the market is very much in the utopian tradition. The economists and managers are the servants of god. Like medieval scholastics, their only job is to uncover the divine plan. They could never create or stop it. (Saul 1997, pp. 124–25)

The financial market has a mythological cycle, which naturalises its cultural position. The supposition that there is a cycle, but that its workings are unsure, means that metaphor needs to be used to complete its form. 'Myth prefers to work with poor, incomplete images' (Barthes 1989 [1957], p. 137), such as the financial market, which has neither an origin, nor a closure, so the cycle completes it by giving it a rhythmical signification.

The absence of an actual referential in the market cycle means that the concept of the cycle itself can be saturated with numerous conflicting histories and metaphors. Once again the *Economist* historicises the cycle by introducing a historical connection and swiftly problematising it: 'The bible records that seven years of plenty were followed by seven lean. People with a literal bent might take this as evidence that the business cycle has been around for even longer than the 200 or so years during which economists have tracked the regular alternations between boom and bust' (18 Mar. 1995, p. 14).

This is a problematic piece of deductive journalism. I wonder whether a reader would seriously attempt to make a connection (as this piece does) between biblical narratives and the veracity of the business cycle, a metaphorical structure. Is the writer trying to suggest that literal readings are erroneous? From a metaphorical perspective, this writer is actually insinuating biblical narrative into the economic arena, simply by suggesting the comparison.

Lowenstein observes that 'financial cycles are apparent only in retrospect. As it unfolds, each swing of the market, cloaked in the vestments of the moment, appears unique' (1996, p. 232). The punctuation of the cycle's itinerary by booms and busts cannot be discerned from either the perspective of the present or the future. But there are still terms for these moments. In trader's parlance, 'bottomish' '[describes] a market that has fallen to a level that indicates an imminent reversal of the downward trend' (Carew 1988, p. 26), and conversely 'toppy' describes a market 'that has reached a level that equals either as previous or expected high, so that the next move forecast is downward' (Carew 1988, p. 244). The *Economist* trivialises the October 1997 stock market fiasco by satirising the 'bottom' metaphor. Entitled 'Mind Your Bottom', the piece, consistent with the issue's Editorial, ridicules traders' debasing metaphors: apparently a trader said there was no need to worry, the fall was simply 'a systematic meltdown of testing new bottoms' (*Economist*, 1 Nov. 1997, p. 82). Other observers called it either 'bottom fishing', or the 'breaching of the quadruple bottom' (*Economist*, 1 Nov. 1997, p. 82).

The cycle is a striking metaphor; providing conceptual boundaries as well as being a crutch based on historical precedents. The notion of cycles in history is not uncommon, but it is now used to structure a mythology of the financial markets. A number of recent texts bring the fragility of the cycle and its cognitive effects together. In fact, there is a whole literary genre of texts—popular apparently with traders in New York—which deals with the threatening aspects of the financial markets. For example, Mackay's *Extraordinary Popular Delusions and the Madness of Crowds*, has been a best–seller on the Street for years. Fridson, the (1996) managing director of Merrill Lynch, confirms this: 'If one works on Wall Street for any length of time, ultimately he or she is directed to the book' (in Mackay 1996 [1841], p. 2). Buchan's analysis is that the book 'tends to be re-issued in the United States at the peak of bull markets or just after they have broken' (1997, p. 107), and my edition is a case in point, it was issued in the bull market of 1996.

Ravi Batra's (1987) *The Great Depression of 1990* is said by Kurtzman to have played a significant part in the Wall Street 'crash' of 1987, because its forecasts made traders feel nervous, thereby contributing to the 1987 crisis (1993, p. 114). Texts such as these have a wide trader readership and in some ways they contribute towards the volatility of the markets as they perform an oracular function. Baker reminds us that it is rumour as much as money that makes the financial markets move (1995, p. 6).[8] The question is, which comes first, the crash or the warning, the chicken or the egg?

Brummett's article, 'Popular Economic Apocalyptic: The Case of Ravi Batra' points out the popularity of this genre for assisting readers in modifying the perceived chaos of financial markets. He draws upon other titles as well: Abert's *After the Crash*, Ruff's *How to Prosper during the Coming Bad Years*, and Smith's *The Coming Currency Collapse*. Clearly these three titles are focused on the apocalyptic, and it is Brummett's opinion that the apocalyptic genre, having departed from its religious roots, now arises in times of perceived chaos and 'in response to subjective confusion about how to account for change' (1990, p. 155). He continues, 'apocalyptic's arguments take two forms. First, it offers its audience an explanation for what is happening, which restores order in their lives. Second, it insinuates political and social prescriptions into its discussion of the coming change' (Brummett 1990, p. 156). The apocalyptic shares both the explanatory and diagnostic functions of market metaphors.

From this perspective, the cycle could be viewed as a rhetorical device for asserting predictability. But this is not always the case. The cycle leads to destruction *and* salvation. Because the return of the same is a fundamental aspect of the cycle, absolute destruction is prevented from occurring, but is always imminent. As a temporal metaphor, the eternally recurring nature of the cycle occasionally facilitates explanations for monetary behaviour (an upswing is imminent), but this is accompanied by a sense of monetary determinism: there is no end in sight, so the process is continuous. 'Where will it end?' asked the *Bulletin* of the Asian market crisis on 4 November 1997 (front page). According to Millman (1995, p. xi), 'the financial markets are non–linear', and therefore there can be no beginning, middle, or end; the cycle metaphor effectively precludes any sense of determination.

Batra is a self–styled guru of market forecasting who confronts government monetarists. He writes, 'some of [the economic cycles] deal with variables commonly regarded as "exogenous" or random in economic theory. Money supply is a case in point. It is supposed to be determined by the Federal Reserve System. But it turns out to have had a rhythmical cycle, which can be traced as far back as the birth of the American nation' (Batra 1987, p. 21). Here Batra is alluding to the idea that money determines its own cycle and thus the cycle is a metaphor useful for explaining money's behaviour outside human agency. But he also draws upon an American mythic paradigm, drawing money and America together in genealogical terms.

Apparently trained by an Indian seer, Batra feels he is in tune with historical rhythms, that he has a unique vision. 'The centerpiece of my philosophy of history is [the] idea that history follows a certain pattern' (Batra 1987, p. 24). This patterning follows the apocalyptic reasoning closely according to Brummett: 'for an audience which cannot see order in confusing events and which no longer knows how to understand experience, apocalyptic argues that a Plan is indeed working through and determining what happens in history' (1990, p. 157). But the plan is part of money's mythology—it ignores accidents from the past, those lurches and stumbles by which we were propelled to the present.

There is no recollection involved with the market: every action seems to exist in isolation. Remembrance of things past, such as 'Black Monday', are absent. In some ways this is because the market is constantly changing, and according to Saul it suffers from selective amnesia: 'The market did not and does not learn because, being devoid of disinterest, it has no memory' (1997, p. 120). Saul contrasts 'interested' thinking (corporatism and self-interest) with 'disinterest', or debate: 'Common sense or ethics or even the memory of past speculative booms ought to have been invoked against this dangerous disorder. What is coming, bit by bit, is an intuitive reaction from the public who, although they have been allowed to understand little of what is going on, nevertheless sense that we are slipping down a dangerously delusionary road. They sense that this complex global market cannot be a limitless abstraction' (1997, p. 190).

The cycle metaphor is a fabrication, forming a substantial footing for market mythology. Batra is deluding his readers (particularly traders) by making them believe that they are the custodians of history and the managers of the future. If Kurtzman is right about the effect Batra's book had on the mood in Wall Street, then surely the cycle was broken because the depression occurred too early: in 1987, not 1990. In effect, forms of prediction and rumour found in texts such as these have a disruptive effect on the cycle itself.

The metaphor of an economic cycle takes past events and hurls them into the future. If one believes in cycles then prediction is viable, and profit can be made from 'up' and 'down', as suggested in *Bombardiers*. So why can't we all harness the cycle for our own benefit and make lots of cash? McCloskey's critique of the expert is pertinent here: 'If you're so smart, why ain't you rich?' (1990, p. 4).

Readers know that real time cannot be altered by means of temporal myths and metaphors (such as the cycle). Neither can the damage the markets can cause be delimited by spatial metaphors (as texts like *Bombardiers* reveal). Nevertheless the cycle retains a great deal of appeal for readers and experts alike, both by encouraging risk management and by ordering chaos. Container metaphors, such as those in *Bombardiers* or Smith's highway and channel metaphors provide a degree of stability. Nevertheless, outside language the bad times do have real ripple effects, because money actually circulates outside the boundaries of economics and market discourses. Market corrections are always anticipated, and are more likely to occur in the month of October than any other, simply because October has been given a mythological status.[9] If enough investors believe the warnings, then they become self–fulfilling prophecies (*Weekend Australian* 18 Oct. 1997, p. 11). As we have seen, Batra's text itself stirred up realised prophetic portents. But, 'Why the market should know about 10th anniversaries let alone care about them, is anyone's guess' (*Australian* 29 Oct. 1997, p. 26). The reason is because the market is composed of real people who are not always rational, who have imperfect knowledge, and who are subjects of their own mythology.

The cycle is noticeably punctuated by signals of instability, and this is where the circle metaphor is dropped in favour of metaphors of noise such as 'boom', 'bust', 'crash', and 'burst'. The temporal element of the cycle is suspended, and a different metaphorical translation comes to the fore. Sound plays a significant role in market trading as Wark's chapter 'Noise' suggests (1994, pp. 167–228). Traders respond to mounting noise by increasing their trading volume. In addition, the more indices are reported, the more trading activity increases.

But outside the trading pits, the sound cannot be heard. According to Lewis, we are now experiencing a 'Silent Boom': money is more readily available nowadays, we just do not bother with or catch the fanfares (12 Jan. 1997, p. 10). But like all other aspects of money and the market, distinctions are rarely clear-cut. A special edition of the *Australian Financial Review* described the October 1997 correction as silent *and* loud: crowds watched computer screens outside the stock exchange (29 Oct 1997, p. 2). Apparently they were dumbstruck when shares lost A $1.6 billion in value in the space of twenty minutes. Meanwhile, on the inside, traders were assaulted by a 'wall of sound': shouting, phone calls, and squawk boxes.

According to Schwager (who has interviewed many successful traders in *Market Wizards* and *New Market Wizards*), a good trader has the ability to uncover patterns or shapes in the market, undiscernible to most. Much like Batra, some of these traders feel they have an affinity with the market. Raschke is one of Schwager's only female interviewees; she is known amongst traders for her short-term strategy on (mainly) stock index futures. Raschke makes an aesthetic connection between music and the markets in *New Market Wizards*. 'There is no better satisfaction,' she writes, 'than playing a piece well, whether the *instrument* is the piano or the markets [my emphasis]' (Raschke in Schwager 1994, pp. 309).

[I have] an ability to perceive patterns in the market. I think this aptitude for pattern recognition is probably related to my heavy involvement with music. In college, I had a dual major of economics and musical composition. Musical scores are just symbols and patterns. A musical piece has a definite structure: there are repeating patterns with variations. Analogously, the markets have patterns, which repeat with variations. Musical pieces have quiet interludes, theme development, and a gradual crescendo to a climax. The market counterparts are price consolidations, major trends, and runaway price moves to major tops or bottoms. You must have patience as a musical piece unfolds and patience until a trade sets up. In both music and trading, you do best when you're relaxed, and in both you have to go with the flow. (Raschke in Schwager 1994, pp. 306–37)

Like Batra, she can sense the vibrations of the market peaks and troughs.

The abstract nature of the market enables a range of confusing spatial and temporal metaphors to be applied to it. Time and space are both curbed and let loose. The metaphors I have identified contribute numerous mythological significations for the market. But some texts also personify the market, giving it (usually) human characteristics. Thus, rather than simply constructing comparisons, vivification enables behavioural comparisons that in turn enable market observers to diagnose and predict events.

MR. AND MRS. MARKET

According to another of Schwager's traders, Eckhardt, the market can be a challenger. Experienced traders feel that the markets have certain unique qualities: 'Very often the feeling is that "they are out to get you," which is simply a personalization of the process. The market [behaves] like a tutor who is trying to instill poor trading techniques. Most people learn this lesson only too well' (in Schwager 1994, pp. 134–35).[10]

Characterisations, like metaphor, are evidence of the need to create form out of uncertainty. In addition, these characterisations create an amorphous character out of unpredictable individual actions. In broad terms rationality is a trait attributed to the market as a whole (after Smith), and irrationality is applied to individuals such as Leeson who constitute the market. Wark's critique of market ideology emphasises this point: 'rationality is attributed to the market itself rather than the actors in it' (1994, p. 187). But the idea of the market as a character persists, despite its inconsistencies, and so it is a difficult issue to analyse, because perceptions of the market shift from day to day. Characterisations in this case refer to types of *collective* actions, such as bullish, bearish, or sick; after all the market is composed of numerous people, it is not a single character. An emphasis on rationality ignores situation, and considers that the sum is the same as the parts of which it is made up. It is Kindleberger's belief that 'the action of each individual is rational, or would be, were it not for the fact that others are behaving in the same way' (1978, p. 34). This is where the herd character comes in.

Muddled characterisations conflict somewhat with the idea that bullish and bearish are distinct market moods or tendencies. Bulls move the market up, thrusting with their horns, whereas bears lie low, hibernate. Bulls cannot become bears, so markets can only ever be *either* bullish or bearish, not both. Characterisations are actually descriptions of the movements of 'the herd' (a collective noun that is either erroneously applied to bears, or implies that all market players are animals), and herds are often unpredictable. According to these types of characterisations, 'Financial booms and crashes are exemplary forms of history, for they appear to present an empirical or measurable psychology' (Buchan 1997, p. 107).

Readers must always be aware that the market is composed of people and hence the market only 'goes' where the people composing it determine. But the idea that nobody knows where the market is heading makes the market capricious and unaccountable.

'The market is dominated by waves of sentiment and herd behaviour like anxious sprinters before the starter's gun, everyone breaks at once to get a good start in the race to avoid losses. If this speculative frenzy were confined to Wall Street, we could simply treat it as a macabre form of entertainment but, unfortunately, it is not. The crash will have serious implications for the real economy' (*Australian* 29 Oct. 1997, p. 13). It did in 1997 in Asia, and 1998 in Russia.

One could try to create a unified character out of the market, as some people do. Frequently this involves forcing the market into either a male or a female characterisation. Graham and Dodd, for example, who are admired by Buffett as market–analyst gurus adopt a unified character: Mr. Market. Decidedly male, Mr. Market 'stands for' the whole. We find that 'Mr. Market is very obliging indeed. Every day he tells you what he thinks your interest is worth' (in Lowenstein 1996, p. 36). So Mr. Market is a discernible, obliging character. But he has mood swings, becoming 'gloomy—actually, seriously depressed' (Graham in Lowenstein 1996, p. 152). The market is sometimes buoyant and pumped up. Generally showing great fortitude, the male market is barely moved: nothing scares it (*Wall Street Journal* 1 Nov. 1996, p. C1), it will not 'be spooked' (*Wall Street Journal* 1 Nov. 1996, p. C1). When strong, the market has been 'on steroids', says the *Wall Street Journal* (20 Dec. 1996, p. C2), signifying an overabundance of testosterone and financial muscle. Thus, while man is knowable, he is simultaneously pumped up and unpredictable.

The market is always 'nervous' and 'ultra sensitive', it responds to many voices (and sounds) (Coombs cited in Strange 1989 [1986], p. 39). In other words, the individuals who compose the market each contribute to a volatile infrastructure. The market has temperamental mood swings, comparable to the unpredictability of schizophrenia, and readers are expected to be diagnosticians of the market. Metaphors of bearing down and depression proliferate—'markets suffering the deepest gloom' (*Business Review Weekly* 30 Jan. 1995, p. 48). Depression is generally the result of inactivity, but tennis can usually be called upon to cure moments of lethargy. It counteracts inactivity by encouraging buoyancy, bounce–backs, rallies (*Wall Street Journal* 20 Dec. 1996, p. C1). But too much rallying makes the market '[act] weak at the knees' (*Wall Street Journal* 13 Dec. 1996, p. C1). Like doctors, we observe symptoms as readers, but there are many and varied antidotes (hence the wildly differing panaceas encountered within economic discourse).

In Forster's terms, flat characters do not develop and have few traits. Round characters, on the other hand, develop and change, and their actions are sometimes a cause of surprise. If the market is male, rational, and hence predictable, then it is flat. But the contradiction in this characterisation is that 'the stock market *is* a crowd', and therefore a personality or a unit that is made out of a collection of decisions (Lowenstein 1996, p. 103). So, if we consider the collective, we find a puzzling array of threatening tendencies, amounting to a kind of volatile mixture of irrational actions.

Baker introduces a selection of characterisations of the market as irrational: 'the Market moves like a lunatic head–butting the buttons in a lift; it's like being handcuffed to a blind man who knows where to go but not how to get there. The Market is a black, grey, bull, bear, trading sideways, [it is a] choppy rollercoaster' (1995, p. 5). In other words, the market 'moves in unpredictable ways' (Baker 1995, p. 5).

It is important to note that Baker frames the market around a male agent. Portraits of the market as a single entity, rather than a collection of people, denominate, and thus the market is seen as male. In terms of personalities, the market is metonymic (as we have seen in one respect in *Bombardiers*). Often however, a collection of men is perceived to act as one obscure woman. The irrational aspect of the market persona is unpredictable, mysterious, 'like a woman' (Smith 1968, p. 20). 'The market is like a beautiful woman—endlessly fascinating, endlessly complex, always changing, always mystifying' (a fund manager cited in Smith 1968, p. 20). For the generation born in the late twentieth century, 'the Market has been a kind of parent. Sometimes the wicked stepmother, sometimes the fairy godmother' (Baker 1995, p. 1). Castells claims that the offspring of the market is profit: '*global financial markets, and their networks of management, are the actual collective capitalist, the mother of all accumulations* [Castells' emphasis]' (1998, p. 343). The market as woman is infinitely complex and indeterminate, perhaps corresponding more with market mythology than its male counterpart.

When we read that 'markets are always changing, and they are always the same', our understanding is both obscured and explained (Schwager 1994, p. xi).

The market as we have seen in the analysis of metaphor is constantly shifting: it has a space, but no place, and it is constantly active and outstretched, errant, and imprisoned. In a similar vein, the market is inconsistently personified, and its traits vary wildly; on the one hand it is like an umpire, ruthless in some instances, but always fair and just, as Strange sardonically remarks (1989 [1986], p. 76). The characterisation of fairness relates to the invisible hand hypothesis: ultimately the market will correct itself according to reasonable supply and demand balance, so that 'markets cure their own diseases' (Mayer 1993, p. 242). Overvalued shares will ultimately fall, as they have been doing in Asia since October 1997. In these instances the market is viewed as a sick patient: either with 'indigestion' (*Wall Street Journal* 16 Aug. 1996, p. C1), or 'if Wall Street sneezes, Australian shares catch a cold' (*Bulletin* 22 Jul. 1997, p. 16). The market is a character analysed in order to explain the health and 'mood' of economies and the nation. If the financial markets are healthy, then the economy must be and vice versa.

In numerous instances the market is perceived to privilege money value over and above other kinds of value (such as honesty). Measuring value in purely pecuniary terms enables shifting benchmarks, because money itself has a constantly changing value in our contemporary markets. In this way, monetary value has acquired an arbitrary nature, and this is heavily resisted by many observers. For Buchan, 'Value is mere sensation and we feel a generous action is precious, and a sudden view of mountains and a handsome face, and such sensations of non–money value have survived as painful residues' (1997, p. 280). Sensation, material, and the experiential are frequently perceived to be more valuable than abstract and capricious forms of currency.

Adam Smith believes that 'a series of market decisions does add up, believe it or not, to a kind of personality portrait' (in Lowenstein 1996, p. 60)—an untenable assertion in relation to the market as I have shown from this diverse selection of characterisations. Smith upholds this double–edged analysis when he says that 'the crowd is a composite personality. In fact, *a crowd of men acts like a single woman*' (1968, p. 23). At times the market is a mystifying female, and at others a rational male. As with so many of the texts I have considered in this work, no representation is ever settled; in fact, contradiction seems to be the imperative behind money's continuing vitality. As Nietzsche says of Apollo and Dionysus, there is always an 'antagonism' between the surface figure (the rationalised male concept) and the nonimagistic (the unknowable female) (1967 [1872], p. 33). It is precisely because of the conflict between description (which attempts to pin down the market) and its counterpart, the uncontrollable, that I have had enormous difficulty knowing where to finish points in this section. The processes of equivalences and conflicts are endless, like the economic cycle, with form and concept constantly playing hide and seek. The market, like money itself, is paradoxically represented as woman and man: both secretive, hidden, and mysterious (the feminine, and the Dionysian), and rational, a knowable figure (the masculine, and the Apollinian). But the tendency is to try to make the Apollinian dominate, and this impulse is intrinsic to money's mythology. In a mythological system, characters play a vital role, but the characterisation of incomprehensible phenomena (such as the market) reveals a tendency towards figuration. What these characterisations in fact do is demonstrate a degree of confusion and uncertainty about the roles of money and its markets, whilst simultaneously forming a portrait of our culture.

NOTES

1. As this feature is twenty seven pages long, it is too lengthy to quote in full. References to the article in this section will only include page numbers.

2. As I have explained, some heroic characters are rich and strong, and (by implication) rational, whereas Leeson is weak minded and prone to attacks of nausea.

3. Kurtzman maintains that these changes are largely due to 'Melamed's efforts' (1993, p. 149): 'Melamed's decision to trade currency futures was based on the change in the nature of money' (1993, p. 149).

4. A spot is 'a foreign exchange market term meaning "now" or "immediate" and refers to the current, prevailing rate of exchange, as opposed to a "forward" rate' (Carew 1988, p. 227).

5. The full sentence reads: 'The material consequences of this apparently abstract digression on time and capital are increasingly felt in economies and daily lives around the world: recurrent monetary crises, ushering in an era of structural economic instability and actually jeopardizing European integration; the inability of capital investment to anticipate the future, thus undermining incentives for productive investment; the wrecking of companies, and of their jobs, regardless of performance because of sudden, unforeseen changes in the financial environment in which they operate; the increasing gap between profits in the production of goods and services and rents generated in the sphere of circulation, thus shifting an increasing share of world savings to financial gambling; the growing risks for pension funds and private insurance liabilities, thus introducing a question mark into the hard–bought security of working people around the world; the dependence of entire economies, and particularly those of developing countries, on movements of capital largely determined by subjective perception and speculative turbulence; the destruction in the collective experience of societies of the deferred–gratification pattern of behavior, in favor of the "quick–buck" common ideology, emphasizing individual gambling with life and the economy; and the fundamental damage to the social perception of the correspondence between production and reward, work and meaning, ethics and wealth' (Castells 1996, p. 436).

6. References to the text in this section will only include page numbers.

7. Mayer tells us that new financial instruments were invented every week in the late 1980s, and some of these were only traded 'a handful of times' (1993, p. 172).

8. Baker mentions an incident when the Tokyo stock market dropped more than $5 billion in two minutes when the singer Lonnie Donnegan's death was announced. 'Ask a Japanese person to say "Lonnie Donnegan". Then ask him to say "Ronald Reagan". *That's why*' (1995, pp. 2–3).

9. The markets 'crashes' of 1929, 1987, and 1997 all occurred in October.

10. According to Schwager, at the time he was interviewing Eckhardt, the latter 'was working on a book about the nature of time. [H]is basic premise is that the passage of time is an illusion' (1994, p. 104). His pseudo-paranoia about the market is itself recognisably illusory.

Coda:
Throwing Sand in the Wheels

Money has a resounding mythology, that echoes and amplifies the centrality of money in our culture. Everywhere we turn, money values determine our thinking, because of the returns inherent in the ubiquity of money's signs. I have shown how—in an eclectic range of texts—money is historicised, naturalised, and characterised, partly because it lacks reference. Money's mythologies enforce common–sensical, but distorted, sets of significations from which there is little escape in our culture.

The financial market is as unregulated as its tropes, perhaps because mythologies respond to, as well as structure, ideologies in the world outside language. Barthes concludes his *Mythologies* with the assertion that 'mythology is certain to participate in the making of the world' (1989 [1957], p. 170). My concluding remarks focus on the way that money's mythologies (as I have shown them) do have an effect outside discourse. The money sign and its various significations are not necessarily true or false, but they do '[sanction] actions' (Lakoff and Johnson 1980, p. 158). Money's mythologies support the naturalisation of the market, which is not necessarily historically justified. Money has far–reaching effects, because it is poorly *and* freely delineated—it is a bridge, a cushion, as well as a designator of character.

Money is thought to be able to change our lives, even though it is nothing but an idea that 'operates according to the meanings we attach to it' (Rowe 1998, p. 382), and currently most meanings are economic, so many people view the world according to money's significations. Western cultures, as well as readers' and traders' behaviour, are measured by metaphorical rises and falls in the GDP, the GNP, and national current accounts. Indices such as the Dow Jones, the Hang Seng, the Nikkei Dow, the consumer price index, and the retail price index are also dominant cultural yardsticks, which are frequently privileged above people's everyday fundamental needs. But money alone is an inadequate determinant of culture.

The financial markets, upon which readers depend for their monetary well-being, are built on an insubstantial mythological foundation. As Derrida explains it, 'The focus or the source of myth are always shadows or virtualities which are elusive, unactualizable, and nonexistent in the first place. Everything begins with structure, configuration, or relationship' (1993 [1978], p. 286). Leeson obliquely acknowledges money's virtuality, and its wavering configuration, when he remarks, 'all the money we dealt with was unreal: abstract numbers which flashed across screens or jumped across the trading pit with a flurry of hands' (1996, p. 56). In other words, money has little stability; it is as easily lost as it is made in the financial market. Money provides us with numerous structures and relations, such as the capitalist, the economy, and the villain. 'And yet, this is what we must seek: a reconciliation between reality and men, between description and explanation, between object and knowledge' (Barthes 1989 [1957], p. 174).

From an economic viewpoint money has an openness; as a 'medium of exchange' there is no difference between an index rate future, a coin, or salt—each of these can be called 'money'. The openness of the money sign supports the structures of the free market system and money's metaphorical nature has significant implications outside discourse for money–management. The free market philosophy essentially loosens monetary bounds, materially and conceptually. Whilst money is not an object that existed prior to language, there is little relief from its signs and value systems. For some, such as Soros, money literally is no object—his hedge fund can gamble with loaned money, which he puts to work on national currencies. His gains far exceed necessity, and so money is ideologically immaterial to him.

Since the deregulation of the market in the 1970s, the financial markets have generally discarded readers' interests, in a fit of over–creativity, and the inventiveness of people within the market, such as Melamed, is unprecedented. Smith's economic wheel no longer simply refers to circulation. We now have Daedalian economies characterised by exponential growth: the Dow Jones index has grown elevenfold in a very short span of human history, and meanwhile the world is a finite ecological space. Economics seems to have lost its (etymological) economic restraint. The wheel is either spiralling out of control, or needs reinventing, because its axes benefit a very small number of people, and most mythologies I have identified, particularly in my final chapter, are recreated by, and supportive of, the unequal and disparate effects of the market.

Perhaps we could rethink 'economic rationalism' (for lack of better terminology), on the grounds that it is supported by nothing more than mythologies that lend the system a natural and historical justification. The illusion that the market is self–regulating is fostered by its naturalising metaphors, such as the cycle. But the market is constructed out of unregulated sets of second–order systems, which have no real foundation. Several commentators I have mentioned, such as Kurtzman, Strange, and Partnoy, believe that intervention should be called for, because innovations, born out of deregulation, are not monitored. 'As the derivatives market has grown, it has become more volatile and dangerous [and] current proposals before Congress are for *less,* not more, regulation' (Partnoy 1997, p. 252). But the *Australian Financial Review* resignedly points out that 'markets will always move up and down. When they do, there will be those who call for sand to be put in the wheels' (30 Oct. 1997, p. 20). I endorse Partnoy's position, because my work has enabled me to identify an unregulated monetary system (mythologically and legislatively), which like a runaway train needs to have (metaphorical) sand thrown in its wheels to halt its progress. Crashes such as the one in 1987 occurred, according to the *Sydney Daily Telegraph*, because 'we had no point of reference' (29 Oct. 1997, p. 11), but what the newspaper fails to realise is that money never did have a reference. The money market is currently an excessively open system, and its metaphors parallel its indeterminacy, but we continue to believe in its efficacy, because characters like Soros reinforce money's ideologies.

The funds used in derivatives, as well as hedge funds, have to come from somewhere, and as Partnoy explains, 'Morgan Stanley's [various trades] may originally have been from a check you wrote to make your mortgage payment' (1997, p. 218). It is the general reader's money—whether he or she be in Mexico, the United States or Japan—that is gambled with in the markets. An article in *Le Monde Diplomatique* points out that many banks are now investing money deposited by readers in volatile markets (Nov. 1998, p. 3). Therefore, 'Financial crisis is threatening to spread to the real economy', which means repercussions for you and me (*Le Monde Diplomatique* Nov. 1998, p. 3).

I have shown how many texts mythologise the rich, often at the expense of the reader, who is subordinate to the mythologies of economic and cultural instrumentalism. A recently released text, entitled *The Millionaire Next Door*, for example, has apparently 'hit a nerve across the United States, smashing onto the bestseller lists in *The New York Times*, *Business Week* and the *Wall Street Journal*. It looks at who the rich are, what they do, where they shop, what they drive, how they invest, where their ancestors come from, how they got rich and how to become one of them' (*Mary Ryan Bookshop Good Book Guide* 1998, p. 12). Furthermore, the text's cover indicates that it was written by Thomas J. Stanley, Ph.D., and William D. Danko, Ph.D., thereby lending its tenets a degree of authority. As a culture, we continue to laud the rich, and market players who make a killing from trading, such as Buffett. And the consequences of this aspect of money's mythology is highlighted in *Le Monde Diplomatique*: 'Now here's a statistic you might have missed. The joint wealth of the world's three richest individuals is greater than the combined domestic product of the 48 poorest countries—a quarter of all the world's states' (Nov. 1998, p. 1). We admire the rich at the expense of a focus on the poor, and in this sense, not only does the mythology support obscene inequality, it also, as Barthes maintains, impoverishes consciousness (1989 [1957], p. 154), as well as immobilising 'values, life, destiny, etc.' (1989 [1957], p. 167).

Every single text I have cited in this work has contributed to money's mythologies, be it Marx's butterfly, the TAB advertisement, or Buchan's railway-shunting yard. Readers can either accept money's mythologies, or 'demystify' them by unravelling their construction, and questioning their effects (Barthes 1989 [1957], p. 171). What many commentators neglect to notice when they are confused by the complexities and the distortions of money's mythologies is that 'only human beings know about money. We invented it' (Rowe 1998, p. 12), and we are in the middle of this constant process. It has not been my intention to suggest alternative systems; I have simply exposed some of money's mythological significations for readers. Demystification, and regulation of the money markets are possible, and they do not entail an arrest of cultural creativity.

Perhaps only the experience of severe economic problems would instigate an interrogation of money's spiralling mythologies. If we question what mythologies people sanction in our everyday cultural experience, we can identify both the flimsiness and the unwarranted importance of money's mythologies in the early twenty–first century, and not be seduced by the ideas that money itself has an ability to transform our lives, and that it alone can cure our ills.

References

Adams, D. (Community Liaison Officer, Channel 7, Queensland). Letter to author, 15 Apr. 1997.

Adams, P. (radio). 'Late Night Live' ABC Radio National, Australia, 18 Aug. 1997.

Aristotle. *The Rhetoric and the Poetics of Aristotle*, trans. W. Rhys Roberts and E. P. J. Corbett, the Modern Library: New York, 1984.

Armstrong, D. M. *Belief, Truth and Knowledge*, Cambridge University Press: Cambridge, 1973.

Attwood, B. (ed.). *In the Age of Mabo: History, Aborigines and Australia*, Allen and Unwin: St. Leonards, NSW, 1996.

Australian. 15 Jul. 1997, p. 14.

————.29 Oct. 1997, p. 13.

————.29 Oct. 1997, p. 26.

————.18 Nov. 1998, p. 12.

Australian Financial Review. 8 Jun. 1995, p. 17.

————.'The Brave New World of Leverage', 7 Sept. 1995, p. 32.

————.21 Sept. 1995, p. 28.

————.21 Sept. 1995, p. 45.

————.'Special Report: Financial Computing', 25 Sept. 1995, pp. 27–33.

————.19 Aug. 1997, p. 44.

————.28 Oct. 1997, p. 12.

————.28 Oct. 1997, p. 16.

————.29 Oct. 1997, p. 2

————.30 Oct. 1997, p. 20

————.14–15 Mar. 1998, p. 6.

Baker, M. *A Fool and his Money,* Orion: London, 1995.

Barthes, R. *S/Z,* trans. R. Miller, Hill and Wang: New York, 1974.

————.*Image—Music —Text*, trans. S. Heath, Fontana: London, 1982 [1977].

————.*The Rustle of Language,* trans. R. Howard, Blackwell: Oxford, 1986 [1968].

————.*Mythologies,* trans. A. Lavers, Grafton: London, 1989 [1957].

Batra, R. *The Great Depression of 1990,* Simon and Schuster: New York, 1987.

Baudrillard, J. *Jean Baudrillard: Selected Writings*, ed. M. Poster, Polity Press: Cambridge, 1989 [1972].

Bauman, Z. *Intimations of Postmodernity*, Routledge: New York, 1992.

Begg, D. et al. *Economics,* 3rd ed., McGraw–Hill: London, 1991.

Benjamin, W. *Illuminations,* ed. H. Arendt, trans. H. Zohn, Schocken Books: New York, 1969.

Bennetts, R. *The Stockmarket as Easy as ABC*, ABC Books: Sydney, 1995.

Blanchard, M. E. *Description: Sign, Self, Desire*, Mouton: The Hague, 1980.

Bloom, W. *Money, Heart and Mind*, Penguin: Harmondsworth, 1996.

Bolla, P. de. *The Discourse of the Sublime*, Basil Blackwell: Oxford, 1989.

Bradley, A. C. *Shakespearean Tragedy*, Macmillan: London, 1971 [1904].

Bretton, H. L. *The Power of Money: A Political–Economic Analysis,* State University of New York Press: Albany, 1980.

Bronson, P. *Bombardiers,* Secker and Warburg: London, 1995.

Bruce, J. B. *Money of Australia*, Kangaroo Press: Kenthurst, NSW, 1992.

Brummett, B. 'Popular Economic Apocalyptic: The Case of Ravi Batra', *Journal of Popular Culture*, vol. 24, no. 2, pp. 153–63, 1990.

Buchan, J. 'Fie On't!', *London Review of Books*, 23 Mar, p. 24. 1995.

————.*High Latitudes*, Harvill Press: London, 1996.

————.*Frozen Desire: An Inquiry into the Meaning of Money*, Picador: London, 1997.

Buffett, W. *Warren Buffett Speaks: Wit and Wisdom from the World's Greatest Investor*, ed. J. C. Lowe, Wiley: New York, 1997.

Bulletin. 'Back in the Fast Lane', 22 Jul. 1997, pp. 14–17.

————.4 Nov. 1997, front page.

Business Review Weekly. 30 Jan. 1995, p. 28.

————.'How Maximum Pessimism Turns up Trumps', 30 Jan. 1995, p. 48.

————.20 Jan. 1997, p. 33.

Business Week. 'The Future of Money', 12 Jun. 1995, pp. 36–49.

————.'The Burden of Being a Misunderstood Monopolist', 22 Nov. 1999, p. 48.

Calder, J. *Heroes: From Byron to Guevara*, Hamish Hamilton: London, 1977.

Carew, E. *The Language of Money*, Allen and Unwin: St. Leonards, NSW, 1988.

Cassirer, E. *Language and Myth*, trans. S. K. Langer, Dover Publications: New York, 1953 [1946].

Castells, M. *The Information Age: Economy, Society and Culture. The Rise of the Network Society*, Blackwell: Oxford, 1996.

————.*End of the Millennium*, Blackwell: Oxford, 1998.

Cawelti, J. G. *Adventure, Mystery, Romance*, University of Chicago Press: Chicago, 1976.

Chambers, R. *Story and Situation: Narrative Seduction and the Power of Fiction*, University of Minneapolis Press: Minneapolis, Minn. 1984.

Chatman, S. *Story and Discourse*, Cornell University Press: Ithaca, N.Y., 1980.

Clason, G. S. *The Richest Man in Babylon*, Signet: New York, 1988.

Courier Mail. 29 Jan. 1997, p. 17.

————.'Goodbye Greed', 18 Oct. 1997, pp. 1, 4.

————.29 Oct. 1997, p. 41.

————.29 Oct. 1997, p. 42.

————.3 Oct. 1998, p. 61

Crawford, T. *The Secret Life of Money: How Money Can Be Food for the Soul*, Allworth Press: New York, 1994.

Cribb, J. *Collins Eyewitness Guides: MONEY*, Collins: North Ryde, NSW, 1990.

Davies, G. A. *History of Money*, with foreword by G. Tonypandy, University of Wales: Cardiff, 1995.

Davies, H. *Living on the Lottery*, Little Brown: London, 1996.

Derrida, J. 'Structure, Sign, and Play', in *Writing and Difference*, trans. A. Bass, Routledge: London, 1993 [1978].

Dictionary of Modern Economics. MIT Press: Cambridge, Mass., 1986.

Digicash. http://www.digicash.nl, http://193.78.226.2/, http://www.digicash.com/, 1995.

Dodd, N. *The Sociology of Money*, Polity Press: Cambridge, 1994.

Economist (survey). 'World Economy: Fear of Finance', 19 Sept. 1992, pp. 5–44.

————.10 Sept. 1994, p. 76.

————.'So Much for the Cashless Society', 26 Nov. 1994, pp. 23–27.

————.'Let the Digital Age Bloom', 25 Feb. 1995, pp. 13–14.

————.11 Mar. 1995, p. 13.

————.18 Mar. 1995, p. 14.

————.1 Apr. 1995, p. 74.

————.'Wall Street: Survey', 15 Apr. 1995, pp. 3–30.

————.'Wall Street and the Economy: Look Out Below', 6 Jul. 1996, pp. 21–23.

————.'Wall Street's Twists and Turns', 20 Jul. 1996, pp. 63–64.

————.21 Dec. 1996, p. 12.

————.21 Dec. 1996, p. 14.

————.21 Dec. 1996, p. 17.

————.21 Dec. 1996, p. 50.

————.The Visible Hand: Big Government is Still in Charge', 20 Sept. 1997, p. 17.

————.1 Nov. 1997, p. 15.

————.1 Nov. 1997, p. 82.

Eleven AM (video recording). Channel 7, Queensland, 28 Oct. 1997.

Eliade, M. *The Myth of the Eternal Return*, Princeton University Press: Princeton, N.J., 1971 [1954].

————.(ed.) *Encyclopedia of Religion,* Macmillan: New York, 1987.

Emmison, M. '"The Economy": Its Emergence in Media Discourse', in *Language, Image, Media*, ed. H. Davies and P. Walton, Blackwell: Oxford, 1983.

Fay, S. *The Collapse of Barings*, Random House: London, 1996.

Fitzgerald F. S. *The Great Gatsby*, Penguin: Ringwood, 1990 [1926].

Fontana Dictionary of Modern Thought. 2nd ed., Fontana: London, 1990.

Forceville, C. *Pictorial Metaphor in Advertising*, Routledge: London, 1996.

Forster, E. M. *Aspects of the Novel*, Edward Arnold: London, 1974 [1927].

Frankel, S. H. *Money: Two Philosophies*, Blackwell: Oxford, 1977.

Frey, S. *The Takeover*, Michael Joseph: London, 1995.

————.*The Vulture Fund*, Michael Joseph: London, 1996.

————.*The Inner Sanctum*, Michael Joseph: London, 1997.

Friedman, M. 'Old Wine in New Bottles', in *The Future of Economics*, ed. J. D. Hey, Blackwell: Oxford, 1992.

Galbraith, J. G. *Money: Whence It Came, Where It Went*, Bantam: New York, 1975.

Ganssman, H. 'Money—A Symbolically Generalized Medium of Communication? On the Concept of Money in Recent Sociology', *Economy and Society*, vol. 17, no. 3, Aug., pp. 285–315, 1988.

Gapper, J., and Denton, N. *All That Glitters: The Fall of Barings*, Hamish Hamilton: London, 1996.

Garten, J. E. 'The Gradual Revolution', *New York Times Book Review*, 8 Feb., p. 7, 1998.

Gates, B. *The Road Ahead*, co-written by N. Myhrvold and P. Rinearson, Penguin: Harmondsworth, 1996 [1995].

Geertz, C. *The Interpretation of Cultures*, Basic Books: New York, 1973.

Genette, G. *Narrative Discourse*, trans. J. E. Lewin, Cornell University Press: Ithaca, N.Y., 1980.

Glaser, H. 'Theory of Metaphor', paper presented to University of Queensland, 20 March 1997.

Gold Lotto (advertisement). May 1997, Brisbane.

Gross, D. *Forbes Greatest Business Stories of All Time,* John Wiley and Sons: New York, 1996.

Gross, D. S. 'Tales of Obscene Power: Money, Culture, and the Historical Fictions of E. L. Doctorow', in *Money Talks: Language and Lucre in American Fiction,* ed. R. Male, University of Oklahoma Press: Oklahoma City, 1980.

Hagstrom, R. G. *The Warren Buffett Way,* Wiley: New York, 1994.

Hamilton, A. *The Financial Revolution,* Penguin: Harmondsworth, 1986.

Hart, K. 'Heads or Tails? Two Sides of the Coin', *Man,* vol. 21, pp. 637–56, 1986.

Harvey, D. *The Condition of Postmodernity,* Blackwell: Oxford, 1994.

Heyne, P. *The Economic Way of Thinking,* 7th ed., Macmillan: New York, 1994.

Hinckley, K. and Hinckley, B. *American Best Sellers,* Indiana University Press: Bloomington, 1989.

Hindess, B. 'Actors and Social Relations', in *Sociological Theory in Transition,* ed. M. L. Wardell and S. P. Turner, Allen and Unwin: Boston, 1986.

Hourihan, M. *Deconstructing the Hero,* Routledge: London, 1997.

Hunt, L., and Heinrich, K. *Barings Lost: Nick Leeson and the Collapse of Barings plc.,* Allen and Unwin: St. Leonards, NSW, 1996.

Hunter, I. 'Reading Character', *Southern Review,* vol. 16, no. 2, pp. 226–43, 1983.

Jackson, K. 'Ten Money Notes', *Granta* vol. 49, Winter, pp. 67–89, 1994.

———.(ed.). Introduction, in *The Oxford Book of Money,* Oxford University Press: Oxford, 1995.

Jensen, J., and Pauly, J. J. 'Imagining the Audience: Losses and Gains in Cultural Studies', in *Cultural Studies in Question,* ed. M. Ferguson and P. Golding, Sage: London, 1997.

Johnson, M. *The Body in the Mind,* University of Chicago Press: Chicago, 1987.

Kain, C. *The Story of Money,* Troll Associates: Mahwah, N.J., 1994.

Kermode, F. *The Genesis of Secrecy,* Harvard University Press: Cambridge, Mass., 1979.

Kimsey, S. 'The Virtual Flight of the Cyber Trader', *Euromoney,* Jun., pp. 45–46, 1994.

Kindleberger, C. P. *Manias, Panics, and Crashes,* Basic Books: New York, 1978.

Klamer, A. 'As if Economists and their Subject were Rational', in *The Rhetoric of the Human Sciences,* ed. J. S. Nelson, A. Megill, and D. McCloskey, University of Wisconsin Press: Madison, 1987.

Kurtzman, J. *The Death of Money,* Simon and Schuster: New York, 1993.

Lakoff, G. 'Contemporary Theory of Metaphor', in *Metaphor and Thought,* ed. A. Ortony, Cambridge University Press: Cambridge, 1993.

Lakoff, G., and Johnson, M. *Metaphors We Live By*, University of Chicago Press: Chicago, 1980.

Lane, R. E. *The Market Experience*, Cambridge University Press: New York, 1991.

Lash J. *The Hero: Manhood and Power*, Thames and Hudson: London, 1995.

Lash, S., and Urry, J. *Economies of Space and Signs*, Sage: Thousand Oaks, Calif., 1994.

Leeson, N. *Rogue Trader*, co-written by E. Whitley, Little Brown: London, 1996.

Le Monde Diplomatique, Nov. 1998, p. 1.

————.Nov. 1998, p. 3.

Levi–Strauss, C. *Myth and Meaning*, Routledge: London, 1978.

————. *The Raw and the Cooked*, trans. J. Weightman and D. Weightman, Farrar, Strauss and Giroux: New York, 1979.

Lewis, M. *Liar's Poker*, Hodder and Stoughton: London, 1989.

————.'The Silent Boom', *New York Times Sunday Magazine*, 12 Jan., pp. 10–11, 1997.

Light, J. F. 'Review: "Wall Street in the American Novel by Wayne W. Westbrook"', *American Literature*, vol. 53, no. 3, pp. 556–58, 1981.

Lindemann, B. 'Readers and Mindscapes', *Journal of Literary Semantics*, vol. 22, no. 3, Dec., pp. 186–206, 1993.

Litt, T. 'Adventures in Capitalism', in *Class Work*, ed. M. Bradbury, Hodder and Stoughton: London, 1995.

Lodge, D. 'The Rhetoric of *Hard Times*', in *Twentieth Century Interpretations of Hard Times*, ed. P. E. Gray, Prentice–Hall: Englewood Cliffs, N.J., 1969.

Lowenstein, R. *Buffett: The Making of an American Capitalist,* Orion: London, 1996.

McCloskey, D. *If You're So Smart*, University of Chicago Press: Chicago, 1990.

————. *Knowledge and Persuasion in Economics*, Cambridge University Press: Cambridge, 1994.

————.'Metaphor in the Dismal Science', paper presented to *Narrative and Metaphor conference*, Auckland University, New Zealand, July 1996.

Mackay, C. *Extraordinary Popular Delusions and the Madness of Crowds*, with an introduction by M. S. Fridson, ed. M. S. Fridson, John Wiley and Sons: New York, 1996 [1841].

McLellan, D. *Karl Marx: A Biography*, Macmillan: London, 1995.

McManamy, J. *CRASH!:Corporate Australia Fights for Its Life,* Pan: Sydney, NSW, 1988.

Maestro, B. *The Story of Money*, Clarion: New York, 1993.

Male, R. (ed.). *Money Talks: Language and Lucre in American Fiction*, with a foreword by R. Schliefer, University of Oklahoma Press: Oklahoma City, 1980.

Marx, K. *Capital,* vol. 1, trans. B. Fowkes, Penguin: Harmondsworth, 1990 [1867].

————.*Capital,* vol. 3, trans. D. Fernbach, Penguin: Harmondsworth, 1991 [1894].

————.*Capital,* vol. 2, trans. D. Fernbach, Penguin: Harmondsworth, 1992 [1885].

Mary Ryan Bookshop Good Book Guide. Issue 51, Dec., p. 12, 1998.

Mayer, M. *Nightmare on Wall Street,* Simon and Schuster: New York, 1993.

Mauss, M. *The Gift: Forms and Functions of Exchange in Archaic Societies,* W. W. Norton and Co: New York, 1967.

Melamed, L. *Escape to the Futures,* John Wiley and Sons: New York, 1996.

Messent, P. *New Readings of the American Novel,* Macmillan: London, 1990.

Millman, G. J. *Around the World on a Trillion Dollars a Day,* Bantam: London, 1995.

Moffitt, M. *The World's Money,* Simon and Schuster: New York, 1983.

Money of the World. Issue 1, Orbis Publishing: London, 1998.

Mueller, I. (Chief Executive, Channel Nine, Queensland). Letter to author, 2 Apr. 1997.

Negroponte, N. *Being Digital,* Hodder and Stoughton: London, 1996.

New Republic. 'Unsweet Smell of Success', 18 Oct., pp. 29–38, 1999.

New Scientist. 'Money Is Dead: Long Live E-Money', 8 Apr., pp. 26–30, 1995.

New York Times. 'Interest in the Divine', 9 May 1997, p. B1.

————.28 Feb. 1998, p. D3.

————.'What Goes Up May Keep Going Up', 5 Apr. 1998, p. 3.

Nietzsche, F. *The Birth of Tragedy,* in *The Birth of Tragedy and The Case of Wagner,* trans. W. Kaufmann, Vintage Books: New York, 1967 [1872].

————.*The Gay Science,* trans. W. Kaufmann, Vintage Books: New York, 1974 [1882].

————.'On Truth and Lie in a Nonmoral Sense', in *Philosophy and Truth,* ed. and trans. D. Breazeale, Humanities Press: Atlantic Highlands, N.J., 1992 [1873].

Park, U. K. 'East Asian Economic Crisis in Global Context', paper given to *Asia Crisis and Its Implications for Australia Conference,* Griffith University, Qld., 4 March 1998.

Parkin, S. *Trade Secret,* HarperCollins: Sydney, 1996.

Partnoy, F. *F.I.A.S.C.O.,* Norton: New York, 1997.

Perlman, E. *Three Dollars,* Picador: Sydney, NSW, 1998.

Philips, D., and Tomlinson, A. 'Homeward Bound', in *Come on Down?* ed. D. Strinati and S. Wagg, Routledge: London, 1992.

Propp, V. *Morphology of the Folktale,* University of Texas Press: Austin, Texas, 1968.

Rabinowitz, P. J. 'The Turn of the Glass Key: Popular Fiction as Reading Strategy', *Critical Inquiry*, vol. 11, Mar., pp. 418–31, 1985.

Radway, J. 'Women Read the Romance: The Interaction of Text and Context', *Feminist Studies*, vol. 9, no. 1, Spring, pp. 53–78, 1983.

Rawnsley, J. *Going for Broke: Nick Leeson and the Collapse of Barings Bank*, HarperCollins: London, 1996.

Reid, I. *Narrative Exchanges*, Routledge: London, 1992.

Rhinehart, L. *The Search for the Dice Man*, HarperCollins: London, 1994.

Ricoeur, P. *The Rule of Metaphor*, trans. R. Czerny, Routledge: London, 1986 [1978].

Ridpath, M. *Free to Trade*, Heinemann: London, 1995.

———.*Trading Reality*, Heinemann: London, 1996.

———.*The Marketmaker*, Michael Joseph: London, 1998.

Rimmon–Kenan, S. *Narrative Fiction: Contemporary Poetics,* Methuen: New York, 1983.

Roberts, J. *$1000 Billion a Day*, HarperCollins: London, 1995.

Rohn, W. Goldman. *The Microsoft File: The Secret Case against Bill Gates*, Times Books: Hong Kong, 1998.

Rorty, A. O. 'A Literary Postcript: Characters, Persons, Selves, Individuals', in *Identity, Character and Morality: Essays in Moral Psychology*, ed. O. Flanagan and A. O. Rorty, MIT Press: Cambridge, Mass., 1990.

Rowe, D. *The Real Meaning of Money*, HarperCollins: London, 1998.

Saul, J. Ralston. *The Unconscious Civilisation*, Penguin: Ringwood, 1997.

Schon, D. 'Generative Metaphor and Social Policy', in *Metaphor and Thought*, ed. A. Ortony, Cambridge University Press: Cambridge, 1993.

Schwager, J. D. *The New Market Wizards*, HarperCollins: New York, 1994.

Shell, M. *Money, Language & Thought*, University of California Press: Berkeley, 1982.

Sieburth, R. 'In Pound We Trust: The Economy of Poetry/The Poetry of Economics', *Critical Enquiry*, vol. 14, Autumn, pp. 142–72, 1987.

Simmel, G. *The Philosophy of Money*, trans. T. Bottomore and D. Frisby, Routledge: London, 1990 [1900].

Skinner, R. Introduction, in *The Wealth of Nations* by A. Smith, Penguin: Harmondsworth, 1979.

Smith, Adam [pseudo]. *The Money Game*, Random House: New York, 1968.

Smith, A. *An Inquiry into the Nature and Causes of the Wealth of Nations*, Penguin: Harmondsworth, 1986 [1776].

Smith, R. 'Money: Ever Wonder Where the Phrase, "In God We Trust," Came From?' *Millionaire,* vol. 2. no. 1, pp. 14–16, 1997.

Soros, G. *Soros on Soros*, John Wiley and Sons: New York, 1995.

Spooner, J. D. *Sex & Money*, Houghton Mifflin: Boston, 1985.

Strange, S. *Casino Capitalism*, Blackwell: Oxford, 1989 [1986].

Sutherland, K. 'Fictional Economies: Adam Smith, Walter Scott and the Nineteenth-Century Novel', *English Literary History*, vol. 54, no. 1, pp. 97–127, 1987.

Sydney Daily Telegraph. 29 Oct. 1997, p. 11.

TAB (advertisement). April 1997, Brisbane.

Thomson, D. 'follow the money', *Film Comment*, July/August, pp. 20–25, 1995.

Thomson, F. P. *Money in the Computer Age*, Pergamon Press: Oxford, 1968.

Time. 14 Sept. 1998, front cover.

————.14 Sept. 1998, p. 48.

Toffler, A. *Third Wave*, Collins: London, 1980.

————.*Power Shift*, Bantam: New York, 1990.

Trading Places (motion picture). Dir. J. Landis, CIC, 1983.

Veblen, T. *The Theory of the Leisure Class*, Unwin: London, 1970 [1899].

Vico, G. *Vico: Selected Writings*, ed. and trans. L. Pompa, Cambridge University Press: Cambridge, 1982.

Wallace J., and Erickson, J. *Hard Drive: Bill Gates and the Making of the Microsoft Empire*, John Wiley and Sons: New York, 1993.

Wall Street (motion picture). Dir. O. Stone, CBS Fox, 1987.

Wall Street Journal, 16 Aug. 1996, p. C1.

————.27 Sept. 1996, p. C2.

————.11 Oct. 1996, p. C19.

————.18 Oct. 1996, p. A7A.

————.25 Oct. 1996, p. A9D.

————.25 Oct. 1996, p. B10.

————.1 Nov. 1996, front page.

————.1 Nov. 1996, p. C1.

————.8 Nov. 1996, p. B5A.

————.11 Nov. 1996, front page.

————.15 Nov. 1996, p. C2.

————.13 Dec. 1996, p. C1.

————.20 Dec. 1996, p. C1

————.20 Dec. 1996, p. C2.

Wang, X. 'Derrida, Husserl, and the Structural Affinity between the "Text" and the "Market" ', *New Literary History*, vol. 26, pp. 261–82, 1995.

Wark, M. *Virtual Geography*, Indiana University Press: Bloomington, 1994.

Weekend Australian. 18 Oct. 1997, p. 1.

————.18 Oct, 1997, p. 11.

————.18 Oct. 1997, p. 20.

Wells, L. 'Judith Williamson, *Decoding Advertisements*', in *Reading into Cultural Studies*, ed. M. Barker and A. Beezer, Routledge: London, 1992.

Were, J. B. and Son. 'Australian Economic and Investment Outlook', March Quarter 1998, p. 62.

West, M. *Vanishing Point*, HarperCollins: New York, 1996.

Wharton, E. *The House of Mirth*, Penguin: Ringwood, 1993 [1905].

Williams, J. (ed.). *Money: A History*, with a preface by A. Burnett, British Museum Press: London, 1997.

Williamson, J. *Decoding Advertisements*, Marion Boyars: Boston, 1978.

———.*Deadline at Dawn*, Marion Boyars: Boston, 1993.

Wolfe, T. *Bonfire of the Vanities*, Picador: London, 1988.

Wolfson, M. H. *Financial Crises: Understanding the Postwar U.S. Experience*, M. E. Sharpe: New York, 1994.

Zephaniah, B. 'Money (rant)', in *The Oxford Book of Money*, ed. K. Jackson, Oxford University Press: Oxford, 1995.

Index

About the Author

ANNA KASSULKE is a writer and cultural critic living in London and Brisbane.